FAITHFUL IMPRESSIONS

The Thrivent Financial Collection of Religious Art

Dear Richard,
    Thank you for
starting such a wonderful
collection. I am grateful
for the privilege of
sharing in these
incredible works of art
with you.

          James R Wehm

Dearest Richard,
    With my deepest gratitude
for all of the wonderful,
enjoyable, and illuminating
years we spent working
together! You will forever be
in my heart and have my
sincere thanks and appreciation.
this book would not be without you.

          Joanna

FAITHFUL IMPRESSIONS

THE THRIVENT FINANCIAL COLLECTION OF RELIGIOUS ART

JOANNA REILING LINDELL

WITH CONTRIBUTIONS BY
JAMES R. WEHN

Curator, Thrivent Financial Collection of Religious Art
Thrivent Financial for Lutherans
625 Fourth Avenue South
Minneapolis, MN 55415

Editor: Laura J. Westlund
Designers: Gayle Jorgens and Stanley Wai
Photographer: Robert Fogt
Publishing and production management: Jim Bindas—Books & Projects LLC

Faithful Impressions was designed with Adobe InDesign CS4 software. The font is Bembo.
Printed and bound in the United States by Quad/Graphics Commercial and Specialty
Group, the book was produced with sheet-fed printing on Jefferson Velvet paper.
The bindings of 1,000 hardcover and 500 paperback copies were Smythe sewn.

Distributed by Thrivent Financial for Lutherans

ISBN: 978-0-615-41632-8 (hardcover); 978-0-615-42929-8 (paperback)

Cover: Hendrik Goltzius, *The Adoration of the Shepherds* (detail), 1598–1600. Engraving.
End sheets: Albrecht Dürer, *The Last Supper* (detail), 1523. Woodcut.

CONTENTS

FOREWORD

The Thrivent Financial Collection of Religious Art holds a special place in the arts community. With its focus on religious-themed works, the collection draws interest from art scholars, educators, and aficionados. Now, for the first time, the collection's major pieces have been catalogued in one volume.

For nearly three decades, the Thrivent Financial Collection of Religious Art has been home to works from world-renowned artists. Today it is one of the country's leading corporate art collections. As represented by the selections in this book, the collection is composed of a cross-section of names and media, from a copperplate by Rembrandt to George Bellows's *The Crucifixion* painting.

Given Thrivent Financial's long-standing connection to the Lutheran church, one might expect that its art collection would comprise solely works by Lutheran artists. Indeed, the rich history of Lutheran art is featured prominently in the collection. But the Thrivent Financial Collection of Religious Art expands its scope to include myriad forms of religious works, with notably strong holdings in religious art.

Why has Thrivent Financial for Lutherans chosen to invest in great works of art? From its beginnings, Thrivent Financial has been committed to improving the lives of our members, their congregations, and their communities. That commitment goes beyond providing financial products and services to support for important educational and historical endeavors.

As a faith-based organization, Thrivent Financial recognizes the powerful connection between art and religion. This connection can be found in places of worship around the world, whether a stained glass window in a small church in America's heartland or an ornate ceiling fresco in a towering European cathedral. For centuries, artists have used their craft to inspire, question, and provoke. At Thrivent Financial we believe the artist's contribution is worth celebrating—and preserving.

Many individuals were involved in the creation of this book. They all deserve sincere thanks, but the people most responsible are our members: because of them Thrivent Financial is able to support the arts and give back to the community. Our members are at the center of everything we do, and this book is a tribute to them.

Brad Hewitt
President and CEO
Thrivent Financial for Lutherans

PREFACE

Thrivent Financial for Lutherans is home to a truly unique corporate art collection. While most corporate collections focus on contemporary secular art, Thrivent Financial owns a specialized collection devoted to religious art ranging from the Middle Ages to the mid-twentieth century. Founded and in large part assembled by Reverend Richard L. Hillstrom, the collection encompasses biblical subjects and related images, such as portraits of influential religious leaders. The vast majority of the eight hundred objects in the collection are prints and drawings. Many are by the most famous artists of Western civilization, including Albrecht Dürer, Rembrandt, and Picasso. Many are by artists whose names are no longer familiar to nonspecialists but who were, nonetheless, outstanding artists of their time and well worth knowing.

Since selections from the Thrivent Financial Collection of Religious Art are displayed in an ongoing series of free exhibitions in galleries at Thrivent Financial's home office, Minnesota is quite fortunate to be the collection's home. Yet Thrivent Financial makes every effort to share the collection with even wider audiences. A splendid example of this outreach is the exhibition *Pursuit of Faith: Etchings by Rembrandt,* recently held at the University of Michigan, Dearborn. Thrivent Financial lent all of the art in the exhibition, including twenty-five etchings by Rembrandt along with one of the artist's original copper printing plates. I can testify that the faculty and student team that carried the project from research to publication and exhibition had a life-changing experience. My own institution, the Minneapolis Institute of Arts, often benefits from Thrivent Financial's

generous loans of works of art that add depth to our exhibitions. I would be remiss were I to fail to mention the tremendous collegiality of the fine curators of the Thrivent Financial Collection of Religious Art, Joanna Reiling Lindell and James R. Wehn: both have a passion for increasing their knowledge of the collection and for making the collection available to the broadest audiences possible.

Faithful Impressions is meant as an introduction to the rich holdings of the Thrivent Financial Collection of Religious Art. It suggests the range and quality of the collection as a whole. The curators rightly focused on the history and the highlights of the collection when compiling this catalogue. My hope is that as you look at the beautiful and engrossing—perhaps sometimes strange—images, you will want to read about them and learn about the artists who made them, their sources of inspiration, their ways of imparting meaning, and the circumstances in which they lived and worked. I hope you will also enjoy the sheer pleasure of seeing highly expressive works of art made on an intimate scale yet intended for large audiences. Many of these artworks are challenging, for they were made by brilliant minds in faraway places during times long gone. But they are equally rewarding as they reveal new worlds to those who open their minds and hearts to them. In these images we often witness others who face the same tests as we do in living as imperfect beings trying to find our way in the spiritual realm.

Tom Rassieur
John E. Andrus III Curator of Prints and Drawings
Minneapolis Institute of Arts

ACKNOWLEDGMENTS

Faithful Impressions was truly a labor of love for many people. During all the years I have been fortunate to serve as curator of the Thrivent Financial Collection of Religious Art, there was discussion about creating a catalogue…"someday." The efforts of many people made this project possible.

I am extremely grateful to Julie Reidhead at Thrivent Financial for Lutherans, who was instrumental in supporting and guiding this project; I could not ask for a more wonderful colleague. Likewise, the support and guidance of Kirsten Spreck at Thrivent Financial has been for many years unflagging and enjoyable. Susan Zima, Jennifer Vaillancourt, Josh MacCaffrey, Ann Hartel, Kim Lochner, Dave Rustad, and Denise Nygaard all provided assistance with the creation and promotion of *Faithful Impressions.*

To James R. Wehn, associate curator of the Thrivent Financial collection, my colleague, dear friend, and cohort on this project: your very fine work on numerous aspects of this catalogue, from managing the photography to entry writing, was essential and reveals your inspired passion for prints, and I thank you.

Jim Bindas, our marvelous project manager, was always on task and upbeat in his skilled guidance of this book from the earliest stages to completion; thank you, Jim. Designers Gayle Jorgens and Stanley Wai are a remarkably talented and enjoyable team, and their artistic skills created this stunning final product. Editor Laura Westlund was wonderfully meticulous, steadfast, and expert in her careful reading of the text. Thank you also to our tremendous photographer, Robert Fogt, and to Charles Walbridge, who helped ensure the reproductions were gorgeous.

Thank you to Alan Baglia, Artists Rights Society; Rebecca Melenka, Lia Melemenis, and Melanie Kjorlien, Glenbow-Alberta Institute; and Andreas Fluck, Nolde Stiftung Seebüll, for their assistance obtaining copyright permissions for artworks outside the public domain.

A host of esteemed scholars and friends gave us support, productive discussions, and opinions of great import. Tom Rassieur, in addition to his friendship, continual conversation, and collaboration on all topics related to Rembrandt and many other favorite printmakers, contributed an excellent preface to open this book. Rachel McGarry's insight on many drawings in the Thrivent Financial collection was illuminating. Shelley Perlove joined us in lively discussions relating to our Rembrandts. Sandra Hindman and Maria Saffiotti-Dale offered observations on the illuminated manuscripts. Lisa Dickinson Michaux, whose mentorship and friendship have been invaluable, long encouraged the creation of this book. To Bernard Derroitte, a cherished friend and colleague who expertly opined on nineteenth-century works in the collection, inspired in me over the years a deep appreciation for the graphic purity of prints as well as the joy of collecting.

Sincere gratitude also goes to a remarkable scholar and mentor, the late Mary Towley Swanson, who was instrumental to both my academic and professional pursuits. My graduate advisor, Shelly Nordtorp-Madson at the University of St. Thomas, was always ready to discuss obscure medieval and early modern topics—and provide much laughter. I am indebted to Sherry Jordon for supporting my earliest interest in religious prints and theology; likewise to Young-ok An for sparking my passion for nineteenth-century studies. I also thank Glenn Moomau for inspiring in me a lifelong desire to write.

Thank you to my family for their enthusiasm and excitement for this project. My mother, Ruth, spent many devoted hours with my children as I researched and wrote this book. My extraordinary husband, Justice, whose support and love are unending, and our children, Viola and Oliver, bring joy to each day and patiently adapted to my long working hours. Each word here is imbued with my love for you three.

My most heartfelt thanks must be expressed to Reverend Richard Lewis Hillstrom. Without his vision, determination, and great love of art, this catalogue, and the Thrivent Financial collection itself, could not have been possible. Reverend Hillstrom's zeal for collecting and for works on paper was contagious and passed to me very quickly when I began working with him, and the connoisseurship and appreciation I learned at his side are gifts I will hold dear always.

Finally, to every inquisitive visitor to the Thrivent Financial Collection of Religious Art, this book is ultimately for you.

Joanna Reiling Lindell
Curator
Thrivent Financial Collection of Religious Art

THE THRIVENT FINANCIAL COLLECTION OF RELIGIOUS ART

Joanna Reiling Lindell

HUNDREDS OF RICH IMPRESSIONS of history and culture from eight centuries of Western religious art are represented in the Thrivent Financial Collection of Religious Art. From a late-thirteenth-century hand-painted miniature on vellum depicting St. Helena with the "true cross" (Plate 1) to seventeenth-century copperplate etchings by Rembrandt van Rijn (Plate 57) to a twentieth-century lithograph by Pablo Picasso (Plate 89), this collection's historical breadth and significance are remarkable. Comprised of more than eight hundred works, it is unique among corporate art collections nationally for its focus on religious subject matter and works on paper. This collection is a vital, shared part of Thrivent Financial's heritage, faith base, and commitment to supporting the arts, culture, education, and the community.

The Thrivent Financial Collection of Religious Art has received national and local media recognition for its excellence. *Art + Auction* magazine listed the collection among its "Top 101 Active Corporate Art Collectors" in 1988, and local arts editor for the *Star Tribune* newspaper, Mary Abbe, described it as "one of the Twin Cities' great artistic treasures."[1] Many works from the collection have been studied by scholars in Europe and the United States, with their research published in academic books and journals. For twenty-nine years, the art collection has served the Twin Cities and greater regional areas as a source of spiritual enrichment, artistic pleasure, and art historical and theological education and research. It is often considered a great hidden treasure because people are sometimes surprised such marvelous works of art are tucked away in a seventeen-story corporate building in downtown Minneapolis. Yet the collection has reached many thousands of viewers,

through scholarly and public exhibitions, loans, gallery talks, lectures, and other educational programming. Our hope and plan is to preserve, share, enjoy, and learn from this magnificent collection for many years to come.

The Company

A collection of religious art is appropriate for Thrivent Financial for Lutherans given its long history and strong connections to Scandinavian Lutherans in the Midwest. For its first nineteen years, from 1982 until 2001, the collection was known as the Lutheran Brotherhood Collection of Religious Art; the name changed along with that of the organization when the two fraternal benefit societies Lutheran Brotherhood and Aid Association for Lutherans merged to create the largest fraternal benefit society in the United States. A fraternal benefit society is a not-for-profit organization that not only offers insurance and investment opportunities to its members but also promotes the well-being of its members and the public through various educational, social, patriotic, charitable, and religious programs and activities. Members of a fraternal benefit society share a religious, ethnic, or vocational bond: in the case of Lutheran Brotherhood, Aid Association for Lutherans, and Thrivent Financial for Lutherans, this bond is a belief in the Lutheran faith.

This Lutheran heritage has deep roots throughout the entire history of these organizations. Aid Association for Lutherans was established in 1902 as a result of efforts by German Lutherans in Appleton, Wisconsin; Lutherans throughout eastern Wisconsin were recruited in order to obtain the requisite five hundred members for the business's state charter. Lutheran Brotherhood was founded in Minnesota after the 1917 merger convention of the Norwegian Lutheran

Opposite: Pablo Picasso, *David et Bethsabée* (detail; see Plate 89), 1947. Lithograph.

Pablo Picasso © 2011 Estate of Pablo Picasso / Artists Rights Society (ARS), New York.

Left: Thirteenth-century Italian Master, *St. Helena with the True Cross* (detail; see Plate 1), c. 1290. Gouache and ink on vellum.

Notes

1. "Corporate Chart: Our Top 101 Active Corporate Art Collectors," *Art + Auction* XI, no. 3 (October 1988): 168–75. Mary Abbe, "The Saints: Image and Devotion in Religious Prints," *Star Tribune* (Minneapolis–St. Paul), December 23, 2007, 4E.

Church of America. Lutheran insurance commissioners Jacob Preus from Minnesota and Herman Ekern from Wisconsin proposed a not-for-profit mutual aid society, Luther Union; after much debate, the proposal passed, and three years later, in 1921, the organization was renamed Lutheran Brotherhood. The grassroots campaigns for both organizations were motivated by a concern for the security of Lutherans, and primarily the companies offered life insurance to protect Lutheran families.

The name Thrivent Financial for Lutherans was approved by members after the corporate merger in 2001. Thrivent Financial united the combined 183-year history of the two fraternal benefit societies and remains a faith-based, not-for-profit membership organization. This Fortune 500 financial services corporation now has nearly 2.6 million members and manages more than sixty-one billion dollars in assets.[2]

The organization's acquisition of art extends beyond the Thrivent Financial Collection of Religious Art. A corporate art collection begun by Lutheran Brotherhood and Aid Association for Lutherans is separate from the Thrivent Financial Collection of Religious Art and includes a great variety of paintings, sculptures, ceramics, textiles, and other art objects. Many of these pieces were purchased or commissioned for corporate centers or offices. Members may be familiar with such memorable works on display in Minneapolis as the Viking ship model and the Reformation window, a stunning creation in stained glass by the renowned Pickel Studio. Although distinct from the Thrivent Financial Collection of Religious Art, the corporate collection also demonstrates the organization's support of the arts and its priority to enhance the workplace of its employees and the experience of visitors to Thrivent Financial with the presence of art.

2. Additional information about the history and current status of Thrivent Financial for Lutherans is available on the organization's web site at www.thrivent.com.

The Collector

Reverend Richard Lewis Hillstrom, a Lutheran minister and art collector, is responsible for collecting the majority of the works in the Thrivent Financial Collection of Religious Art and served as its founding curator. When he began to build the collection in 1981, he was already a great connoisseur of art and a recognized collector. He had been developing his own personal collection of primarily American drawings, prints, paintings, and sculpture for almost forty years. He was involved with several local museums and had close friendships with many artists and art dealers throughout the United States and Europe. His colleagues at Lutheran Brotherhood trusted his expertise and substantial experience when appointing him to establish this collection of religious art.

Born and raised in Dassel, Minnesota, Hillstrom left this small town to attend Gustavus Adolphus College in St. Peter, Minnesota. After his graduation in 1938, he moved to Rock Island, Illinois, to study at Augustana Seminary. In 1942 he was ordained a Lutheran minister, and he served a congregation in Indiana until 1947; during this period he began collecting art. He returned to Minnesota in 1947 to serve as assistant pastor at Mount Olivet Lutheran Church in Minneapolis, and in 1952 he accepted a ministerial position at Bethesda Lutheran Medical Center in St. Paul, where he served as chaplain and then director of chaplaincy services until his retirement in 1981.

While he was a young minister, Hillstrom traveled the world and slowly built his personal collection. Befriending dealers and artists yet always remaining the frugal Swedish Lutheran pastor, he negotiated the price of works he desired, occasionally arranging payment plans and sometimes waiting years to buy a piece he loved. His tales of buying Old Master prints and drawings on the streets of Paris for dollars in the 1940s and of visiting with American artists Birger Sandzén and Elof Wedin as he contemplated which of these artists' works to purchase are entertaining and astounding. He lived on the modest income of a pastor and carefully planned and saved for his regular travels and art purchases. He considered his collection a great source of enjoyment and a preservation of culture, as well as a sound investment. Indeed, his personal collection and the Thrivent Financial collection have both proved appreciably successful investments, a fact Hillstrom believed was appropriate and complementary to the financial services focus of the organization. Yet he reflected recently that for himself and for Thrivent Financial for Lutherans this art collection reveals more about the reputation of the corporation than about its financial aspect: "The company is not just there to make or manage dollars and cents, but to actually make a contribution to the community through this cultural vehicle."

In 1978 Hillstrom was elected a trustee of the Minnesota Museum of American Art in St. Paul and was chair of its collections committee. He served on the Board of Trustees at the Minneapolis Institute of Arts from 1994 until 2000 and participated in its accessions and development committees. From 2000 to 2006, he served as a nontrustee member of the accessions committee until he resigned at the end of that term for health reasons. He supported the creation of the Print and Drawing Curatorial Council at the Minneapolis Institute of Arts in the early 1980s and was an active board member of this group. He even promoted a dynamic art program at the Bethesda Lutheran Medical Center, regularly organizing art shows and sales there.

Donating works from his own collection to local arts institutions is important to Hillstrom. He gave many artworks to the Minneapolis Institute of Arts, the Minnesota Museum of American Art, and the American Swedish Institute. The bulk of his personal collection was donated to the art museum of Gustavus Adolphus College. His significant contribution to this museum comprises much of its permanent collection, and the museum was named the Hillstrom Museum of Art, a notable tribute to his generosity and his many years of studying and collecting art. He also helped establish an endowment for purchasing works on paper for the permanent collection of the Minneapolis Institute of Arts. He has been an influential and much loved figure in the Twin Cities arts community for decades, and his gifts create a legacy that will maintain and continue his devotion to the arts.

Today, at the age of ninety-five, Reverend Hillstrom remains a rich source of art historical knowledge, strong connections to local and international artists and institutions, and extraordinary stories about his long life dedicated to ministry, travel, and

the arts. The Thrivent Financial Collection of Religious Art is the perfect expression of his dual passions, religion and art, as well as a vibrant statement of Thrivent's commitment to education and the preservation of religious heritage.

FIGURE 1. Reverend Richard L. Hillstrom, Rome, May 7, 1950.

The Collection

In 1981, Lutheran Brotherhood was moving into a new home office at the corner of Fourth Avenue and Sixth Street in downtown Minneapolis. Reverend Hillstrom and individuals working at Lutheran Brotherhood believed this was the ideal time to start a new corporate art collection. Discussions ensued between Hillstrom and Dr. Edward A. Lindell, executive vice president in the Fraternal division, and soon Hillstrom was hired as the company's art consultant and curator. He worked closely with David Swanson, manager of the Advisor Community/Ethnic branch of the Fraternal department, to establish guidelines for the collection within a corporate setting. They hoped the collection would express and support a commitment to art, education, and religious history. By early 1982, the collection was officially begun.

This initial team had a specific vision: the collection would represent only religious subject matter. This focus was ideally suited to Lutheran Brotherhood's historical ties to the Lutheran church, and Hillstrom and his colleagues knew that a religious collection would set itself apart from other more secular corporate art collections. Another distinctive aspect would be the collection's emphasis on works on paper, or prints and drawings. Originally, Hillstrom planned to acquire several artistic media, including paintings and sculpture, but it soon became apparent that for storage and preservation reasons a concentration on works on paper would be more appropriate for a corporate environment. The

relating to Christ, and works from the time of the Protestant Reformation. Throughout the collection a wide range of religious and theological material is represented, from the Stations of the Cross to depictions of great cathedrals, the saints, and scores of scriptural and noncanonical religious subjects.

The first piece that Hillstrom acquired

FIGURE 2. *The Passion* exhibition on display in the Thrivent Financial Religious Art Gallery, Minneapolis, 2010.

five paintings in the collection are exceptions among the more than eight hundred prints and drawings. The Thrivent Financial Collection of Religious Art may be unique in the world for featuring works on paper devoted to religious subject matter.

European prints and drawings from the early modern period (the fifteenth to the late seventeenth centuries) comprise the largest portion of the collection. These Old Master artworks highlight artists of the northern and southern Renaissance and Baroque eras, as well as early prints and miniatures from the late medieval period. Sixteenth-century Italian drawings are abundant in the collection, and holdings from the nineteenth and twentieth centuries are strong as well, notably nineteenth-century European religious drawings and twentieth-century German and European expressionist prints. Thematic areas that developed include the Passion, scriptural and biblical topics, Marian iconography, imagery and iconography

for the new religious art collection was a lithograph by American artist George Wesley Bellows, *Crucifixion of Christ* (Figure 3). Two years later, in 1984, Bellows's painting of the same subject (his only known religious painting) was also acquired (Plate 86). Hillstrom had long admired the work of Bellows, whose art, including another impression of the *Crucifixion of Christ* lithograph, was in his personal collection. Bellows is considered one of the most influential American artists of the twentieth century; he and other members of "the Ashcan School" in New York City (also known as "The Eight") sought to express artistic realism through depictions of urban life. *The Crucifixion* is large in scale and visually powerful, and the early acquisition of this painting demonstrated the historical breadth of the collection, which would include dramatic modern works as well as more traditional religious art from the fifteenth through eighteenth centuries.

Certain prints are vital inclusions within any significant print collection, and the Thrivent Financial collection is fortunate to own impressions of two of Albrecht Dürer's well-known masterprints: *Knight, Death, and the Devil* (Plate 12) and *St. Jerome in His Study* (Plate 13). Other central works or series in the oeuvre of Dürer represented wholly or in part in the collection are his revolutionary *Apocalypse* series (Plate 8) and his marvelous sets of the *Large Passion* (Figure 18), the *Engraved Passion* (Plate 11), and *The Life of the Virgin* series (Plate 10). These series were important in Dürer's time for being highly collectable, devotional, and educational. Holding many such sets enhances the scholarly potential of a private collection: we can view the entire set of these prints today and attempt to emulate and understand the original function- ality, aesthetic enjoyment, educational and devotional aspects, and multiple and artistic qualities of the series, both in individual works and through the unity of these works together as a series.

Hillstrom utilized several avenues for collecting. He subscribed to auction catalogues and participated in national and international art auctions, and he spread the word about the new collection among art dealers in the United States and Europe with whom he had previously worked. His fine reputation as a collector preceded his role as a curator and collector for Lutheran Brotherhood, and dealers were eager to offer exceptional pieces that would be appropriate for the new collection. Unique preparatory drawings and sketches by such renowned artists as John Singer Sargent, Eugène Delacroix, Sir Edward Coley Burne-Jones, and Jean-Auguste-Dominique Ingres were ideal, marvelous contributions to the collection. Hillstrom's keen eye was also responsible for the acquisition of works of historical and theological importance. *Protestant Satire on the Eucharist* (Figure 35), a small roundel drawing by German artist Sebald Beham that depicts a specific theological issue during the Protestant Reformation, was an excellent addition to the collection's Reformation holdings.

Any collector can tell you that choosing a single favorite work of art is difficult, yet certain works do stand out as Hillstrom's

FIGURE 3. George Wesley Bellows, *Crucifixion of Christ*, 1923. Lithograph.

favorites. He enjoys series or sets of prints, perhaps for the stories they tell and their frequent close connection to Scripture. He considered Dürer's *Apocalypse* series, arguably one of the most influential sets of prints in Western art, essential for the collection. The monumentality of the print series is further showcased in Max Pechstein's *The Lord's Prayer* (Plate 81), a series held in complete in the Thrivent Financial Collection of Religious Art. Hillstrom also loved James J. Tissot's gorgeous *The Prodigal Son in Modern Life* series (Plate 76) and Domenico Tiepolo's *Flight into Egypt* (Plate 39), a staggering twenty-seven plate set expanded from one brief scriptural reference. As Hillstrom charm- ingly commented, "The Bible said, essentially, 'They went to Egypt' [Matthew 2:14], but Tiepolo figured out about twenty-six other things they did along the way!" Indeed, the print series format is ideal for the visual and thematic expansion of the imaginative nature of such rich stories of humanity. Hillstrom also treasured *First Communion at Mont St. Père* by Léon Augustin Lhermitte (Figure 6), a beautiful large charcoal drawing depicting children's first receipt of the sacrament; Lhermitte's gentle handling of the lace on the young girls' veils feels simultaneously sumptuous and delicate.

Both the organization (first Lutheran Brotherhood, then Thrivent Financial for

Above: FIGURE 4.
Albrecht Dürer,
St. Jerome in His Study,
1514. Engraving.

Right: FIGURE 5.
Max Pechstein, *Our
Father, Who Art in Heaven,*
from *The Lord's Prayer*
series, 1921. Hand-colored
woodcut.

Max Pechstein © 2011 Artists
Rights Society (ARS), New York /
Pechstein Hamburg / Toekendorf /
VG Bild-Kunst, Bonn

Lutherans) and the curators have always
sought to share the holdings of the collection,
making the artworks available for viewing and
study. A primary duty of a collection
is preservation and conservation, to ensure
the care of the art, but equally important
is the duty and privilege to promote the
art through educational programming and
exhibitions. The Thrivent Financial Collection
of Religious Art is a source of ongoing scholarship, as its curators and other art historians
use it to research academic and theological
topics. Providing access to the art is further
accomplished through in-house and loaned
exhibitions, gallery talks and lectures, and a
number of tours and study sessions. Hillstrom
and others in the company also maintained a
strong conviction that the collection should
be seen and appreciated by members of
the fraternal organization and by our larger
community. In the late 1980s a program was
established to send works from the collection
to Lutheran congregations throughout the
United States, and for more than ten years

Hillstrom facilitated these small exhibitions.
Hundreds of churches of all sizes hosted
these exhibitions at no cost, and the Thrivent
Financial collection reached many thousands
of members and nonmembers, frequently
traveling to areas that did not have a local
museum or access to fine art.

Through the years Hillstrom encouraged
an important relationship for the collection
with the Minneapolis Institute of Arts. The
curators of the museum's Print and Drawing
department were friends and colleagues
whom Hillstrom often consulted on significant purchases. The Thrivent Financial
collection has loaned numerous works to the
MIA, and Thrivent Financial for Lutherans
provides considerable support and gifts to the
MIA for special exhibitions. Most recently
Thrivent Financial partnered with the
museum as the 2010 sponsor of Public Tours,
a program of free, docent-led, daily tours
of the museum's collection, demonstrating
its desire to extend its curatorial vision and
emphasizing its enthusiasm to promote the
arts, education, and culture in our community.

Today, the original vision is continued
and vastly expanded with dozens of tours,
gallery talks, lectures, and exhibitions each
year. In 2008 a lecture series was initiated to
coincide with in-house exhibition openings.
Guest lecturers speak on topics related
to the current exhibition in the gallery;
these successful events bring members and

nonmembers from the Twin Cities into the Thrivent Financial corporate center to view the collection and learn about the art. Educational programs remain crucial to the collection's curatorial goals and serve as an expression of the fraternal benefit society heritage of Thrivent Financial for Lutherans.

The in-house galleries on the second floor of the Thrivent Financial corporate center hang approximately forty to sixty works in one or two themed exhibitions at a time. Showing works from the collection with accompanying didactic labels is a priority for the collection curators, who rotate the works to highlight theological and art historical scholarship and themes, as well as to protect the art and maintain its continued preservation. Recent exhibitions include *Familiar Image, Sacred Impressions: The Reformation and Beyond, The Saints: Image and Devotion in Religious Prints, Made to Fit: The Meaning of Dress in Religious Prints, The Passion: Five Hundred Years in Art,* and *Modern Impressions: Color and Expression in Twentieth-Century Religious Prints.*

Reverend Hillstrom had never worked with an assistant curator or curatorial assistant until I joined him as assistant curator in 2001. He retired from the collection in 2005 at the robust age of ninety, and I became its curator. James R. Wehn joined me as assistant curator in 2008. I aim to preserve and enhance much that Reverend Hillstrom created, while implementing educational and scholarly programming and research to maximize the potential and reputation of this notable collection.

With his legacy of two outstanding art collections as well as donations to many art institutions, Richard Hillstrom demonstrated his great passion for art and his truly generous spirit. A self-taught art connoisseur, he lived the essential principle of collecting: you must genuinely love what you collect. After all, you look at your art day after day, so it must give you pleasure. Thrivent Financial for Lutherans is proud to follow Reverend Hillstrom's fine example and delight in its exceptional collection of religious art, continuing its commitment of the past thirty years to preserve, share, and enjoy these beautiful and important works of art.

Above: FIGURE 6. Léon Augustin Lhermitte, *First Communion at Mont St. Père,* 1884. Charcoal.

Left: FIGURE 7. Richard Hillstrom in the Thrivent gallery, 2000.

Notes

The author enjoyed the great privilege of working with former curator and collector Reverend Richard Lewis Hillstrom for four years before he retired from the collection. Much of the information about the collection's history was gathered from Hillstrom's and the author's recollections as well as from a formal interview conducted with Hillstrom by the author in September 2009 in preparation for writing this book. Direct quotations, unless otherwise noted, are from that interview.

THE RELIGIOUS PRINT

Joanna Reiling Lindell

 RELIGIOUS ART HAS HELD OUR fascination and devotion for centuries. Art with religious subject matter has told us stories about who we are, what we believe, and what we feel. As visual and emotional beings, we have often found art to be as perfect an expression as possible of God's grace and beauty. Whether from a natural human yearning for spirituality or due to the influence of organized religion in culture and society, much art throughout the history of human civilization has been religious. Prior to the early modern period in Western history, a great percentage of art was religious; as secular imagery became more pervasive in Western art from the sixteenth century onward, some types of religious subject matter did decline but by no means were diminished or overcome by secular art. Religious imagery has even been fervently renewed in later centuries, and secular and religious themes are often combined in an intriguing interplay. By retelling familiar biblical stories through the visual arts, poetry, or literature, Christians continually reassert and redefine their beliefs about their place in the world and their sense of spirituality. After all, religious stories are essentially about origin and culture as much as devotion, and great value can be gleaned from nonreligious components of religious art as well. Many different cultures and religions in the history of the world have expressed their beliefs through art; this catalogue and the Thrivent Financial Collection of Religious Art focus on Jewish and Christian themes.

The Thrivent Financial collection represents a significant gathering in the United States of solely religious works on paper and paintings from the thirteenth through the twentieth centuries, simultaneously preserving and sharing the rich, varied history of Western art, religion, and culture

as much as theological and spiritual tenets. Amassed from eight centuries, the collection's more than eight hundred works delight and inspire. Through them, we can trace interesting trends, stylistic and cultural developments, and, above all, the enduring messages of Christianity. Because the Thrivent Financial collection primarily comprises works on paper, this catalogue concentrates on the artistic media of prints and drawings.

Printed images are important in the history of art and have a distinct history separate from other media. Invented in northern Europe during the fifteenth century, Western printmaking offered a new and efficient way to make and reproduce visual information. Book illustrations, along with text, could be quickly and consistently created with a printing press, rather than by painstakingly hand-copying each page. Printed images were affordable and more accessible to a broader segment of the population, especially those unable to purchase or even see paintings or illuminated manuscripts. The popularity of printed images quickly increased, and as early as the sixteenth century collectors began accumulating both secular and religious prints. Printmaking offered early modern artists an opportunity to be recognized as stylistically innovative outside the older disciplines of sculpture or painting. Albrecht Dürer, for example, was an excellent painter, but his extraordinarily skillful woodcuts and engravings make him truly exceptional in a survey of Western art. Similarly, in the seventeenth century, despite the fame of his painting, Rembrandt van Rijn was able to achieve in his etchings a level of spontaneity, whimsy, and emotional drama and intimacy that surpassed nearly all previous printmaking accomplishments. The history of the religious print, including shifts in function, meaning, and execution, is a complex topic that cannot

Opposite: Rembrandt van Rijn, *The Hundred Guilder Print*, c. 1648 (detail; see Figure 11). Etching, drypoint, and engraving.

Left: Albrecht Dürer, *The Man of Sorrows*, from the *Engraved Passion* (detail; see Plate 11), 1509. Engraving.

be fully explored in this brief survey. *Faithful Impressions* highlights works from the Thrivent Financial collection to illustrate aspects of this rich history.[1]

Through the centuries, source material for artists producing religious subject matter was diverse. The primary source has long been the canonical Scriptures, the accepted collection of Holy Scriptures in the Christian church. The exact canonical Scriptures changed through time as books and materials were added or removed for political and theological reasons. The Old Testament (also called the Hebrew Bible) and the New Testament compose this historical source called the Holy Bible. Different translations of the Bible were used in different regions and at different times.

Apocryphal and noncanonical writings and tradition constitute another major source of religious subject matter. Over the centuries the Bible developed from more books than are included in the accepted canon. Books and stories not in today's Bible would have been familiar to many Western artists; such stories were widely known and believed, and the church even taught them at times. Passed down through oral tradition, they became deeply ingrained in society and would have been known to many individuals at any given time. One important example, *The Golden Legend* or *Legenda Aurea* by Jacobus de Voragine, was a medieval sourcebook first published around 1260 C.E. that compiled centuries of existing and detailed oral tradition and writings about the lives of the saints. This book, and its stories, was immensely popular for hundreds of years and was reprinted multiple times in several languages. Many religious prints derive their subject matter directly or indirectly from *The Golden Legend,* since accounts of the lives of the saints were not included in the accepted canon of Holy Scripture.

Individual artists and their patrons are another source of religious art through commissions. The church has historically been the primary patron for the design and execution of such art, which often decorated churches. Wealthy, elite members of society also became significant historical sponsors of religious art. Whether paintings, sculpture, stained glass, frescoes, mosaics, or works on paper, ecclesiastical and private commissions of religious art have long expressed and been intended for spiritual devotion, theological teachings, advancement of technical skill, and aesthetic enjoyment.

The Original Print

Original prints differ significantly from the photographic reproductions most common in our contemporary era.[2] Printmaking has long embraced new technology, often with highly positive results, but in response to widespread misconceptions and questionable practices related to "prints" after the advent of photographic reproduction, organizations devoted to the practice and study of original prints attempted to specify a clear definition of an original print. The Print Council of America published the pamphlet *What Is an Original Print?* in 1961, which outlines the following criteria:

> An *original print* is a work of art, the general requirements of which are:
>
> The artist alone has created the master image in or upon the plate, stone, woodblock or other material, for the purpose of creating the print.
>
> The print is made from the said materials, by the artist or pursuant to his direction.
>
> The finished print is approved by the artist.[3]

This definition should not exclude the fact that printmaking can be a collaborative process that may involve more than one person. The artist may not always directly participate in the creation of the matrix, the block or plate, but the conceptual intention of the artist and the work's content should be of an original nature.[4]

The original print has the potential to be a powerful, personal object. To hold a piece of paper in one's hand, or gaze on it in a book or album, can elicit a close connection. The subject depicted on paper can be tangible and solid but also intimate—seen only by the eyes of one particular viewer, or small group of viewers, in a given moment. Because of this personal and individual relationship, works on paper can be very influential and persuasive communicators of ideas. Admiring a glorious stained glass window in a vaulted cathedral or examining a large-scale painting

Notes

1. Both single-sheet printed images and printed book illustrations are relevant to our discussion. They often commingled function and influence, though their differences must be noted as their creation and collection exhibit many distinctions.
2. Photographic or facsimile reproductions available since the twentieth century are problematic to the modern understanding and marketing of original prints. As Linda C. Hults discusses in *The Print in the Western World: An Introductory History* (Madison: University of Wisconsin Press, 1996), the ability to create countless numbers of such reproductions, with no alteration whatsoever in the quality of the image, and then even sign and edition such "prints," undercuts and bears false witness to the nuanced, unique nature of the original print itself (8–9).
3. Print Council of America, *What Is an Original Print?* (New York: Print Council of America, 1961), n.p.
4. Hults, 9.

or fresco is often moving and fulfilling, but the immediacy of the experience of enjoying a print or drawing is altogether different. The touch of the paper; the faintly sweet, sometimes musty scent; thick ink settled permanently into the richly textured or feather light paper—all of these sensual qualities enhance the viewing of a work on paper. Prints delight for their aesthetic, visual qualities; inspire with their myriad meanings and interpretations; and astound with their intricate, stunning technical qualities. Collectors have been captivated by this nuanced and varied media throughout history.

Prints and drawings also appeal for their accessibility. Prints are available to viewers not only in a physical, touchable sense but monetarily as well: they have always been more affordable and available for more people to view than other media. Essentially pieces of paper, prints are likewise highly transportable; they are capable of expressing an idea or image (religious or otherwise) across the world simultaneously. Although religious subject matter is highly important in the history of art and Christianity, the religious print or drawing was never only about religion or theology. As time went on, secular components or little details from daily life were depicted within religious scenes, sometimes intentionally, sometimes not. These features reveal much about the art but also about life at the time of the work's creation.

Early Prints: The Fifteenth and Sixteenth Centuries

Before the advent of printed woodblock images (c. 1425) and the printing press (1453) in Europe, hand-painted miniatures and illuminated manuscripts were the popular artform on paper for religious and secular subjects.[5] Works ranged in quality and function, but the finest could be embellished or illuminated with gold or silver and painted with rare and expensive pigments. These books and manuscripts might require years to produce and were commissioned by wealthy members of society, often including clergy. Such images illustrated religious and musical texts, as well as small and large-format devotional books. The earliest artwork in the Thrivent Financial collection is *St. Helena with the True Cross* by a late thirteenth-century Italian Master, c. 1290 (Plate 1): this miniature is an example of the common church-centered religious imagery of the medieval period, often restricted in use or viewing only to clergy or the elite.

Relief printing developed from the long-standing practice of stamping woodblock images onto textiles, combined with the growing popularity of paper after the existence of paper mills in Europe since the thirteenth century.[6] The first printed religious images in Europe appeared by the second quarter of the fifteenth century in central Europe and southern Germany.[7] These woodblock prints were made from a relief printing method. Intaglio printmaking, the other primary method, likely began in the 1430s in Germany.[8] These early prints were prevalent years before the printing press was invented.

In the fifteenth and early sixteenth centuries, Germany became the center of print culture. The printing press had the most profound effect on Western civilization as any invention up to that time. One of the first books printed with moveable type in a press was a Latin Bible completed in 1454 in Mainz, Germany, by Johannes Gutenberg. By the end of the century, hundreds of cities and towns across the continent had printing presses. The intense growth in printed literature was aided by the concurrent development of humanism, a philosophical and intellectual movement with Italian origins that migrated to Germany by the late fifteenth century.[9] Valuing knowledge, language, and classical ideals in art and literature, humanism emphasized the individual over medieval dogma.[10] The thirst for knowledge inspired by humanism and the reproduction of the printed word and image from the printing press had a transformational cultural effect and opened exciting avenues for the creation of prints.[11] A middle class emerged during the first quarter of the sixteenth century, and the medieval guild system began to be replaced by individual enterprise.[12] The ability to rapidly disseminate new ideas through print media was immensely influential, and this period in Europe was characterized by artistic realism and detail, great interest in nature and science, and a strong reshaping of ideas about the individual's place in the world.

Notes

5. Before paper was in widespread use in Europe, specially prepared animal skins, called vellum, served as the support for certain kinds of artwork, such as miniatures, books, and illuminated manuscripts. Vellum was usually prepared from the skin of young calves or sheep.

6. Jeffrey Chips Smith, *The Northern Renaissance* (London: Phaidon Press, 2004), 242.

7. Peter W. Parshall and Rainer Schoch, *Origins of European Printmaking* (New Haven: Yale University Press, 2005), 1. Printed images from woodblocks existed in other cultures and areas of the world centuries prior to the development of the woodblock print in Europe.

8. Ibid.

9. Christiane Andersson and Charles W. Talbot, *From a Mighty Fortress: Prints, Drawings, and Books in the Age of Luther, 1483–1546* (Detroit: Detroit Institute of Arts, 1983), 32.

10. Ibid., 32–33.

11. For a thorough discussion of the impact of printmaking on Western society, see Elizabeth L. Eisenstein, "Some Conjectures about the Impact of Printing on Western Society and Thought: A Preliminary Report," *Journal of Modern History* 40, no. 1 (March 1968): 1–56.

12. Andersson and Talbot, 30.

Martin Schongauer was the first print-maker to develop the medium of engraving into one able to stand "independent of the arts of the goldsmith or even the painter."[13] Two prints by Schongauer in the Thrivent Financial collection, *Christ before Pilate* and *Christ in Limbo* (Plate 6), evince this artist's technical mastery and innovation. Schongauer transformed the religious print into a more engaging, dense, and lifelike medium that was capable of eliciting deeper devotional potential as well as admiration for the technical components of the engraving.

The early modern print workshop was a bustling center of creation and commerce. Workshops were businesses as much as they were sources of great art; innovation and expression were central aims for many artists and workshops, but so was making money. Artists of every level of reputation and skill belonged to this system at this time, whether as the master, apprentice, or craftsman. The master in a workshop was the name and the draw for commissions, but many others would also touch a work. The earliest woodblock prints in Europe, simpler in form and technique, were likely created in each stage of production by one artist, but from the fifteenth century the artist/master/printmaker would create a print's original design, then the artist or another craftsman would transfer the original drawing onto the matrix before it would ultimately be cut, etched, or engraved, and finally prepared and printed by different people. Some artists were more involved than others in the complete process of artistic creation and production.

Prints have layered meanings and functions that often changed over time. In the fifteenth and sixteenth centuries, their uses were both practical and profound, as "devotional or intellectual aids; talismans; decorations for furniture or walls; playing cards; announcements of local events; explanations of portents, such as a two-headed calf or a bright comet; satirical or polemical commentaries; and, of course, works of art."[14] The print also reproduced other works of art. Most early prints were not made as a result of specific patronage; rather, they were created for the open market.[15]

Many printmakers promoted and sold their prints and sets of prints to other artists and craftsmen. Sets of religious prints depicting the Apostles, the Virgin, or the Passion could become models for iconographic programs for other artists' work.[16] Religious subject matter endured as the most common and popular type in various artistic media, and workshops could greatly benefit from sourcebooks or models about how to depict such figures and events. Prints depicting saints in open space with their iconographic attributes, such as Israhel van Meckenem's *St. Stephen* (Figure 8), demonstrated to other artists traditional artistic representation of specific religious figures.

Collectability was another primary function for prints. Many early print-makers marketed their print sets or series to be sold in full or with the expectation that a collector would ultimately buy the entire set, thereby appealing to a range of economic incomes.[17] Serious and amateur print collectors could be enticed to acquire a complete series or gradually work toward this goal. Some single-sheet prints and sets were expensive; sometimes artists would create different versions of a print or series—some small in format and lower in price, some large and more sophisticated and technically impressive, accompanied by a higher price. Albrecht Dürer's *Engraved Passion* (Figure 9, Plate 11) was a refined series of the highest quality that was made with a more elite clientele in mind. Prints were still a much more affordable artform for collectors at any level. For example, six sets of Dürer's *Engraved Passion* sold for three florins, slightly more

FIGURE 8. Israhel van Meckenem, *St. Stephen*, c. 1480. Engraving.

Notes

13. Michel Melot, Antony Griffiths, and Richard S. Field, *Prints: History of an Art* (New York: Rizzoli, 1981), 139.
14. Smith, 242.
15. Ibid.
16. Susie Nash, *Northern Renaissance Art* (New York: Oxford University Press, 2009), 134.
17. Ibid., 137.

than what he paid for a "portmanteau [large suitcase] for two florins, four stiver."[18] Dürer famously dispatched his wife and mother to sell his prints at fairs across Germany, and he sold or gave away many of his prints during travels throughout Italy and the Netherlands. Scholars are increasingly recognizing that these cultural and economic aspects of early printmaking contribute significantly to the understanding and history of Western culture.

The most obvious and perhaps enduring function of religious prints is as devotional media. Early print artists were often working from their own agenda and probably seriously considered the potential salability of a print. Yet the church and other religious entities such as monasteries were vital patrons for religious prints. A monastery or particular pilgrimage site might commission prints to their specifications to commemorate a religious event or for pilgrims to purchase as a souvenir from their visit. Such prints could operate not just devotionally but also as a conduit for conferring God's grace, offering a vehicle for the imagination of the early modern viewer to, for example, experience immersive empathy for Christ in his agony during the Passion. Through the literal act of empathetically looking at these prints, a Christian could find redemptive power, grace to combat sinful nature, and avoid eternal damnation. A simple image of the Madonna holding the Christ child could be equally powerful to the pious viewer in facilitating meditation and prayer (see Figure 10).

The power of the human gaze on such religious prints was very real to early modern viewers: to look upon an image of Christ, the Virgin Mary, or a saint was to communicate through prayer and worship. Religious mysticism and spiritual pilgrimage had long been essential devotional practices in Western Christianity. Demand for devotional prints was high in part because many individuals could not read.[19] One member of the clergy clearly expressed the spiritual passion and action such prints might inspire: "in a published sermon of the late fifteenth century, a famous preacher of Strasbourg Cathedral, Johann Geiler von Kaisersberg, urged his audience, 'If you cannot read, then take one of those paper images on which the meeting of Mary and Elizabeth is

painted. You can buy one for a penny. Look at it, and think how happy they were and full of hope, and come to know that in your faith! Then show your extreme reverence for them; kiss the picture on the piece of paper, bow down before it, kneel in front of it, call upon the Virgin, give alms to a poor person for her sake!'"[20] Inexpensive religious prints offered vital means of devotion and even theological education, as the imagery could serve as

FIGURE 9. Albrecht Dürer, *Christ before Pilate*, from the *Engraved Passion*, 1509. Engraving.

FIGURE 10. Albrecht Dürer, *Virgin and Child Crowned by One Angel*, 1520. Engraving.

Notes

18. Albrecht Dürer, *Dürer's Record of Journeys to Venice and the Low Countries*, ed. Roger Fry (New York: Dover Publications, 1995), 40, 55.
19. Many religious prints do appear to have been made for a largely literate audience, as evidenced by the frequent incorporation of text, often Latin. Peter Schmidt, "The Multiple Image: The Beginnings of Printmaking, between Old Theories and New Approaches," in Parshall and Schoch, 43.
20. Smith, 243–44.

universal language. Devotional prints used for personal prayer and reflection were common and had positive benefits for the creation of religious imagery, though naturally such quotidian practice meant that many papers did not survive.[21]

Printed by the thousands, inexpensive early religious woodcuts that usually depicted saints or relics were sold at pilgrimage sites and church festivals.[22] At a time when many Christians believed veneration of an icon or relic had redemptive or curative powers, prints also served as surrogates for the original objects.[23] A large woodcut of Christ's head, crowned with thorns, by Sebald Beham c. 1520 (Plate 21) draws on this tradition and expresses a powerful devotional potential.

As the intaglio printing techniques of engraving and etching developed, religious prints started to compete with painting in complexity and quality. Although still less expensive than a painting, very fine intaglio prints commanded the attention of collectors among an elite class of royalty, scholars, merchants, and artists. Wealthy and well educated, this group delighted in masterful, innovative representations of religious scenes, and printmakers such as Albrecht Dürer and Lucas van Leyden flourished in the early modern period.

Dürer's *Apocalypse* series (1498; Plate 8) and three *Meisterstiche,* or masterpieces— *St. Jerome in His Study* (1514; Plate 13), *Melencolia I* (1514), and *Knight, Death, and the Devil* (1513; Plate 12)—highlight a turning point in religious printed imagery and were momentous examples of the spectacular technical advances and complex compositions that this artist presented to the world. Dürer valued each element involved in printmaking and culturally elevated the medium's entire professional process and output. His oeuvre reflects huge shifts in Western culture through humanist ideals, major theological changes, and careful study of the natural world, and his influence and innovation in printmaking is perhaps matched only by Rembrandt van Rijn in the seventeenth century.

Educational and devotional functions for the religious print often intertwined. Print series were an ideal format to teach theological and scriptural concepts. Series that depicted scenes from the Passion may have included devotional text or prayers and could inspire compassion in devout viewers as they contemplated Christ's suffering. The ability to tell lengthy stories in series format combined with the accessibility and transportability of prints to make a medium well suited for religious instruction. Noncanonical and apocryphal stories and ideas were also often recorded and retold in religious prints.

The Protestant Reformation in Germany was successful in large part because of advances in print culture. Central changes in religious art at this time include the wider emergence and growth of secular imagery, shifts in portraiture, and the patronage of works. The market for art expands as there are more buyers from the emerging merchant or middle class. Specific theological and cultural issues debated during this period led to major changes in art. Prints were employed to promote political and theological propaganda, both mild and extreme, on all sides of the Protestant Reformation. Portraits of Reformation figures (several of which can be seen in this catalogue) became important not only for the contemporary religious movement but also in the history of the religious print. Images of saints and relics in religious prints declined and shifted from the time of the Reformation due to concerns over misdirected worship of them. But such imagery experienced renewal during the Counter Reformation as proponents revived the imagery of the cult of the saints.[24]

Woodcuts could be printed hundreds or even a thousand times before serious wear on the block appeared. Imagine the enormous influence one woodcut (let alone hundreds) could have on any number of cultural or political issues compared with the former method of creating works on paper by hand. Engravings and etchings could also be printed many times before significant breakdown in the plate, although their multiple potentiality was less than that of a woodblock. Highly portable and distributable, prints circulated the same ideas and images across Europe, encouraging discussion and extending the dissemination of ideas and change in a rapid new way.

Notes

21. Ibid., 244. The "privatization of piety" has long been cited as an originating cause for the emergence of the printed image in Europe. Prayer and worship in a private space, with the aid of such early religious prints, was certainly a significant component to the development of the print; Peter Schmidt, however, argues such devotional practice happened as often in a church as in private spaces and that this thesis of origin for the print is inadequate (Schmidt, 50–51).

22. Antony Griffiths, *Prints and Printmaking: An Introduction to the History and Techniques* (Berkeley: University of California Press, 1996), 16–18.

23. Parshall and Schoch, 62.

24. Schmidt, 47.

Not all prints in the history of the medium have sought to explore new interpretations of subject matter, offer social and moral commentary, or even illustrate texts. Some religious prints were executed, at least in part, to demonstrate technical mastery of the artist and to publicize artistic styles. By the end of the fifteenth century, printmakers were imitating the prints of other artists. The "reproductive" print is not a photomechanical reproduction in the modern sense but rather a type of original print that is replicative because it reproduces or copies another original artwork. The monumental example of Agostino Carracci's *The Crucifixion* (Plate 32) remains a complex model of the reproductive print. Some artists creating a different type of reproductive print sought not to copy an earlier work but instead hoped to emulate or pay homage to one or to its artist. At the end of the sixteenth century, Hendrik Goltzius engraved a series of six prints that he called the *Meesterstukje,* or master engravings, as a tribute to his technical virtuosity and to establish himself as next in a line of great printmakers.[25] *The Circumcision* (Plate 47) from this series shares many iconographic elements with Dürer's version of the same subject and imitates Dürer's composition and handling of the burin.

The Dutch Republic

Many reproductive prints were produced in the Dutch Republic during the seventeenth century. This was also a time of extraordinary innovation and brilliance in nonreproductive religious and secular prints, in particular as seen in the work of Rembrandt van Rijn. The Baroque era in the Netherlands is called the Golden Age: by the seventeenth century, incredible wealth, extraordinary artistic talent, and prosperous commerce were realities in the Dutch Republic. The rising merchant class was altering many aspects of culture and society—and had income to spend on art. Innovations in art included the expanding genre scene and the Dutch landscape tradition, often portrayed with a new defined sense of atmospheric space, realism, and increasing secular imagery, as well as religious imagery with secular components. Rembrandt and his contemporaries made numerous religious works of art; indeed, religious controversy[26] in the Dutch Republic contributed to the creation and popularity of certain kinds of religious subject matter.

Rembrandt filled his works with psychological depth and masterly light and shadow. At the height of his career, he was the most successful artist in Holland. He depicted beggars and street merchants as often as he

FIGURE 11. Rembrandt van Rijn, *The Hundred Guilder Print,* c. 1648. Etching, drypoint, and engraving.

Notes

25. Hults, 125.
26. Shelley Perlove and Larry Silver extensively discuss the religious climate and Rembrandt's involvement in it in *Rembrandt's Faith: Church and Temple in the Dutch Golden Age* (University Park: Pennsylvania State University Press, 2009).

Notes

27. Prior to the Reformation, the Catholic church stressed the equal importance of Scripture and church tradition (encompassing oral tradition, clerical teachings, and noncanonical source material) as the authority for Christians. Martin Luther, with other reformers, emphasized that Scripture alone ought to inform the Christian's life. Scripturally based subject matter certainly becomes more prevalent after the Reformation, but Protestant denominations took different positions on the subtleties of such theology, and the European Counter Reformation also had an enormous effect on the religious image in art.

28. Tim Barringer notes in *Reading the Pre-Raphaelites* (New Haven: Yale University Press, 1999) that in England, despite modern challenges to religion, "the Victorian age remained profoundly Christian... Protestantism was central to English national identity" (109).

did wealthy individuals or the Virgin Mary and Christ. His prints express emotion, action, and humanity in a way that elicits feeling rather than simply looking, and he presents the human and divine so flawlessly that we are left wondering which is which. Rembrandt's influence within the history of art, and specifically in the history of printmaking, is so imposing it can scarcely be articulated. His originality and innovation are astounding, and history will undoubtedly continue to laud his legacy.

Rembrandt created a remarkable number of religious works, many of which were inspired by earlier artists and traditions. He was an extremely experimental etcher who made varied, stunning prints, many of which are examined in this catalogue. His prints illustrate how religious subject matter shifts in this period in northern Europe. Scripturally based subject matter flourishes, likely due to the dominance of Protestant denominations and their adherence to Scripture as the main authority for Christianity.[27] Rembrandt is also responsible for bringing a highly personal quality to the religious print, which would develop further in later centuries. As secular imagery became more prevalent, the potential variety and influence of new interpretations of religious subject matter also expanded. Rembrandt merges divine subjects with everyday secular ones, making the material more accessible and offering fresh interpretations of traditional subjects (see Plate 61, his *Flight into Egypt*). Like artists centuries before him, Rembrandt draws not only on Scripture for his source material but also on noncanonical sources, including Jewish traditions and Scripture and apocryphal Christian texts and traditions. The religious print in the seventeenth century dramatically incorporates secular components, fresh interpretations of traditional subject matter, greater realism, and the resurgence of strong biblical topics. Technical innovation in the medium of etching (including Rembrandt's use of drypoint and etching) forever changes the look and execution of prints. New visual textures and new meaning for private devotion of the religious print for the wealthy merchant class further alter the function of religious prints, and—as we will see

even more in the nineteenth century—the religious print becomes more personal.

Also in the seventeenth century and into the eighteenth, an elegance of line and a lyrical sense of grace are conveyed in many Italian religious prints, beautifully appropriate for conveying many theological themes and seen in the work of Giovanni Benedetto Castiglione (Plate 34), Guido Reni (Plate 36), Bartolomeo Biscaino (Plate 35), and Giovanni Domenico Tiepolo (Plates 39 and 40).

Modern Religious Prints

While it is true that the religious print's popularity wanes in certain areas from the eighteenth century on as a result of the overall secularization of Western culture, strong and expressive examples of nineteenth- and twentieth-century religious works on paper abound. During the modern period, religious prints continue to change in style and function. They reflect avant-garde movements or styles, including a move toward greater abstraction and reduction of form and composition. Technical advances in modern printmaking are substantial and frequent, including the introduction or expansion of lithography, the aquatint, mezzotint, and a revival of etching. Realism continues to progress in art, especially for prints. The advances of photography as well as the Impressionist and Postimpressionist movements further affect the development of modern prints and printmaking. Biblical literalism, along with new translations, influences the interpretation of Scripture. Thematically, religious prints become much more personal, often expressing the artist's own religious beliefs rather than those of the church or overarching theological doctrines. While religion was challenged by the growth of modern science and secularization, numerous religious and spiritual revivals in the modern period contribute to the creation of religious art.[28] War and great social and cultural changes in Western society during the nineteenth and twentieth centuries encouraged some artists to create religious imagery as a response to contemporary problems.

The devotional image holds new meaning in the nineteenth century. The image of the suffering Christ, prevalent in the history of devotional prints, becomes more tangible and nuanced by social issues. Édouard Manet's rare etching and aquatint *Dead Christ with Angels* (Plate 73) with its stark forms and hauntingly realistic depiction of the body of Christ was possibly seen by nineteenth-century viewers to represent "a devotion to a new icon of social justice, the image of the suffering people."[29]

In the nineteenth and twentieth centuries, many religious prints and drawings push the iconographic boundaries further by looking to the past while concurrently introducing stylistic and technical innovation. Many avant-garde movements review the past in pursuing their progressive artistic and social aims. For example, the Pre-Raphaelite Brotherhood, an English artistic and literary movement of the mid-nineteenth century, sought to reawaken the past through inspiration from the classical, medieval, and Renaissance periods. The idea of promoting and eliciting social and philosophical change through the arts was a very appealing concept to many artists and arts circles, and often this was achieved through religious art. The large stained glass window study by Pre-Raphaelite artist Sir Edward Coley Burne-Jones, *St. Matthew* (Figure 12, Plate 74), the *Book of Job* series by William Blake (Plate 67, Figures 56–59), and a later lithograph by Pablo Picasso, *David et Bethsabée* (Plate 89) all draw on this notion of looking to the past in progressiveness.

Another influence on the religious (and nonreligious) modern print was the highly collected Japanese woodblock prints with their thick black lines and asymmetrical compositions, as well as their exoticism in Western culture. James J. Tissot's series *The Prodigal Son in Modern Life* (Figure 13, Plate 76, Figures 60–63) exemplifies aspects of Japonisme. Non-Western, African, and Oceanic arts and culture equally influence modern art through many artists' visits to islands and the collection and study of art objects from distant lands. Referred to as primitivism, and evident in multiple examples of twentieth-century art in this catalogue (see "The Twentieth Century"), truly avant-garde styles pushed formal boundaries of art history and facilitated aspects of expressionism through which artists could convey their own personal religious beliefs.

Around the turn of the twentieth century, politics and the effects of materialism and industrialism elicited new avenues of expression for artists who celebrated and lamented modernity. Many artists found renewal and inspiration in the print medium and its historical ties to handmade craftwork and cultural heritage. Prints were ideal for the expression of emotion and spiritual concepts. Later, the devastation brought on by the World Wars profoundly affected artists who served in battle, lost loved ones, and experienced political upheaval and economic hardship. Modern artists explored ideas of spiritual renewal through religious subject matter and attempted to address their concerns and aspirations. Artists of this period utilized bold color, primitivism, and abstracted forms to create modern impressions of the present and future.

During the early to mid-twentieth century, German expressionist artists and printmakers found stylistic and thematic inspiration from German artists of the fifteenth and sixteenth centuries. Partly nationalistic, partly personal, these artists sought to revitalize the raw graphic strength of the woodcut medium. Emil Nolde's woodcut *Prophet* (1912; Plate 82) is a powerful example: this somber face implores us to reflect on the deep faith of this prophet. Nolde enhances the contemplative mood

FIGURE 12. Sir Edward Coley Burne-Jones, *St. Matthew*, 1873. Black and colored chalks, pencil.

Notes

29. Hults, 550. Critics harshly commented on the cadaver-like Christ in the painting (also by Manet) that this print was made after. Some stated that the image represented the "death of the proletariat" (547–49).

by technical means, exploiting and exposing the wood grain to create a textural viewing experience and a strong reference to the German woodcut tradition.

Faithful Impressions and the Thrivent Financial Collection of Religious Art both demonstrate the vitality of the print series in the history of religious prints. Its multiple

format is ideal for the telling of many scriptural episodes, and the repetitive nature of the series is well suited to the strong devotional aspect of prints. The religious print series continues in decidedly modern form with Max Pechstein's set of twelve large-scale woodcuts, *Das Vater Unser* (*The Lord's Prayer,* 1921; Plate 81, Figures 5 and 65–67). On the title page of the series (Figure 65*)*, three men sit humbly in prayer, forming a traditional triangular composition—yet this is the only traditional art historical element about this strongly graphic series, with its thick black lines, primitivist influences, and judicious use of bold color. This powerful series can be thought of as a modern version of the small medieval devotional prayerbook that incorporated images and text. Pechstein's series reflects many modern and progressive characteristics: the large size of the woodcuts allows full visual immersion, and the centrality and style of the text is reminiscent of contemporary advertising posters and avant-garde Cubist collage. The poster size format of this series is

a brilliant reinvention of a traditional religious and artistic devotional experience. Pechstein was a devout Christian, and the crucial role of his faith in his life is evident in *Das Vater Unser.*

The connoisseurship, or discerning appreciation, of works on paper has been a vital aspect of their study for centuries. Thanks to the efforts of print and drawing collectors of the past we have many examples of catalogues raisonnés and scholarly references on aspects of print study such as paper watermarks, collector's marks and accompanying biographies, and notes on the quality and record of various prints' impressions, states, and editions. Each of these elements assists in determining the attribution, art historical significance, and meaning of such works. A distinguished collector may be a scholar of a particular artist or style and may aid in determining the artist or quality of a print or drawing. The collecting by historical and present-day connoisseurs also influences the study and cultural perception of the artworks. Those who appreciate and collect prints and drawings (i.e., individual collectors, dealers, art institutions, private collections) help scholars learn more about them as they also preserve these precious examples of art history. The discerning eye and careful care of the passionate collector or art collection is invaluable to the preservation and study of works on paper. This essay has focused on the religious print, but it must be noted that many original drawings are in the collection as well. Drawings are discussed in each section of the catalogue. Drawings are crucial in the artist's creative process, commonly functioning as studies to aid in composing another artwork, including prints, and share a close relationship with printmaking in the graphic arts.

The pieces of paper featured in this book have been steadfastly held, studied, and prayed on as much as they have been admired and cherished as collectable objects and works of art. Each work on its own expresses aspects of the complex history of the religious image on paper; together, these works, nuanced with the beliefs and traditions of those who created, commissioned, and viewed them, form a collective lineage of the transformations and endurance of the religious image in the West.

Notes to the Reader on the Plates

Faithful Impressions features a selection of prints, drawings, and paintings that highlight the range and breadth of the Thrivent Financial Collection of Religious Art. This representative set of works has been organized into seven sections according to media, geographic region, and time period. Within each section, catalogue entries are generally presented in chronological order. Multiple artworks by an artist are grouped together, and occasionally entries are ordered with consideration to artistic style or school rather than by date.

— At the beginning of each entry, the artist's name, nationality, and lifespan are listed with the artwork's title, date, and media. Dimensions are given height before width, in inches and millimeters. Unless otherwise noted, the dimensions refer to the image size. Whenever possible, works have been reproduced at actual size and are noted as such in the captions.

— Accession numbers appear after the dimensions at the beginning of entries. These numbers start with two digits that represent the year of acquisition, followed by a dash and a numeral indicating the serial order in which the artwork was acquired that year. When a print series has been assigned a common accession number, a point and an additional numeral distinguish individual images within the series.

— When available, identifying numbers are listed from the standard references of an artist's work. Full citations for these reference books and catalogues raisonnés are in the bibliography. Notes at the end of entries also document sources pertaining to the artist or the artwork, and these are also included in the bibliography.

— Watermarks and artists' signatures are noted and described when present. Signatures "in the plate" of a print are not listed.

— When known, provenance and notable exhibition history are detailed at the end of the entries. Lugt numbers and collector's marks, which help determine and record provenance, are listed whenever possible.

— In theological discussions, gendered nouns and pronouns are eschewed in favor of inclusive language for God and humankind.

— Common terms used in the study of prints and drawings are defined in a glossary on page 210.

Secundum lucam.

N illo tempore.
Missus est ange
lus gabriel a deo
in civitatem galilee cui nomen

Miniatures & Early Prints
before 1500

Flemish (Bruges?) Master of the Gold Scrolls, *St. Luke Writing His Gospel* (details; see Plate 4).

PLATE 1. Italian Master,
*St. Helena with the True
Cross,* c. 1290. Gouache
and ink on vellum
(actual size).

Helena, Empress of the Roman Empire, hands the True Cross to her son Constantine, the Emperor. She places in his hands the most vital Christian relic: the cross on which Christ was crucified and the object on which Christians believe humanity was saved through the death and resurrection of Christ. Some scholars believe that Helena was primarily responsible for instilling Christian beliefs in her son, who was renowned for establishing Christianity as the dominant religion of the Roman Empire around 312 C.E., emphasizing the significance of this act of passing the cross. Helena stands on the right in an orange-red gown across from her son in gray-blue, both figures against a deeper blue ground and surrounded by decorative leaf motifs. The delicate decorative forms scattered throughout the miniature are characteristic patterning or ornamentation in works of this period.

St. Helena with the True Cross is the earliest work in the Thrivent Financial Collection of Religious Art. Before the advent of printed woodblock images in Europe around 1425 and the invention of the printing press around 1453, hand-drawn and painted miniatures and illuminated manuscripts were the popular artform on paper for religious and secular subjects. Painstakingly hand-painted miniatures from the medieval and early modern periods ranged in quality and function, but the finest were embellished with gold or silver, painted with rare and expensive pigments, and commissioned by wealthy members of society, including clergy. Such works often illustrated religious and musical texts, as well as small and large-format devotional books.

This miniature is a large initial N cut from a manuscript choirbook on vellum. This choirbook (c. 1290) would have been rather large and was most likely used by clergy during religious services. This miniature likely "illustrated the introit 'Nos autem gloriari' sung at the Mass both on the feast of the Finding of the Cross (May 3) and on the feast of the Exaltation of the Cross (September 14)."[1] The verso of the miniature shows part of three lines of text in a rounded Gothic hand and music on a four-line stave. An inscription on the verso appears to read "Bologna." This relatively small miniature is an example of the common church-centered religious imagery of the medieval period that was from a large work (the choirbook) and restricted in use and view to clergy or the elite.

Tradition tells us that in her search for the True Cross Empress Helena ordered the destruction of a temple of Venus that had been erected on a hill on the site of Christ's tomb near Calvary. The diggers found three crosses, which all believed to be the crucifixion crosses of Christ and the two thieves. Either Helena or Macarius, the Bishop of Jerusalem, brought a sick woman to touch each of the three crosses, and the one that cured her was declared by Helena to be the True Cross. Helena left part of the cross under the protection of the Bishop of Jerusalem, and in 327 C.E. brought part of the cross back to Rome to join other religious relics at her palace, which eventually became the church of Santa Croce in Gerusalemne (Basilica of the Holy Cross in Jerusalem).[2]

The story of the True Cross was retold in detail by Jacobus de Voragine in his *Legenda Aurea* or *The Golden Legend*, published in 1260. This extraordinarily popular medieval sourcebook was a compilation of centuries of writings as well as church and oral tradition; it was republished and translated many times and was a crucial source for artists, clergy, and scholars. *The Golden Legend* and other sources encouraged the profusion of saint imagery in various forms of artistic media and fostered the tremendous popularity of the Cult of the Saints, the widespread devotional and cultural practices of reverence to saints in medieval Europe. Saint imagery could be devotional, meditative, and instructive. Theologically, saints have served as intercessors between God and humanity, and they have long been a popular subject in art, fulfilling essential roles in both art and religious life.

■ JRL

PLATE I

Italian Master, late thirteenth century

St. Helena with the True Cross

c. 1290
Gouache and ink on vellum
6¹¹⁄₁₆ × 6⅜ inches
170 × 157 mm
03-01

Notes

1. R. S. Johnson, dealer information.
2. Jacobus de Voragine, *The Golden Legend: Readings on the Saints*, trans. William Granger Ryan (Princeton: Princeton University Press, 1993), 1: 277.

PLATE 2

Lucca Illuminator or
attributed to Martino
di Bartolomeo,
Tuscany, late
fourteenth century

*St. John the Baptist
Preaching*

Late fourteenth century
Illuminated manuscript
Gouache, ink, gilding
on vellum
7¹⁵⁄₁₆ × 6⅝ inches
202 × 173 mm
95-10

St. John the Baptist is known as the precursor to Christ: his actions preceded and mirrored those of Jesus of Nazareth. He was miraculously born of Elizabeth, a cousin to the Virgin Mary; she was already at an advanced age, and his birth was foretold to his father, Zechariah, a temple priest, by the angel Gabriel (Luke 1:5–24). John the Baptist is best known for his mission of baptizing and preaching along the river Jordan (c. 27 C.E.); he baptized Jesus of Nazareth and many others, and he urged his followers to repent and prepare for the coming of the Messiah (Luke 3:1–22). The solitary life and preaching style that John the Baptist practiced, as well as his diet of wild honey and locusts, suggested a likeness to Old Testament prophets.[1]

Because of these biblical references, St. John the Baptist is commonly depicted in the context of baptism or preaching. Medieval monastic orders readily identified with him and his ascetic life, which may have influenced his frequent appearance as a subject of religious art during the medieval period, since many medieval miniatures and illuminations were created in monasteries. Paintings, stained glass windows, church benches, and sculpture also featured John the Baptist, especially with his traditional attributes of a long cross and animal skins.

In this illumination, vibrantly colored leafy motifs in orange, deep lapis blue, and pink curl and decorate a large initial F. Inside the letter St. John the Baptist stands in three-quarter length, facing the viewer with one raised hand and finger pointed toward heaven and the other hand grasping a tall cross. A highly burnished gold ground balances the deep lapis blue pigment. Delicate white lines accent acanthus leaf shapes and the drapery in John's clothing; his elaborately detailed hair, beard, and clothing evince a sophisticated presentation of form and depth. The illuminator dresses John the Baptist in an apparent undergarment or layer of gray-toned skin, covered by a pink and olive swathe of fabric as the overgarment. The curious dressing of John the Baptist in such skin was popular in the fourteenth and fifteenth centuries and may have been related to medieval drama or a scriptural interpretation of the Gospel that stated he wore the skin of a camel.[2]

The initial is historiated, meaning it is a letter that also includes an identifiable figure or scene. On the verso, part of three lines of text and two lines of music can be seen. The letter is on vellum, specially prepared animal skins (goat, sheep, or calf) used in the same way as paper for writing manuscripts and documents as well as serving as the support for illuminations and miniatures. The time-consuming production of vellum and parchment restricted their use compared to the later, more easily available format of paper. Parchment was the predominant writing material in Europe from the fourth to the sixteenth centuries, at which time the printing press and continued growth of paper mills supplanted its widespread use.

This illumination is part of a group cut from the choirbooks of the Charterhouse in Lucca, Italy, presumably from the Carthusian Abbey of Santo Spirito. This cutting has historically been attributed to Martino di Bartolomeo from Siena, who was active around 1390.[3] The initial was likely from an antiphonary, a large book that contained the sung portions of the Divine Office and was often used by a choir, while hymns were in a separate volume: the antiphonaries included decorated or historiated initials that depicted saints and key events of the liturgical year.[4]

Three additional cuttings from the same manuscript are in the Bernard H. Breslauer Collection of Manuscript Illuminations. The exceptionally long fingers of John the Baptist

---

Provenance

James Dennistoun
(1803–1855), bought
in Lucca in 1838; Mrs.
Herbert Henley-Henson,
granddaughter to
Dennistoun and wife to
the Bishop of Durham,
Auckland Castle; Kenneth
Clark, Lord Clark of
Saltwood, O.M. (1903–
1983), bought c. 1930,
sold at Sotheby's, July 3,
1984, lot 93(4).

Notes

1. David Hugh Farmer, *Oxford Dictionary of Saints* (Oxford: Oxford University Press, 2004), 277.
2. Ibid., 278.
3. William M. Voelkle, Roger S. Wieck, and Maria Francesca P. Saffiotti, *The Bernard H. Breslauer Collection of Manuscript Illuminations* (New York: Pierpont Morgan Library, 1992), 181. In 2009 Sandra Hindman visited the Thrivent Financial collection and viewed *St. John the Baptist Preaching* and stated that the Martino di Bartolomeo attribution for this grouping of cuttings is no longer accepted by some scholars who instead favor the attribution of "Lucca Illuminator." The attribution notwithstanding, this cutting, along with other decorations of initial letters and friezes from the Lucca Charterhouse choirbooks, clearly draws inspiration from the Cathedral choirbooks contemporaneously worked on in Lucca by Martino di Bartolomeo.
4. Michelle P. Brown, *Understanding Illuminated Manuscripts: A Guide to Technical Terms* (Los Angeles: J. Paul Getty Museum, 1994), 11.
5. Voelkle et al., 181.

suggest a stylistic closeness with *Man Receiving Communion*, illustrated in the Breslauer catalogue; the repetition of the smallest illuminated circles is also visible in both cuttings. The two other referenced cuttings from this manuscript lack the very long digits. With such manuscripts, it is common for pages and miniatures to be created by different illuminators.

These works also share the same provenance. The group of cuttings was in the collection of the Scottish antiquary James Dennistoun, "an early connoisseur of Italian primitives" and collector of cuttings from illuminated manuscripts.[5] Later these manuscript cuttings belonged to the art historian Kenneth Clark. ■ JRL

PLATE 2. Lucca Illuminator or attributed to Martino di Bartolomeo, *St. John the Baptist Preaching,* late fourteenth century. Gouache, ink, gilding on vellum (actual size).

PLATE 3

South German Master, fifteenth century

Moses in Conversation with Warriors

c. 1470

Pen and ink with tan, blue, red, green, and light brown wash

3¹¹⁄₁₅ × 5¾ inches
100 × 147 mm

95-16

Watermark: Tour (Tower; close to Briquet 15869–15875)

Notes

1. William M. Voelkle, Roger S. Wieck, and Maria Francesca P. Saffiotti, *The Bernard H. Breslauer Collection of Manuscript Illuminations* (New York: Pierpont Morgan Library, 1992), catalogue number 40.

2. Ibid.

Moses stands among twelve men who are armed with swords and other weapons. He wears the iconic dress of a biblical prophet, and his long robe and red cloak contrast with the fifteenth-century clothes and armor of the men around him. The scene is probably intended to illustrate a passage from the book of Exodus; however, because the drawing has been cut from its original context within a handwritten manuscript, it is difficult to be sure which one. Exodus 12:3, in which Moses instructs the Hebrew people to prepare for the last of God's plagues on Egypt and to flee into the wilderness, is inscribed in German calligraphy on the verso, or back, of the paper, but whether this scene appeared in the book before or after the verso text is unknown. The men with Moses may represent the leaders of the twelve houses of Israel, which could explain the variety of attire. That most of them are armed may also allude to a later verse, Exodus 13:18: "The Israelites went up out of the land of Egypt prepared for battle."

The attribution of this work to a German artist is based on the German script and on the drawing's stylistic resemblance to other illustrated religious texts from the same period. Very similar New Testament illustrations in other collections have been linked to a German lectionary written in a Swabian dialect.[1] *Moses in Conversation with Warriors* may be a sister leaf to these other miniatures as it is not uncommon for Old Testament readings to be included in a lectionary. It seems equally plausible that these miniatures were painted in a workshop that produced more than one religious book. Not all of these illustrations are by the same artist, even though they are sketched and colored with the same technique.

Unlike the other miniatures in the Thrivent Financial Collection of Religious Art, *Moses in Conversation with Warriors* is painted on paper rather than vellum. Manuscripts on paper became possible in Europe with the establishment of paper mills in the fourteenth century and grew in popularity during the fifteenth century. Because paper cannot easily support the heavy pigments that were painted on vellum, ink and watercolor were used on this paper instead. This artist brushed the colored washes so that areas of blank paper would create the effect of light and enhance the sense of three-dimensional shapes.[2]

A watermark of a tower indicates that the paper was probably made in Germany between approximately 1442 and 1471, so the illustration was painted sometime after 1442. Several elements within the image corroborate that the painting was likely created in the second half of the fifteenth century. The full armor on the man to the left of Moses is typical of the gothic style worn in this period, especially the helmet, a *sallet*, identified by the extension of metal over the nape of the neck. Foot armor, or *sabatons*, was usually pointed during the latter half of the 1400s, and the shape of the blade on the large halberd (the second battle axe from the right) is also consistent with the late fifteenth century.

Although the artist's name, the location of his workshop, and the date of the drawing are uncertain today, *Moses in Conversation with Warriors* remains an intriguing handmade example from a time when books were increasingly printed with moveable type and illustrated with woodcuts. Curiously, this work has also been taken from a Bible or liturgy written in the vernacular German language, instead of the more common Latin.

■ JRW

PLATE 3. South German
Master, *Moses in
Conversation with Warriors*,
c. 1470. Pen and ink
with tan, blue, red, green,
and light brown wash
(actual size).

PLATE 4

Flemish (Bruges?)
Master of the Gold
Scrolls, fifteenth
century

*St. Luke Writing
His Gospel*

Mid-fifteenth century[1]
Illuminated manuscript
Ink and gold on vellum
7⁷⁄₁₆ × 5⁵⁄₁₆ inches
189 × 135 mm
92-29

Provenance

Paul Graupe, Berlin; Kurt
Arnhold, Dresden, 1928.

Notes

1. In 1992, at the time of
   acquisition, art dealer
   R. S. Johnson dated this
   work c. 1430–50; in
   2009, during a visit to
   the collection, Sandra
   Hindman dated it
   c. 1450–75.
2. David Hugh Farmer,
   *Oxford Dictionary of
   Saints* (Oxford: Oxford
   University Press, 2004),
   329.
3. Michelle P. Brown,
   *Understanding
   Illuminated Manuscripts:
   A Guide to Technical
   Terms* (Los Angeles: J.
   Paul Getty Museum,
   1994), 23–24.
4. Ibid., 24.
5. Jules Lubbock,
   *Storytelling in Christian
   Art from Giotto to
   Donatello* (New Haven:
   Yale University Press,
   2006), 10.

St. Luke diligently writes his Gospel at a special desk with metal rods in the scriptorium. A small winged ox lies next to him; the ox is a traditional attribute for Luke, perhaps because of the mention of a sacrifice in the temple at the beginning of his Gospel.[2] Latin text, possibly from Luke's writings, flows from the mouth of the ox and reads "Santus Lucas." The patterned floor, vaulted ceiling, and shadowed pitcher on the table create a simple form of perspective and depth of space for this enclosed room. Though a storm rages outside the small window, the space seems brightened by Luke's illuminated halo. This miniature is a page that illustrated the Gospel sequence of St. Luke in a Book of Hours; it appears to be the first chapter of Luke, verse 26. This sheet includes a full decorated border that is characteristically Flemish in style: blues, greens, browns, and peaches color various floral motifs accented with burnished gold. Additional text appears on the verso.

The Book of Hours was used by individuals for private devotions. Such books contained the Little Office of the Blessed Virgin as their central text, along with other devotional or church texts such as a liturgical calendar and litany of the saints.[3] Books of Hours were very popular in Europe in the medieval and early modern periods, varying in quality depending on the budget of the patron. They commonly featured illuminated miniatures that illustrated the different texts; the saints, the Virgin, and Christ were frequently depicted.[4] This Book of Hours that included *St. Luke Writing His Gospel* was done in the style of the Master of the Gold Scrolls.

St. Luke is one of the four Evangelists

PLATE 4. Flemish (Bruges?) Master of the Gold Scrolls, *St. Luke Writing His Gospel,* mid-fifteenth century. Ink and gold on vellum.

who lived in the first century. He wrote two canonical books, the Acts of the Apostles and the Gospel of Luke. He was a Greek physician and a disciple of St. Paul. Luke is revered for his literary contribution; his Gospel emphasizes the compassion of Christ and includes the well-known parables of the Good Samaritan and the Prodigal Son.

St. Luke holds particular significance in the history of art because since the medieval period he has been considered the patron saint of painters. As early as the fifth century people believed that St. Luke painted a portrait of the Virgin Mary in person.[5] This act not only provided subject matter for religious art but has been used as a justification for the artistic tradition in the Christian faith. The creation of religious art has been challenged at times in Western religious history, and the tradition of St. Luke's artistic activities exemplifies the value and importance of art in the Christian tradition.
■ JRL

Martin Schongauer is generally considered the most skilled and influential engraver of the late fifteenth century. He is the first of the earliest engravers for whom historians have been able to establish at least a partial biography. Born around 1450 in Colmar, Germany, he began a classical education at the University of Leipzig in 1465, but he left his studies soon after to pursue artistic interests. During his lifetime Schongauer was known primarily for his panel paintings and frescoes, very few of which are extant. But today impressions of 116 of his engravings have survived, evincing his importance to the development of intaglio printmaking in northern Europe.

Schongauer brought to the copperplate a painter's sense of composition and form, and he adapted his burin technique to better mimic natural shapes. Rather than adhering to a rigid pattern of parallel lines and cross hatches, he subtly modeled his lines to describe the texture of the object, attaining with the burin a natural spontaneity traditionally achieved with pen and ink.[1] *Ecce Homo* reflects this mature engraving style. Notice, for example, the way in which he has modeled the dog snarling by the steps with stippling and a variety of fluid, serpentine lines that belie both the texture of the fur and the animal's underlying musculature.

Taken from the description of Pilate's trial of Christ in John 19:2–8, Schongauer's *Ecce Homo* is one of twelve scenes from a series illustrating Christ's Passion. With the Latin words "ecce homo," commonly translated "behold the man," Pilate presents Christ in a robe and wearing a crown of thorns to an angry crowd shouting for his crucifixion. Pilate was both fearful of the mob and uncertain of Christ's guilt. In the engraving Pilate lingers in the doorway behind Christ, metaphorically standing on the threshold as he questions the throng to which he will soon surrender an innocent man.

In the right foreground, the prominent figure with a rope over his shoulder informs the viewer what will happen next in the story. This man, who appears in several scenes from the series, is always a catalyst of the action, leading Christ toward his crucifixion. He wears a short doublet with no hose or pants, a vulgar way for a man to dress in the fifteenth century; the frill on his hem and sleeves is a sign of frivolousness and low morals. A fifteenth-century viewer of *Ecce Homo* would identify this man as a villain, even before noticing the hammer in his right hand, which suggests that he will be the one who later nails Christ to the cross.

■ JRW

PLATE 5

Martin Schongauer, German, c. 1450–1491

Ecce Homo

c. 1480

Engraving

6⁵⁄₁₆ × 4⁷⁄₁₆ inches
160 × 112 mm

96-14

Hollstein 25

Note

1. David Landau and Peter W. Parshall, *The Renaissance Print, 1470–1550* (New Haven: Yale University Press, 1994), 50–51.

PLATE 5. Martin Schongauer, *Ecce Homo,* c. 1480. Engraving (actual size).

PLATE 6. Martin
Schongauer, *Christ in
Limbo,* c. 1480.
Engraving (actual size).

PLATE 6

Martin Schongauer, German, c. 1450–1491

Christ in Limbo

c. 1480

Engraving

6⅞₆ × 4⅜₆ inches
163 × 115 mm

99-30

Hollstein 29

Watermark: Bull's head with St. Anthony cross (Briquet 15227)

Like *Ecce Homo* (Plate 5), Martin Schongauer's *Christ in Limbo* is in his Passion series. This scene, which occurs between Christ's crucifixion and his resurrection, originates in popular legends rather than in the Bible. Schongauer's composition is loosely based on a telling of the story in the apocryphal Gospel of Nicodemus, which is retold by Jacobus de Voragine in *The Golden Legend*. According to this latter text, after Christ died he descended toward the dark underworld in a blaze of "gold and royal purple sunlight." Biblical figures suffering in purgatory proclaim Christ's glory, while Satan and his demons tremble in fear. Lacking color, Schongauer's engraving simply yet effectively represents the brilliance of Christ with only a crossbeam halo and a victory banner in a field of white space.

As related in *The Golden Legend*, Christ reaches out to Adam, who is kneeling at the front of the crowd, and takes his right hand to lead him to paradise. Next to Adam kneels Eve, who is not mentioned in the legend. Schongauer has put the forbidden fruit, complete with bite marks, in her hand, perhaps to help identify the figure of Adam and remind the viewer of the original fall of humankind that God promised would be forgiven through Christ. On Eve's left, wearing an animal hide, is John the Baptist, who heralds Christ's arrival in limbo in the story by remembering the day he baptized Christ and declaring, "Behold the Lamb of God!"[1]

Because of their mobility, Schongauer's prints were more accessible to other artists than his paintings were. His motifs were recognized and studied throughout Europe by artists across disciplines and media. His unique representation of devils and beasts also had a notable influence on later printmakers. The grotesque demons featured in *Christ in Limbo* inspired similar monsters in Jacques Callot's *Temptations of St. Anthony* (Figure 14) and Albrecht Dürer's own scenes of *Christ in Limbo*.
■ JRW

Note

1. Jacobus de Voragine, *The Golden Legend: Readings on the Saints,* trans. William Granger Ryan (Princeton: Princeton University Press, 1993), 223.

FIGURE 14. Jacques Callot, *Temptations of St. Anthony* (full image and detail), 1635. Etching.

PLATE 7

Israhel van Meckenem, German, 1445–1503

The Beheading of John the Baptist

c. 1480

Engraving

8⅜ × 6⅛ inches

213 × 155 mm

99-17

Hollstein 366

Notes

1. National Gallery of Art, Alan Shestack, and Lessing J. Rosenwald, *Fifteenth-Century Engravings of Northern Europe from the National Gallery of Art* (Washington, D.C.: National Gallery of Art, 1967), n.p.
2. Nanette B. Rodney, "Salome," *The Metropolitan Museum of Art Bulletin,* New Series, 11, no. 7 (March 1953): 190.
3. The daughter of Herodias is not named in canonical Scripture; however, the name Salome is used in apocryphal texts.
4. James Laver, *Costume and Fashion: A Concise History* (New York: Thames and Hudson, 2006), 68–70.
5. Ibid., 72.

Israhel van Meckenem was the most productive printmaker of the fifteenth century, with more than six hundred prints attributed to him. Yet less than one-fourth of these compositions are his invention. Many are copies of prints created by several of his contemporaries, including Martin Schongauer and the younger artist Albrecht Dürer. Meckenem also acquired and retooled the worn plates of other engravers, primarily those of the Master E.S., giving him the opportunity to expand his workshop into a lucrative publishing enterprise. City records suggest that Meckenem lived and worked most of his life in Bocholt, Germany, where he was also a prosperous goldsmith.[1]

The Beheading of John the Baptist is one of Meckenem's original works, and the composition alludes to Meckenem's background as a goldsmith as well as to the origins of engraved prints among the decorative arts. He has incorporated architectural tracery to frame two episodes from the story, in much the same way that niches in Gothic architecture, altarpieces, or reliquaries were filled with religious narratives. In Meckenem's print, the central column and arches simultaneously appear both a part of Herod's palace and outside the picture plane. The beheading of John the Baptist (Matthew 14:1–12 and Mark 6:17–29) was a popular medieval narrative.[2] The themes of intrigue and violence, played out through a dramatic chain of events, fostered an ideal subject for serial representation.

The biblical story begins with Herod's imprisonment of John the Baptist for declaring that it was against the law for Herod to marry Herodias, the wife of his brother, Philip, while his brother was alive.

At a banquet in honor of Herod's birthday, the daughter of Herodias, Salome, dances for Herod and his guests.[3] Pleased, Herod promises his stepdaughter anything she wants, and at Herodias's bidding Salome asks for the head of John the Baptist on a platter—a request that Herod is bound to honor. Meckenem chose to depict two episodes from the story, and Salome appears in both. On the left, she holds out the platter to receive John's severed head, a dramatic embellishment not included in the Bible. On the right, Salome presents the head to Herod and her adulterous mother in the banquet hall where musicians blow horns and dogs enjoy table scraps.

Meckenem has effectively set Herod's festival in a medieval European royal court. The costumes, which appear outlandish to a modern eye, are derived from aristocratic fashions of the fifteenth century. The delightful collection of hats, shoes, sleeves, and dresses reads like a costume book popular during this period. The extremely long sleeves, short doublets, and tight hose on the musicians in the right foreground became the mode in the second half of the 1400s.[4] Each musician's doublet has a different style of sleeve; so excessive is the material on the right musician's sleeves that they must be knotted behind his back to keep from dragging on the floor. The long pointed shoes, called *poulaines,* were also fashionable in the fifteenth century.[5] A sign of lavishness, *poulaines* were subject to sumptuary laws, which attempted to regulate acceptable displays of extravagance by social class or profession. Even longer are the peculiar double-pointed slippers that peek out from Salome's dress in both scenes.

■ JRW

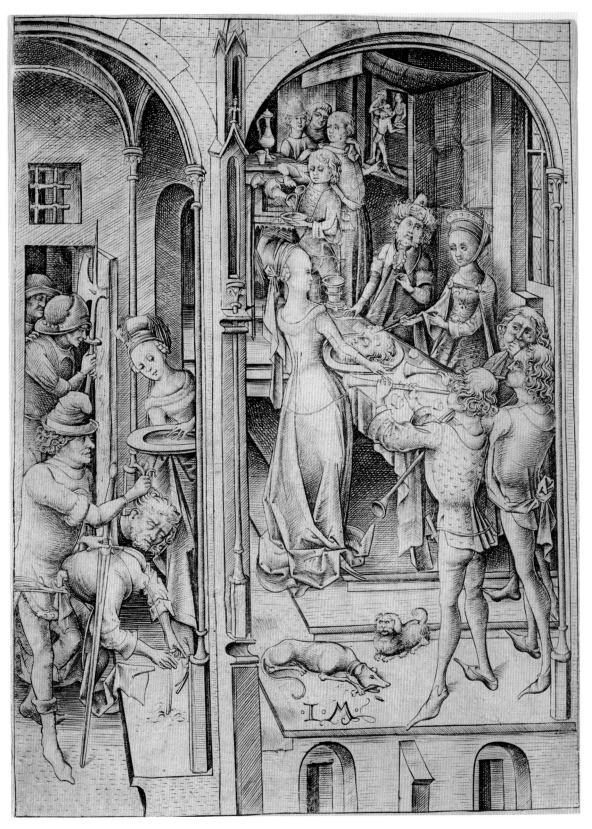

PLATE 7. Israhel van
Meckenem, *The Beheading
of John the Baptist,* c. 1480.
Engraving (actual size).

ALBRECHT DÜRER

PLATE 8

**Albrecht Dürer,
German, 1471–1528**

*The Four Horsemen
of the Apocalypse,*
from the
Apocalypse series

1498 (1511 edition)

Woodcut

15½ × 11 inches
394 × 277 mm

83-16

Bartsch 61–75,
Meder 164–178

Watermarks: Tower
and crown, flower with
triangle

Albrecht Dürer's revolutionary set of prints depicting the Revelations of St. John the Divine represents one of the most influential and innovative contributions to the history of printmaking. The full-page format of these impressive woodcuts was groundbreaking when first published in 1498, and *The Apocalypse* was the first book in the West to be both illustrated and published by a recognized, major artist.[1] By this time, Dürer was established as a master and had begun to cultivate a strong reputation throughout Europe. The extraordinary level of quality of the illustrations and the printing also makes this series truly remarkable in the history of Western art.

The impetus for creating a series on the Apocalypse was likely influenced in part by cultural fervor over the imminent half-millennium.[2] Depictions of the Apocalypse were not a new subject for printmakers and artists. Dürer's godfather, Anton Koberger, was a very successful printer in Nuremberg who also probably printed this series; he had printed a bible in 1483 from which Dürer found inspiration for motifs, ideas, and typeface.[3] Illustrated publications prior to *The Apocalypse* contained pages that included both type and illustrations on the same page, but Dürer's *Apocalypse* featured large, full-page illustrations. Several editions and single sheets were printed of this popular series. The series included fifteen woodcuts, with a new frontispiece added for the 1511 edition. The first edition, quite rare today, was printed with German text in 1498. Latin text editions were printed in 1498 and again in 1511. The 1511 edition was published and sometimes bound with Dürer's 1511 editions of his *Life of the Virgin* and *Large Passion* series.

The *Apocalypse* prints were regarded by Dürer and his contemporaries as monumental in technical skill and historical scope. With this series Dürer began to radically shift artistic and cultural perceptions of the woodcut and the print, emphasizing that each was an independent medium capable of the quality and level of skill inherent to engravings and even panel paintings. By boldly cutting his monogram on each block, Dürer forcefully announced his artistic identity and proudly claimed the work as his own.[4] Until this time, woodcuts were regarded and produced more or less anonymously and with far less sophistication, considered in the arena of craftsmanship rather than individual artistic production. Woodcuts were historically produced with the involvement of several people: a designer/artist, a cutter, a printer, and finally a publisher. Dürer identifies himself as the publisher of this series in the colophon, and many scholars believe he also cut the blocks.[5] Thus, Dürer firmly declared full responsibility for the creation of this superb series, leaving little doubt as to how he begins to build an immense legacy in the history of Western art.

The Four Horsemen of the Apocalypse is the most famous of the woodcuts from this series, and it has become one of the most important and recognizable prints in the history of the medium. Technically, Dürer created a stunning interplay of horizontal lines with contrasting diagonals. The scene is simultaneously visually compact and comprehensive, suggesting the universality and power in such an image and story. In St. John's Revelation, a lamb with seven eyes and seven horns opens seven seals of a scroll it has taken from Christ.

Provenance

Gottfried Eissler (1862–1924); Hennes Meyer. Each impression in this set has a hand-notated consecutive number in brown ink on the lower right margin, indicating the coherence of this set from an earlier period.

Notes

1. Giulia Bartrum, *Albrecht Dürer and His Legacy: The Graphic Work of a Renaissance Artist* (Princeton: Princeton University Press, 2002), 124.
2. Ibid., 125.
3. Ibid.
4. Christiane Andersson and Charles W. Talbot, *From a Mighty Fortress: Prints, Drawings, and Books in the Age of Luther, 1483–1546* (Detroit: Detroit Institute of Arts, 1983), 240.
5. Ibid.

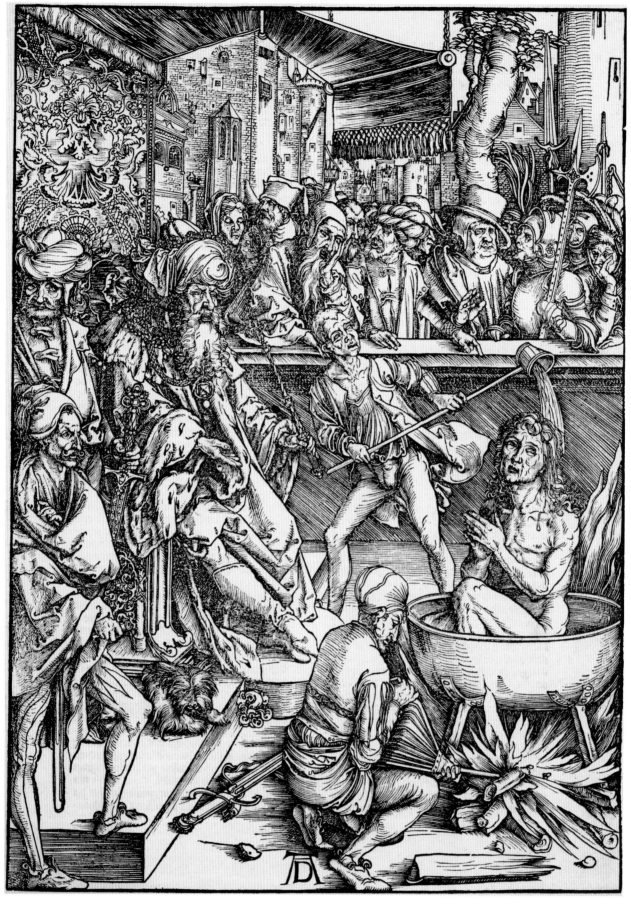

FIGURE 15. Albrecht Dürer,
*Martyrdom of
St. John the Evangelist,*
1498 (1511 edition).
Woodcut.

With the opening of each seal, a horse and rider of terrible consequence—and symbolic destruction of humanity—appear. This woodcut shows a dramatic moment in the story: the first crowned horseman, holding a bow and arrow on the far right, represents the "Conqueror"; next to him with a raised sword is "War"; the central figure trailing behind him holding the scales of justice is "Famine"; and finally the bottom figure on the pale, sick horse is "Death" (Revelation 6:1–8).[6] Bodies are trampled under the thundering horses' hooves, which compositionally overlap and build upward into the scene, conveying the powerful force of movement intended. Dürer succeeds in creating a harrowing and impressive visual companion for this moment in the story.

The woodcuts in this series illustrate dramatic chapters in the Book of Revelation. *Martyrdom of St. John the Evangelist* (Figure 15) shows the attempted torture and religious persecution of John in a boiling cauldron of oil (he escapes unscathed). This print displays astounding technical intricacy for the woodblock matrix, resulting in a marvelous interplay of patterning, texture, and depth. The process of engraving with a burin more easily produces thinner, undulating, and expressive lines; when cutting a woodblock, the ability to taper each line with a knife to create the sophisticated lines found in this series is held only by a master cutter.[7] Dürer successfully achieves this technique, while maintaining astounding energy and malleability of line and form in each of the active, dramatic prints. These images appear alive and complex far beyond the solid nature of the woodblock matrix and antecedents' work.

■ JRL

Above: FIGURE 16. Albrecht Dürer, *St. Michael Fighting the Dragon*, 1498 (1511 edition). Woodcut.

Below: FIGURE 17. Albrecht Dürer, *The Sea Monster and the Beast with the Lamb's Horns*, 1498 (1511 edition). Woodcut.

Notes

6. Bartrum, 31.
7. Andersson and Talbot, 240.

PLATE 9

**Albrecht Dürer,
German, 1471–1528**

St. Eustace

c. 1501

Engraving

13⅞ × 10³⁄₁₆ inches
352 × 259 mm

94-19

Bartsch 57, Meder 60,
Hollstein 60

Watermark: High crown

Notes

1. Dagmar Eichberger, "Dürer's Nature Drawings and Early Collecting," in *Dürer and His Culture,* ed. Dagmar Eichberger and Charles Zika (Cambridge: Cambridge University Press, 1998), 27.
2. Giulia Bartrum, *Albrecht Dürer and His Legacy: The Graphic Work of a Renaissance Artist* (Princeton: Princeton University Press, 2002), 142.
3. David Hugh Farmer, *Oxford Dictionary of Saints* (Oxford: Oxford University Press, 2004), 187.

Intricacy and attention to the tiniest details are endemic to Albrecht Dürer's skillful engravings, and *St. Eustace,* the largest that he executed, exemplifies these qualities. Nearly every centimeter is meticulously filled. From the expanse of the landscape, to the city in the upper left, and the various plants and animals inhabiting the space, we still find the reverent Eustace and the powerful stag in the scene. This engraving forces the viewer to look carefully and seek the crucifix and the saint amid such abundant detail, characteristic of northern Renaissance art.

For Dürer, who rigorously studied nature, such a religious theme gave him opportunity to demonstrate the close connection he saw between truth and nature, as well as his thoughtful, and almost scientific, rendering of God's creatures. Dürer believed the practice of accurately depicting nature was vital for artists, nature being God's perfect creation and inspiration: "life in nature manifests the truth in these things…therefore observe it diligently, go by it and do not depart from nature arbitrarily, imagining to find the better by thyself, for thou wouldst be misled."[1] Many extant drawings and studies by Dürer of animals and plants show how sensitively and seriously he studied nature. A superb study for this engraving's dogs exists in Windsor Castle, The Royal Library collection, titled *A Greyhound.*[2]

The initial visual cues in this engraving draw the viewer's eye to the animals in the foreground (the beautiful dogs and horse) before we seek the man and his vision of the Crucifixion between the stag's antlers. This scene is a revelation of God's presence in nature. God's creation is everywhere in the overwhelming abundance of nature, but one must also seek God in the minutiae. The viewer is invited to look intensely into this dense landscape and is rewarded with tiny visual treasures, such as two lovely swans in the water behind Eustace and a very small mounted knight in a far off clearing just above Eustace's horse's head. By reflecting visually into this image, the viewer can fall deeply into the detail of the landscape just as Eustace fell into his conversion.

St. Eustace is best known as the patron saint of hunters. The years when this Roman martyr lived are unknown, but churches dedicated to Eustace in Rome date from as early as the eighth century, and there are also ancient dedications in England.[3] Eustace is commonly depicted in the wilderness because his legend is associated with tales of a man who meets a stag that prompts his conversion to Christianity. Between the stag's antlers was a small image of the Crucifixion, which stopped Eustace and presumably brought him to his knees, as Dürer figures him here. A curiosity can be seen in Dürer's placement of Eustace within the Nuremberg landscape: the saint is indeed kneeling before the stag, but at first glance the perspective appears off and he seems floating, with his head level to that of his horse, rather than firmly placed on the ground. Even if the perspective is somewhat inaccurate in this relatively early engraving for Dürer, perhaps he placed Eustace this way intentionally, slightly aloft by the power of this moment of spiritual revelation.

Eustace's legend has been historically connected to that of a Roman general under Emperor Trajan who experienced a similar conversion, though no sound historical evidence confirms that the two men were the same. His legend is also closely tied to that of St. Hubert. All three figures have been conflated at various times throughout history, and this engraving has been erroneously called "St. Hubert" because of the legends' similarity. Dürer, however, referred to this engraving as "the Eustace" multiple times in his diaries.

■ JRL

PLATE 9. Albrecht Dürer,
St. Eustace, c. 1501.
Engraving.

PLATE 10. Albrecht Dürer,
The Marriage of the Virgin,
from *The Life of the Virgin*
series, c. 1503–5. Woodcut.

Mary and Joseph's hands are joined as they stand with their families, a priest, and others milling in the temple. Both figures' heads are slightly bowed in reverence to one another and to this momentous occasion. The clasping of their hands is skillfully placed in the center of the composition, drawing the eye inward toward the receding, detailed architectural space. There is an intimacy and sense of actual place in this woodcut, as with the others in this series, Albrecht Dürer's *The Life of the Virgin*. With wincing eyes, furrowed brows, soft faces (as well as those lined with maturity), the figures here seem to express individual personalities and emotions in a very human manner.

The telling of the marriage or betrothal of Mary derives from an apocryphal book, *The Gospel of the Birth of Mary,* a Latin text that either originated in the medieval period or, as a preface to the book suggests, was compiled by St. Jerome from an original Hebrew version.[1] The detailed life of Mary is later retold in *The Golden Legend,* an extremely popular medieval sourcebook published in 1260 and compiled by Jacobus de Voragine, the Archbishop of Genoa. *The Golden Legend* recorded and further reinforced legends about the lives of the saints, Mary, and Christ, and Dürer and his contemporaries would have been familiar with it.

Striking architectural spaces and landscape are incorporated in Dürer's *Life of the Virgin* series. Intricate details adorn arches and columns, framing Mary and Joseph and their onlookers. This series is also notable for the remarkable costume and gestural details of the figures. Beautifully detailed garments and wonderful headdresses and hats add to the ambience and appeal of *The Marriage of the Virgin*. The woman directly behind Mary on the far right side of the woodcut wears clothing and a headdress typical of fashionable, wealthy women in Nuremberg during the artist's lifetime; she wears a heavily pleated, fur-trimmed garment and elaborate headdress called a *Stürz*.[2] In 1500, Dürer completed a number of costume studies (including at least two of this particular figure) that feature women of Nuremberg dressed for various aspects of daily life, such as going to church

or a dance or staying at home.[3] His interest in the costume and dress of various cities remained strong throughout his entire career and enhances the aesthetic appeal and distinctiveness of many of his works.

Dürer's *Life of the Virgin* series includes nineteen woodcuts chronicling the life of the Virgin Mary. Seventeen of the woodcuts, including this one, were created between 1503 and 1505. In 1510 Dürer created the two additional prints, *The Death of the Virgin* and *The Assumption and Coronation of the Virgin,* impressions of which are also in the Thrivent Financial Collection of Religious Art. The entire series was published in 1511, along with accompanying Latin text and a frontispiece. The Latin text was composed by Benedict Schwalbe (Chelidonius), a local Benedictine theologian and friend of Willibald Pirckheimer, who was a close friend and patron of Dürer.[4] At this time Dürer's seminal and extremely popular *Apocalypse* and *Large Passion* series were also reprinted in their second editions. *The Life of the Virgin* was often bound together with these other series. The woodcuts in this series are smaller in format than the other two.

Much religious subject matter in art over the centuries does not derive directly from canonical Scripture but rather from noncanonical scripture, apocryphal material, oral tradition, church tradition, and other sourcebooks such as *The Golden Legend. The Life of the Virgin* series is one example of countless religious prints in the history of the medium that can reinforce and even educate about such noncanonical stories and concepts through their dissemination. This series certainly had a strong devotional function. Dürer dedicated the series to Willibald Pirckheimer's sister; Caritas Pirckheimer (1466–1532) was a gifted scholar of the Latin and Greek languages and the abbess of a Franciscan convent in Nuremberg, St. Clara's, a center of culture as well as contemplative devotion.[5] Further study is needed, yet with this dedication, and in such a setting, perhaps the series was used educationally to reinforce church teachings on the life of the Virgin to the novices and nuns at the convent.

■ JRL

PLATE 10

Albrecht Dürer, German, 1471–1528

The Marriage of the Virgin, from *The Life of the Virgin* series

c. 1503–5
Woodcut
11¹¹⁄₁₆ × 8¹⁄₁₆ inches
297 × 205 mm
98-31
Bartsch 82, Hollstein 194/II
Watermark: Triangle with flowers (Meder watermark no. 127)

Notes

1. "Mary, Gospel of the Birth of," in *The Oxford Dictionary of the Christian Church,* ed. F. L. Cross and E. A. Livingstone (Oxford: Oxford University Press, 2005); http://www.oxford-christianchurch.com, accessed July 11, 2010.
2. Giulia Bartrum, *Albrecht Dürer and His Legacy: The Graphic Work of a Renaissance Artist* (Princeton: Princeton University Press, 2002), 145.
3. Ibid., 144–45.
4. Linda C. Hults, *The Print in the Western World: An Introductory History* (Madison: University of Wisconsin Press, 1996), 89.
5. Bartrum, 164.

PLATE 11

Albrecht Dürer,
German, 1471–1528

*The Man of
Sorrows,* from the
Engraved Passion

1509
Engraving
4¹¹⁄₁₆ × 2¹⁵⁄₁₆ inches
120 × 75 mm
91-24
Bartsch/Meder 3–18

PLATE 11. Albrecht Dürer, *The Man of Sorrows,* from the *Engraved Passion,* 1509. Engraving (actual size).

Each of the superb engravings in Albrecht Dürer's *Engraved Passion* series is a study in the technical virtuosity achieved by this singularly gifted artist. Each small image invites the viewer to lean in and closely examine the work. Like medieval illuminated prayerbooks and Books of Hours, series of prints depicting the Passion served in part as contemplative, devotional tools for their owners and viewers. This particular series was as much a showpiece of the artist's skill as an expression of Christian doctrine.

The Man of Sorrows is a complex representation of devotional piety and theological reflections. In Dürer's time, the sense of sight was a way to connect with the divine, and pious meditation was stressed as a means to salvation. Christ's human nature and suffering were central themes in devotional life, and contemplation could be practiced by viewing prints such as *The Man of Sorrows.* In the image Mary and John gaze up at Christ, who looks outward toward the viewer. From the wound in Christ's side, blood streams directly onto Mary and John in an undeviating connection gained through their devotion. The blood signifies God's grace—thus salvation for humanity—through the sacrifice of Christ. It also alludes to the Eucharist, specifically the theological doctrine of transubstantiation, which states that during communion one consumes the actual blood and body of Christ, which confers grace. In this image there is no mediation or conduit, such as the church, through which the blood must flow to reach the pious individual; rather, grace is gained through direct and personal devotion. This idea fits nicely into the small, intimate format of this devotional print series, but it also anticipates crucial shifts in theological

doctrine and debate that were percolating in Europe, especially in Germany, as part of the imminent Protestant Reformation.

In contrast, Dürer's earlier *Christ on the Cross* (Figure 18) from his *Large Passion* series features angels holding chalices to catch the blood spilling from Christ's wounds. This motif also suggests a Eucharistic message: Christ's blood, spilled to save humanity, is obtained through the Eucharist—but *with* mediation from the church. Among the issues of heated debate around the time of the Reformation were how God's grace was received by Christians and whether the presence of Christ was real or symbolic in the Eucharist. The Eucharist was a primary vehicle for the receipt of grace, but its service of both kinds, bread and wine/body and blood, was restricted to only certain Christians. Martin Luther and other theologians and Christians argued that all Christians must receive the full Eucharist, both bread and wine. Dürer, a scholar and provocative thinker as well as a superb artist, was involved in the leading circles of intellectual and religious debate in Europe during this time of remarkable changes in technology, culture, and religion. His works express the full range of variation in his own and his society's shifting theological and cultural thought. The *Engraved Passion* truly exhibits the important devotional potential of a religious print series.

Dürer's exquisite *Engraved Passion* was another precedent-setting religious print series that also served as a showpiece set of the artist's work for connoisseurs and collectors. Since the fifteenth century, when the earliest prints were made in Europe, the print series has been a popular format for telling religious stories such as Christ's Passion. For the first time, devotional imagery could be published for a mass audience. Many printmakers produced sets of woodcuts, engravings, or etchings that depicted religious subjects and could be sold together or individually. Dürer completed and published several print series of Christ's Passion, a subject he worked on throughout his career in numerous prints and drawings. The small scale of the plates in this series inspired the sixteenth-century artists known as the Little Masters.

There are fifteen plates in the *Engraved Passion,* and an additional sixteenth plate, *St. Peter and St. John,* is often associated with the series because of its small size and commensurate quality, even though it is not a scene from the Passion. The set in the Thrivent Financial collection includes an impression of *St. Peter and St. John.* All of the plates in this series were created between 1507 and 1512. During this period Dürer executed several of his major print series, including the *Life of the Virgin* and both woodcut Passion series as well as the *Engraved Passion.* These years brought increasing personal and professional prosperity to Dürer, who purchased a house in Tiergärtnertor and became a member of the Greater Council of Nuremberg in 1509.[1]

Until the series was completed in 1512, the individual engravings were sold separately. All fifteen engravings were ultimately often given or sold as a set directly by Dürer, as noted multiple times in the diary he wrote during his Netherlandish and Low Country travels.[2] His deliberate distribution of the set to new friends, dignitaries, and artists aided in the dissemination of his art throughout Europe; his potential artistic and historical influence increased as he succeeded in further displaying his talents across the continent. Erasmus of Rotterdam, the famous humanist with whom Dürer visited and corresponded, was among the notable people who received this series.[3]

This series was never intended to be published with text in book form, as occurred with Dürer's woodcut series. Some complete sets of the *Engraved Passion* were bound, and occasionally hand-colored, by collectors in Dürer's time and the centuries that followed.[4] The coloring of such engravings would not have been condoned by the artist: Giulia Bartrum aptly points out that such a practice reveals that collectors sometimes associated the series with devotional prayerbooks that were illustrated with illuminated miniatures, which emphasizes and reinforces our understanding of the extremely high regard of Dürer held in his own time and later.[5]

■ JRL

Notes

1. Giulia Bartrum, *German Renaissance Prints, 1490–1550* (London: British Museum Press, 1995), 11.
2. Ibid., 44.
3. Walter L. Strauss, *The Complete Engravings, Etchings, and Drypoints of Albrecht Dürer* (New York: Dover Publications, 1973), 101.
4. Bartrum, 44.
5. Ibid.

FIGURE 18. Albrecht Dürer, *Christ on the Cross,* from the *Large Passion,* c. 1497–1500. Woodcut.

PLATE 12. Albrecht Dürer,
*Knight, Death, and the
Devil,* 1513. Engraving.

Knight, Death, and the Devil is one of Albrecht Dürer's *Meisterstiche,* or master engravings, along with *Melencolia I* and *St. Jerome in His Study* (Plate 13). Connoisseurs feel these *Meisterstiche,* all of similar size and date, represent the pinnacle of Dürer's oeuvre in terms of technical skill, pictorial composition, and iconographic program. Here, a knight in fine armor sits high on a glistening steed. With battle lance in hand and sword at his side, he gazes resolutely forward as he rides through the woods. Below his mount, a dog runs with equally steadfast intent, while to the side a decaying corpse on an old horse carries an hourglass. An armed and gruesome devil trudges close behind.

In his journals, Dürer referred to this print rather ambiguously as *der Reiter,* meaning "the horseman" or "rider," but since the sixteenth century it has been interpreted in a variety of ways. The Italian biographer and art critic Giorgio Vasari was the first to describe the scene in his second edition of *Lives of the Most Eminent Painters, Sculptors, and Architects* (1568), calling the "armed man on horseback" a representation of human strength.[1] Joachim von Sandhrart, in the seventeenth century, was the first known to have referred to the figure as a "Christian Knight," and the present title *Knight, Death, and the Devil* began to be used during the eighteenth century.[2]

In Dürer's time, written guides to Christian living were rich with soldiers, arms, and armor as metaphors for steadfast faith and wholesome life. One passage from *Handbook of the Christian Soldier* by the humanist scholar Desiderius Erasmus of Rotterdam seems to describe the scene of this engraving: "In order that you may not be deterred from the path of virtue because it seems rough and dreary… and because you must constantly fight three unfair enemies, the flesh, the devil, and the world…"[3] The art historian and iconographer Erwin Panofsky wrote that the figure represents an idealized "Knight of Christ," whose unwavering faith keeps him on a noble path, rejecting distractions from the devil or deadly temptations of the flesh. Offered as evidence is an appeal by Dürer to Erasmus, urging him to speak up on behalf of the Reformation leader Martin Luther, who had purportedly been kidnapped. In Dürer's words, "Hear, you Christian knight, ride forth at the side of Christ, defend the truth, attain the martyr's crown."[4]

A few scholars have pointed out that honorable knights were in decline by the sixteenth century and that good, civilized people would have feared any heavily armed man on horseback.[5] An infamous knight from Rothenberg named Kunz Schott was an enemy of Nuremberg, and he allegedly stole a package of Dürer's prints in a raid. Rather than a "Knight of Christ," Dürer's horseman has thus been interpreted as an armed bandit who plunders travelers along the road.[6] Death and the Devil may be his wicked companions, or they may have appeared to warn him of consequences of his sinful behavior.

However, Christian knights were common in German art at the beginning of the sixteenth century. The gothic arms and armor worn by Dürer's "rider" were present in countless images of St. George. While there is no dragon to fight or princess to save in Dürer's scene here, this knight carries the same type of battle lance and broadsword as St. George. A similarly decorated *sallet* (helmet) and fluted armor can be seen in Dürer's *St. George on Horseback,* engraved in 1508. St. George enjoyed a resurgence in popularity in the early sixteenth century when Emperor Maximilian I attempted to gain support for a crusade to the Holy Land.[7] In 1508, the year Maximilian was crowned Holy Roman Emperor, Hans Burgkmair made two chiaroscuro woodcuts of knights on horseback that were very similar in style: one of St. George and the other of Maximilian. Thus, within the context of the print market at the time, it seems reasonable to assume that viewers of *Knight, Death, and the Devil* would recognize the symbol of a noble knight (perhaps even St. George), only to discover Death and the Devil lurking about instead of a dragon. This personal, quiet moment in the woods reflects the inner fortitude and moral perseverance that must lie at the core of the saint's spirit. By depicting the traditional armor and weaponry of St. George in this engraving, Dürer transforms a heroic dragon slayer into a new, symbolic Christian knight who must rationally and carefully navigate the path between good and evil.

■ JRW

PLATE 12

Albrecht Dürer, German, 1471–1528

Knight, Death, and the Devil

1513
Engraving
9⅝ × 7¹³⁄₃₂ inches
244 × 188 mm

87-22

Bartsch 98,
Hollstein 74,
Meder 74

Provenance

Fürst Karl de Paar (1772–1819); Max Kade (1882–1967).

Notes

1. Giorgio Vasari, *Vasari's Lives of the Most Eminent Painters, Sculptors, and Architects,* trans. Mrs. Jonathan Foster (London: G. Bell, 1891 [1568]), 3: 72.
2. Giulia Bartrum, *Albrecht Dürer and His Legacy: The Graphic Work of a Renaissance Artist* (Princeton: Princeton University Press, 2002), 187.
3. Christiane Andersson and Charles W. Talbot, *From a Mighty Fortress: Prints, Drawings, and Books in the Age of Luther, 1483–1546* (Detroit: Detroit Institute of Arts, 1983), 276.
4. Erwin Panofsky, *The Life and Art of Albrecht Dürer* (Princeton: Princeton University Press, 1995), 151.
5. Andersson and Talbot, 276.
6. Ibid.
7. David Landau and Peter W. Parshall, *The Renaissance Print, 1470–1550* (New Haven: Yale University Press, 1994), 187.

PLATE 13

Albrecht Dürer,
German, 1471–1528

*St. Jerome
in His Study*

1514
Engraving
9¹¹⁄₁₆ × 7⅜ inches
246 × 187 mm
96-13
Bartsch 60,
Meder/Hollstein 59a

FIGURE 19. School of
Joos van Cleve, *St. Jerome
in His Study,* sixteenth
century. Oil on panel.

Notes

1. Christiane Andersson
   and Charles W. Talbot,
   *From a Mighty Fortress:
   Prints, Drawings, and
   Books in the Age of Luther,
   1483–1546* (Detroit:
   Detroit Institute of
   Arts, 1983), 32–33.
2. Ibid., 34.
3. The plant or bush may
   have been a castor bean
   plant, from the Hebrew
   qiqayon. Bruce M.
   Metzger and Roland E.
   Murphy, eds., *The New
   Oxford Annotated Bible,
   with the Apocryphal/
   Deuterocanonical Books*
   (New York: Oxford
   University Press, 1994),
   1189.
4. Linda C. Hults, *The
   Print in the Western
   World: An Introductory
   History* (Madison:
   University of
   Wisconsin Press,
   1996), 92.

Jerome, one of Christianity's most beloved saints, is also one of the most frequently depicted in art. Jerome was a monk and scholar who lived from c. 345 to 420. His translation of most of the Bible's original texts into Latin, along with biblical commentaries interpreting the texts, earned him a momentous legacy within the church. This engraving has become an iconic representation of St. Jerome and is one of Albrecht Dürer's *Meisterstiche,* or master prints (see also Plate 12, *Knight, Death, and the Devil*).

Dürer created these superb prints largely for connoisseurs and collectors. Though they were not intended to be devotional in function, they do contain significant psychological and theological themes. *St. Jerome in His Study* expresses a contemporary ideal of the saint as the model humanist scholar, fulfilling a contemplative life in the service of God. Nuremberg was a center of humanism, an intellectual movement with Italian origins that migrated to Germany by the late fifteenth century; it valued knowledge, language, and classical ideals in art and literature and emphasized the importance of the individual human being over medieval dogma.[1] Many of its proponents were prominent Nuremberg citizens, including Dürer's closest friend and patron Willibald Pirckheimer (1470–1530).

During the Protestant Reformation and the centuries that followed, pervasive saint imagery declined in European art due to concerns about overt worship of saints in favor of God—yet illustrations of Jerome and other specific saints endured. Jerome was often compared to Martin Luther because both men were scholar monks who translated Scripture into the vulgate, the language of the people (Latin and German respectively). This comparison appeared in art created at the time of the Reformation, and this engraving by Dürer was emulated by several other artists, including one example by Monogrammist WS.[2]

Jerome was a devoted scholar and prayerful monk who sought to create an accurate translation of the Bible through study of the original texts and earlier translations. Dürer presents the definitive image of the saint in his 1514 engraving: Jerome's head is bowed attentively over his work in his light-filled room. The lion curled on the floor is the most recognizable attribute for Jerome in art; it derives from the telling of Jerome's life in *The Golden Legend,* in which a story is recounted that Jerome removed a thorn from a lion's paw and the animal then became a lifelong companion to the saint. The cardinal hat hanging on the wall just above Jerome's head is traditional iconography that references the long-held (but likely inaccurate) belief that he was a cardinal. Directly above his head Dürer gives the saint a "halo" of light. Within Jerome's sight is a small crucifix placed on his table and a skull on the windowsill, humble reminders of death and redemption. Dürer's Jerome is working diligently, yet he is also comfortably ensconced in his warm, inviting study. Slippers sit casually by the head of the dog, and books and plush pillows are scattered on hard surfaces. A large gourd hangs from the ceiling; this is a reference to a controversy about the historical translation of the Hebrew word *kikayon,* meaning "gourd." Jerome had translated the word as "ivy" in Jonah 4:6, which describes how the Lord provides a plant (the gourd or the ivy) to spring up and shelter Jonah.[3] The inclusion of the gourd here likely indexes Jerome's scholarly work as well as the divine favor and shelter under which he studied.[4]

From the marvelously detailed wood-planked ceiling to the lifelike wall of windows, Dürer created a truly welcoming and attractive contemplative space. The room is bathed in sunlight streaming in from the beautiful circular patterned windows, which creates lovely designs on the walls. His placement of St. Jerome in this bright space, with these crown glass windows, became a precedent for later interiors in which Jerome would be portrayed. These particular windows can be seen in other depictions of St. Jerome's study, such as a sixteenth-century painting in the Thrivent Financial collection, *St. Jerome in His Study* (Figure 19), a copy of a painting made by Dürer in 1521. This representation was clearly influenced, directly or indirectly, by Dürer's 1514 engraving with its crown glass windows.

■ JRL

Plate 13. Albrecht Dürer,
St. Jerome in His Study,
1514. Engraving.

PLATE 14

**Albrecht Dürer,
German, 1471–1528**

*Madonna
by the Wall*

1514

Engraving

6¾ × 4¹⁵⁄₁₆ inches
146 × 100 mm

87-34

Bartsch 40,
Meder 36

PLATE 14. Albrecht Dürer,
Madonna by the Wall, 1514.
Engraving (actual size).

Albrecht Dürer returned to the subject of the Virgin and Child many times in his career, often in the medium of engraving. Of his numerous depictions of Mary and Christ, *Madonna by the Wall* has been singled out by many critics and historians over the centuries for its visual brilliance, sumptuous texture, and seemingly effortless composition. Deep blacks contrast with glorious silvery contours. Mary's fur-lined, voluminous garments enfold her, her arms tucked around her child. The shape of both figures together mimics the ideal triangular Italian Renaissance compositional device. Mary appears the perfect devoted mother as her plump infant seems to squirm charmingly in her arms, which clasp him tightly; with his head turned away, face slightly grimaced, he looks like a typical fussy infant. Despite this realistic portrayal, his chubby left hand is raised in benediction, leaving no doubt as to his identity. At Mary's waist hangs a large set of keys, a symbol of her station and importance, as traditionally the female head of household would have been in charge of

access to the home and its larders. The city wall against which the Virgin leans is that of Dürer's hometown, Nuremberg. The city's castle can be seen in the background, a view Dürer could enjoy from his own home.[1]

In another fine example of his Madonna and Child engravings, *Madonna with the Pear* (Figure 21), Dürer presents the Virgin gazing lovingly at her calm son as she offers him a pear; here, his right hand is raised in benediction as he looks directly at the viewer. The pear is a substitute for the more typically applied apple in such a scene, a reference to Christ as the Savior of humanity's Fall. The inclusion of such iconography encourages a meditative response from the viewer, who contemplates the import of this child. Dürer included the pear multiple times in his works, and there was a precedent for this fruit in Marian art since at least the medieval period. Mary's draped garments gently envelop her form and are delicately trimmed with fur at the bottom and the neckline. The wealth characteristic of a woman who would have worn such clothing in Dürer's time visually reinforces this figure as an individual of significant social and cultural status. The many folds and creases in Mary's gown not only contribute to the technical mastery of the engraving but also indicate an enormous amount of fabric—an expensive prospect. This engraving accomplishes a balance of soft angular lines with swirling, rounded ones. Dürer incorporates many tapering and varietal lines to achieve the organic, undulating pattern of the gnarled tree trunk offset by the rounded shape of the clouds and two soft arches in the building behind Mary, which harmoniously contrast with the sharper creases and folds of her gown.

It is doubtful the historical Mary would have possessed wealth commensurate with how she is portrayed in these images, but

this tradition in art endows her with fine garments because she is the Mother of Christ. Dressing Mary in elegant clothing has a long-standing history; along with many other iconographic elements, it bestows nobility, reverence, and import on her. In art, Mary is often seated on a plump, tasseled pillow, which protects her from hard surfaces. She is also often shown, as in Dürer's *The Annunciation* from the *Small Passion* (Figure 20), with an open book, representing her literacy, another quality generally expected of aristocratic women in the medieval and Renaissance periods in Europe. The tradition in Marian literature and piety of her ability to read as well as teach others is perpetuated in religious art with multiple visual references to Mary reading.

Mary's role in the history of the Western and Eastern church, culture, and society cannot be overstated. Mariology in Christian theology, literary traditions, and the overwhelmingly prevalent veneration and devotional practices known as the Cult of Mary all contribute to the abundance of rich Marian imagery in the history of art.

■ JRL

Above: FIGURE 20. Albrecht Dürer, *The Annunciation,* from the *Small Passion,* 1510. Woodcut.

Below: FIGURE 21. Albrecht Dürer, *Madonna with the Pear,* 1511. Engraving.

Note

1. Walter L. Strauss, *The Complete Engravings, Etchings, and Drypoints of Albrecht Dürer* (New York: Dover Publications, 1973), 164.

Plate 15

**Monogrammist MZ,
German, active
c. 1500**

Solomon's Idolatry

1501

Engraving

7½ × 6¼ inches
178 × 152 mm

98-06

Bartsch 1

FIGURE 22. Lucas van Leyden, *Idolatry of Solomon,* 1514. Engraving.

King Solomon angered Jehovah when he allowed his wives to turn his heart from God and began to worship their foreign idols (I Kings 11:1–13). In this engraving by the Monogrammist MZ, Solomon kneels prayerfully in a vaulted shrine, while one of his seven hundred wives points his gaze toward a female idol atop an ornamental pedestal designed like a late medieval reliquary, but flanked on all sides with nude women instead of Christian saints.

Solomon's Idolatry, along with other scenes such as Samson and Delilah, Judith and Holofernes, and Aristotle and Phyllis, from both religious and secular literature, was used to illustrate the dangerous potential of women and their ability to lure even the strongest and wisest men to self-destruction. "The power of women" became a popular theme at the end of the fifteenth century, developing from misogynist ideas in theological and philosophical texts that described women as morally weak. Before that time, the scene of *Solomon's Idolatry* was not depicted in art, suggesting that the iconographic representation probably developed expressly to demonstrate this theme of machinating, influential women. The motif used by MZ here seems to have become a standard. Printmakers copied subject matter and designs from one another, and MZ's version is adapted from one made about a decade earlier by the Master of the Housebook.[1] An engraving made by Lucas van Leyden in 1514 (Figure 22) places Solomon and his wife in virtually the same poses, although the setting and the idol are changed. The stilted pose of Solomon's wife in MZ's print is characteristic of his human figures, and in this case aids to accentuate her domination as she towers over the king.

Evidence that might reveal MZ's mysterious identity remains inconclusive. Print connoisseurs and historians speculated as early as the seventeenth century that the Master MZ was Mätthaus Zaisinger, a documented goldsmith and printmaker working in Munich around 1500.[2] An engraved plaque on a reliquary box attributed to Zaisinger in the Andechs monastery church is similar in style to MZ's printed works. Dated 1501, the Madonna and Child with angels on the reliquary are copied after a print of the holy family by Albrecht Dürer.[3] MZ frequently drew inspiration from subject matter in Dürer's prints, and the idol in *Solomon's Idolatry* betrays this influence. The body of the nude statue is based on an engraved figure of Nemesis made by Dürer shortly before MZ's print. MZ may not have intended any particular meaning when he mimicked the figure, but it is conceivable that a sixteenth-century viewer acquainted with Dürer's engraving would have grasped the irony of MZ's pictorial allusion. As a powerful goddess of fortune and retribution, Nemesis reinforces the sixteenth-century idea that Solomon's error was not only breaking God's commandment against worshiping a false idol, but succumbing to the beguiling power of a woman.[4]

■ JRW

Provenance

Comte de Maltzan
(Lugt 3024a).

Notes

1. Christiane Andersson and Charles W. Talbot, *From a Mighty Fortress: Prints, Drawings, and Books in the Age of Luther, 1483–1546* (Detroit: Detroit Institute of Arts, 1983), 313.
2. Ibid., 312.
3. National Gallery of Art, Alan Shestack, and Lessing J. Rosenwald, *Fifteenth-Century Engravings of Northern Europe from the National Gallery of Art* (Washington, D.C.: National Gallery of Art, 1967), n.p.
4. Andersson and Talbot, 312.

PLATE 15. Monogrammist
MZ, *Solomon's Idolatry,*
1501. Engraving (actual
size).

PLATE 16

**Lucas van Leyden,
Netherlandish,
1489/1494–1533**

Ecce Homo

1510

Engraving

11¼ × 17³⁄₁₆ inches
285 × 438 mm

01-17

Bartsch 71,
Hollstein 71

Watermark: Gothic P
(New Hollstein 3a; close
to Briquet 8534)

Lucas van Leyden is the first printmaker
from the Netherlands to achieve an international reputation. Not only did his skill
with the burin rival that of the best German
engravers, his remarkable attention to detail,
inventive compositions, and uncanny ability
to evoke a sense of reality have delighted print
connoisseurs for five centuries. His innovative
approach to the *Ecce Homo,* or Pilate's
presentation of Christ, marks a turning point
in the history of art. Conventional printed
depictions of the story, like that by Martin
Schongauer (Plate 5), were intended for
devotional use and thus presented the viewer
with an iconic, closely framed image of a
suffering Christ and the interaction between
Pilate and the angry mob. In his uncommonly
large version, van Leyden expanded the
scene and placed Christ and Pilate off-center
on a platform within a vast architectural

Christ's trial, but many seem simply to be
going about their daily activities.

This unique composition for *Ecce Homo*
that moves the primary religious action into
the background gives the historical event a
quotidian feeling, thereby humanizing the
biblical scene. Van Leyden used a similar
pictorial construction that same year (1510)
in his *Baptism of Christ* (Figure 23), albeit on a
scale about one-quarter the size of *Ecce Homo.*
Again, large anonymous figures dominate the
foreground, while across the pool Christ and
John nearly blend in with a group of men
waiting to be baptized. Modern art historians commonly recognize van Leyden's *Ecce
Homo* and *Baptism of Christ* as evidence of
his attention to the appearance of reality and
a tendency toward what would become the
Netherlandish genre scene. Generally defined
as a "slice of life" that portrays the activities of
everyday living (often with subtle moral impli-
cations), the genre scene became increasingly
popular through the sixteenth and seventeenth
centuries. Although not a genre scene in the
purest sense with its well-known subject
matter from Christ's Passion, van Leyden's *Ecce
Homo* exemplifies a transition away from traditional religious representation based on icons
toward a more subjective, human narrative.[1]

Van Leyden contributed to the sense
of reality by clothing the figures in an array
of sixteenth-century fashions, which were
illustrated in popular costume books and
early travel guides that described a variety
of ethnic groups for pilgrims to the Holy
Land. Pilate's central tower and platform were
based on the Gravensteen, the old court-
house in Leiden, which still stands today.
During van Leyden's time the Gravensteen
was the site where public executions took
place, giving at least the local viewers of *Ecce
Homo* a familiar landmark appropriate to the

FIGURE 23. Lucas van
Leyden, *Baptism of Christ,*
1510. Engraving.

landscape. The angry crowd is gathered below,
dominating the space closest to the viewer.
Scattered throughout the square, on the streets
and balconies and in the windows of the
buildings, are dozens of figures. Some watch

PLATE 16. Lucas van Leyden, *Ecce Homo,* 1510. Engraving.

story. H. van de Waal and Peter W. Parshall both speculated that the scene might reflect a theatrical production or Passion Play that was commonly performed during religious festivals.[2] Episodes from the Passion were staged in village squares, and the audience traveled from scene to scene, imagining themselves in Jerusalem with Christ.[3] Pious Christians attended these events and used them, as they did meditative texts and printed Passion series, to transcend the physical world and achieve a direct connection with Christ.[4] In this regard, van Leyden's clever juxtaposition of an everyday, material existence with the condemnation of Christ can be seen as a reflection of this moral dilemma. The broad cityscape, the inverted narrative composition, and the intense detail require active participation of the viewer, whose eyes must enter the scene and navigate the busy square, seeking out the true object of devotion. Many of the figures encountered within the scene

steer the viewer's gaze toward Christ, but many do not. Each type of figure offers the viewer a moral decision: to direct devoted attention toward Christ or to become distracted by the material world.

Certainly some of van Leyden's international audience cherished this print for its material qualities. As an extra large copperplate print, it was probably among the most expensive on the market. The exquisite burin work, the naturalistic detail, and the marvelous use of single-point perspective must have made it particularly tempting to wealthy connoisseurs at a time when fine religious prints were collected and valued as much for artistry as for devotional use. Proof that van Leyden's *Ecce Homo* enjoyed widespread appreciation when it was first printed can be seen in paintings by the Italian artists Andrea del Sarto and Jacopo da Pontormo: both men copied buildings from *Ecce Homo* as early as 1517.

■ JRW

Notes

1. Peter W. Parshall, "Lucas van Leyden's Narrative Style," *Nederlands Kunsthistorish Jaarboek* 29 (1978): 217.
2. H. van de Waal, P. Wardle, and R. H. Fuchs, *Steps towards Rembrandt: Collected Articles, 1937–1972* (Amsterdam: North-Holland, 1974), 184; Peter W. Parshall, "Lucas van Leyden and the Rise of Pictorial Narrative," Ph.D. thesis, University of Chicago (1974), 69.
3. Parshall, "Lucas van Leyden and the Rise of Pictorial Narrative," 69; J. van Herwaarden, *Between Saint James and Erasmus. Studies in Late-Medieval Religious Life: Devotions and Pilgrimages in the Netherlands,* Studies in Medieval and Reformation Thought 97 (Leiden: Brill, 2003), 76.
4. Herwaarden, 588.

PLATE 17

Lucas van Leyden, Netherlandish, 1489/1494–1533

Adam and Eve after Their Expulsion from Paradise

1510

Engraving

4¹¹⁄₁₆ × 3⅜ inches

163 × 120 mm

87-36

Bartsch 11, Hollstein 11

PLATE 17. Lucas van Leyden, *Adam and Eve after Their Expulsion from Paradise,* 1510. Engraving.

Eve sorrowfully walks ahead of Adam, who gently prods her onward out of the garden. This scene derives from the book of Genesis from the passage 3:9–24, in which God expels the couple from the garden of Eden after they have disobediently eaten the fruit of the tree of knowledge. They received the punishments of toil over the earth for Adam and painful childbirth for Eve; Adam holds a spade and Eve her firstborn child, both symbols of God's punishment and expulsion as related in Scripture. Further attesting to van Leyden's close reading of the original text, both figures wear rudimentary garments, Adam's clearly made of animal skins. According to Genesis 3:21, God clothed them in skins after they discovered their nakedness in shame, and they subsequently left Eden.

Although the biblical verse that describes the pair actually leaving the garden (Genesis 3:24) does not mention their infant son Cain, this occurs immediately after in Genesis 4:1. Van Leyden's poignant, original interpretation of this episode includes the child. This is a family leaving their home as much as it is Adam and Eve's exit from Eden. The scene recalls depictions of Mary and Joseph's flight into Egypt, even in that Adam appears older than Eve. The suggestion of a family scene here is not surprising given the artist's propensity and innovation for constructing detailed genre scenes and components in his prints (see Plate 16, *Ecce Homo*). Despite the slight departure from the biblical text, this particular interpretation of the story may be a reflection of a religious movement contemporary to van Leyden, Devotio Moderna, which stressed accurate, direct readings of Scripture.[1]

Ellen S. Jacobowitz notes that van Leyden's prints from 1510 on display a strong understanding of the capabilities of the engraving medium. Many decorative details in this work, such as the windswept nature of Eve's flowing hair and the figures' garments, as well as a more sophisticated inclusion of texture and tone in the overall composition, reveal the artist's talent as an engraver.[2]

■ JRL

Provenance

Pierre-Jean Mariette (1694–1774; Lugt 2097).

Notes

1. Ellen S. Jacobowitz and Stephanie Loeb Stepanek, *The Prints of Lucas van Leyden and His Contemporaries* (Washington, D.C.: National Gallery of Art, 1983), 86.
2. Ibid.

PLATE 18

PLATE 18. Lambert Hopfer, *The Conversion of St. Paul,* n.d. Etching on iron (actual size).

Lambert Hopfer,
German,
active c. 1525–50

*The Conversion
of St. Paul*

Etching on iron
5⅜ × 3⅜ inches
136 × 85 mm
00-18
Hollstein 22-I/III

his eventual missionary work and writings. The weighty impact of Paul's conversion on the entire religion and history of Christianity is visually emphasized with powerful imagery in art. In this version, Hopfer presents the event as fiercely overcoming Paul with an image of Christ using a standard to push divine light onto earth toward him. Paul's letters comprise a significant portion of the canonical New Testament; his historical and theological influence within the history of the church is immense, and his conversion has long been popular subject matter for artists.

Lambert Hopfer was the son of the Augsburg artist Daniel Hopfer (c. 1471–1536; see Plate 19). Lambert and his brother Hieronymus Hopfer (c. 1500–1563) continued their father's profession as etchers in Augsburg and Nuremberg. The Hopfer workshop was the first to successfully adapt the practice of etching on armor to etching on metal plates for prints. Ultimately, softer copperplates would be used for etchings, but the Hopfers used iron plates. Two hundred thirty of the Hopfer plates were reissued and printed in Nuremberg in the seventeenth century by David Funck, who added numbers to the prints. *The Conversion of St. Paul* in the Thrivent Financial collection is a splendid early first state impression before the Funck number appeared.

■ JRL

Divine light dramatically erupts from the heavens, striking down in a jagged sheet toward Paul, who falls from his horse. Both Paul and his horse bow to the force of the moment. Belongings spill out of Paul's purse as he raises his arm to shield his face. Missionary, great thinker, writer, and apostle to the Gentiles, St. Paul (died c. 62–65) was a first-century Jew of the Diaspora who was originally named Saul and was from Tarsus. His conversion story is well known and recounted in the book of the Acts of the Apostles. While on the road to Damascus, Paul experienced a vision of divine light and the risen Christ that would forever alter his own life path and influence many others through

Evidence suggests that prints made from etched iron and steel plates developed concurrently with etched armor decoration around the turn of the sixteenth century.[1] Artist Daniel Hopfer from Augsburg, Germany, is credited with inventing this particular printing method, and he certainly was prevalent among contemporary printmakers in the development of etching's potential. Hopfer's experiments using ground and acid to create shape and tone led to a unique style that appears in both his prints and his armor decoration.[2] The ornate floral patterns with putti against dark backgrounds within and around the main arch of *Sculptural Altarpiece* exemplify the "Hopfer style."

Daniel Hopfer's etching commemorates an altar built for the Dominican church of St. Magdalena in Augsburg that was dedicated in 1518. The plaque in the triumphal arch, below the Crucifixion, names the benefactor as Phillip Adler, a successful businessman and one of Augsburg's wealthiest citizens.[3] Adler's eagle-head coat of arms, as well as the heraldry of his wife, Anna Ehem, appears twice on the structure. Pieced together from two separate impressions, *Sculptural Altarpiece* is among Hopfer's largest etchings. Present-day print historians place it in a category of "monumental" prints, which are created with multiple matrices and sheets of paper and then assembled, post-press, to produce an image larger than print technology could otherwise support.[4]

The iconographic program of the altarpiece relates the lineage of the Christian church from the Kingdom of Israel in the Old Testament or Hebrew Bible, through

PLATE 19. Daniel Hopfer,
Sculptural Altarpiece,
c. 1518. Etching on iron.

Christ, to the foundation of the early church in Rome. This chronological progression begins in the predella, or base, of the altar, with the Old Testament figure of Jesse, father of David, who was chosen by the Lord to be King of Israel (1 Samuel 16:1–13). As Jesse sleeps, the thick stem of a tree grows from his belly, a visual reference to Isaiah 11:1–2: "A shoot shall come out from the stump of Jesse, and a branch shall grow out of his roots. The spirit of the Lord shall rest on him."[5] Early theologians equated the Latin word *virga* (shoot) with *virgo* (virgin) and interpreted the verses as a prophecy that Christ, born to Mary, was heir to the royal house of David.[6]

Bustling with activity, the altar's first platform depicts the holy kinship: ancestors of Jesse and Christ's extended family. The Christ child, identified by his cross-shaped halo, stands at the center of the kinship, between Mary (crowned, as the mother of the Son of God) and another woman. Whimsical and innately human, this holy kinship emphasizes Christ's incarnation. One cousin is nursed, while others play among the legs of watchful grandparents, aunts, and uncles. A boy in the left corner has apparently misbehaved and is being spanked. Seemingly an unusual choice for a church altar, this childhood punishment of the time contrasts Christ's ultimate divinity and serves as a lighthearted reminder that Christ became human to redeem the sins of humankind. On the second tier, the program takes a serious turn with a traditional Crucifixion scene beneath a ribbed vault. Mary and John stand on either side of the cross, perhaps a visual reference to John 19:26–27, when Christ

entrusts filial responsibility of his mother to John. On the third tier, the resurrected Christ stands divinely, triumphantly alone, freed from death and offering his blessing to humanity.

Atop the altar, just below an eternal flame, Saints Peter and Paul hold a medallion containing an image of the *sudarium,* a kerchief that wiped Christ's face on the road to Calvary. This miraculous relic believed to be imprinted with Christ's face was kept in Rome and became a highly revered devotional icon as early as 1300.[7] In the hands of the two apostles traditionally associated with the establishment of the apostolic church in Rome, this image of Christ becomes the divine conclusion in the altar's program, legitimizing the Roman Catholic church as the rightful heir of Christ.

Hopfer's print is the most complete extant visual record of Adler's original altar, which was dismantled during a renovation of the St. Magdalena church in 1724. Written descriptions in church records noting Adler's financial patronage reveal only that the altar was constructed with three open tiers and that the columns were made of red marble.[8] The animated, natural quality of Hopfer's figures raises the question whether the print may represent an idealized altar design rather than the finished altar, in which the figures were probably carved in wood and painted to appear realistic.[9] The large print was probably made as a memento for church members or visitors to take home; hung on a wall, it may have functioned as a personal altar for private devotion.

■ JRW

PLATE 19

Daniel Hopfer,
German,
1471–1536

Sculptural Altarpiece

c. 1518

Etching on iron,
printed on two sheets

Lower sheet:
11½ × 8¼ inches
292 × 210 mm

Upper sheet:
12⅝ × 6¾ inches
320 × 172 mm

97-27

Bartsch 21,
Hollstein 28,
Metzger 34

Watermark: Shield with
three stars (Briquet 1463)

Provenance

Franz Gawet (1762/1765–1847); Ambroise Firmin-Didot (1790–1876); Johann Sigmund Bermann (1794–1846).

Notes

1. David Landau and Peter W. Parshall, *The Renaissance Print, 1470–1550* (New Haven: Yale University Press, 1994), 323.
2. Ibid., 324.
3. Christof Metzger et al., *Daniel Hopfer: ein Augsburger Meister der Renaissance: Eisenradierungen, Holzschnitte, Zeichnungen, Waffenätzungen* (Munich: Staatliche Graphische Sammlung, 2009), 355.
4. Larry Silver, Elizabeth Wyckoff, and Lilian Armstrong, *Grand Scale: Monumental Prints in the Age of Dürer and Titian* (Wellesley, Mass.: Davis Museum and Cultural Center, Wellesley College, 2008), 8–9.
5. Gertrud Schiller, *Iconography of Christian Art,* trans. Janet Seligman (London: Lund Humphries, 1972), 1: 15.
6. Ibid.
7. Ibid., 2: 78–79.
8. Metzger et al., 355.
9. Ibid.

PLATE 20

**Albrecht Altdorfer,
German, 1480–1538**

The Fall of Man
from *Fall and
Redemption of Man*

c. 1513

Woodcuts

2¹³⁄₁₆ × 1⅞ inches
72 × 47 mm

89-09.1

Bartsch 1,
New Hollstein w.1,
Winzinger 25

Miniature prints and
print series became
increasingly popular early
in the sixteenth century
as printmakers gained
virtuosity and patrons
collected prints as much
for their novelty and
artistic innovation as for
their subject matter.
The forty tiny woodcuts
in Albrecht Altdorfer's
*Fall and Redemption of
Man* (ten of which are
illustrated here) represent
an extraordinary
achievement in both
artistic expression and
technical craft. Altdorfer
probably created *Fall and Redemption of Man*
in response to Dürer's three popular Passion
series, particularly *Small Passion* (1510), which
featured thirty-seven woodcuts of similar
content.

But Altdorfer's densely illustrated compositions are almost entirely his own design,
with only a handful alluding to those of his
Nuremberg contemporary. The series opens
with *The Fall of Man* (Plate 20), as Eve offers
Adam a piece of forbidden fruit before a
sword-brandishing angel drives them from
Eden in the second scene (Figure 24). Next a
sequence narrates the miraculous conception
of the Virgin Mary, including Joachim and
Anna, parents of Mary, and her presentation
in the temple as a young girl (Figure 25).
Most of the remaining scenes depict the life
of Christ, from his Incarnation through his
Passion and Ascension (Figure 30), before a
touching and prayerful *Death of the Virgin* and
Last Judgment (Figure 31). The closing image
in the set owned by Thrivent Financial shows
the Virgin Mary being crowned by angels
as she holds the Christ child (Figure 32).
Uncut examples in two other collections with
multiple woodcuts printed per sheet suggest
that *Virgin Crowned by Angels* may have been
intended as a frontispiece for the series bound
in a miniature book.[1]

In his hometown of Regensburg,
Altdorfer became a leading artist in the
Danube School, a group of artists working in

PLATE 20. Albrecht Altdorfer, *The Fall of
Man,* from *Fall and Redemption of Man,*
c. 1513. Woodcut (actual size).

Regensburg, Passau, and
Vienna. Their expressive
style and keen interest
in nature led them to
emphasize setting as a
means to convey mood.
Landscape alone became
a worthy subject among
the Danube School, and
later in his career Albrecht
Altdorfer was one of the
first in the history of
Western art to produce
pure landscape paintings.
His use of landscape,
architecture, and light
throughout the *Fall and
Redemption of Man* series
conveys a strong sense of
atmosphere and monumentality, despite the
diminutive size of these woodcuts.[2]

Although the identities of the figures
and their actions are not always at first
obvious, the energized compositions beckon
the viewer to see what is happening in each
scene. When examined closely, the extremely
fine, carved lines reveal a heightened sense of
detail, absorbing the viewer in the reality of
the narrative. Altdorfer's closed construction
in several of the woodcuts further accentuates
the viewer's relationship to the event and
perception of the moment. For example, in
Circumcision (Figure 27), the Christ child is
hardly visible behind the turned back of the
sandek, who holds the infant during the ritual
brit milah. Rather than overtly presenting
the circumcision as done by Dürer and later
by Hendrik Goltzius (Plate 47), Altdorfer
encourages the viewer to peer into the image
and catch a glimpse of the ceremonial knife in
the hand of the *mohel.*

The set of *Fall and Redemption of Man*
in the Thrivent Financial collection boasts
a royal provenance, having been owned
in the nineteenth century by Friedrich
August II (1797–1854), King of Saxony
(reigned 1836–54). His oval-shaped collector's
stamp containing the initials "FA II" topped
by a crown appears on thirty-five of the forty
woodcuts, usually in the lower right corner,
but often this is obscured by Altdorfer's lines.

■ JRW

Provenance

King Friedrich August II,
King of Saxony
(1797–1854; Lugt 971).

Notes

1. Christiane Andersson
   and Charles W. Talbot,
   *From a Mighty Fortress:
   Prints, Drawings, and
   Books in the Age of Luther,
   1483–1546* (Detroit:
   Detroit Institute of
   Arts, 1983), 180.
2. Giulia Bartrum, *German
   Renaissance Prints, 1490–
   1550* (London: British
   Museum Press, 1995),
   188–89; Andersson and
   Talbot, 180.

Left to right, by row:

Figure 24. *Expulsion from Paradise.*

Figure 25. *Presentation of the Virgin.*

Figure 26. *Nativity.*

Figure 27. *Circumcision.*

Figure 28. *Agony in the Garden.*

Figure 29. *Christ Nailed to the Cross.*

Figure 30. *Ascension.*

Figure 31. *Last Judgment.*

Figure 32. *Virgin Crowned by Angels.*

PLATE 21. Sebald Beham,
*Head of Christ, Wounded
with Thorns,* c. 1520.
Woodcut.

PLATE 21

Sebald Beham,
German, 1500–1550

*Head of Christ,
Wounded
with Thorns*

c. 1520

Woodcut

17 × 13 inches

433 × 331 mm

85-60

Bartsch 26 (as Dürer),
Hollstein 184

Intently sorrowful eyes gaze outward amid bold, thick black lines of Christ's anguished face. This image of the head of Christ is borne out of a rich art historical and theological tradition known as the *sudarium,* deriving specifically from Albrecht Dürer's engraving *Sudarium Held by Two Angels* from 1513 (Figure 33), in which two angels hold St. Veronica's relic handkerchief, the sudarium, between them. Dürer's face on this sudarium (a self-portrait) is the inspiration for Beham's striking, enlarged version in this woodcut. Dürer's famous *Self-Portrait,* a painting from 1500, has also clearly influenced the creation of this woodcut—even the detail of reflected windows has been included in the piercing eyes.[1] Such emulation, as well as later intentional falsification of the attribution of this print through the addition of a Dürer monogram, caused *Head of Christ, Wounded with Thorns* to be attributed to Dürer for some time.

The tradition of the sudarium stems from the apocryphal legend of Veronica, which relates that while Christ carried the cross on the road to Calvary, St. Veronica compassionately wiped his brow with her handkerchief. Christ's face was believed to be miraculously imprinted on the handkerchief, and this cloth became known as the religious relic the sudarium, from the Latin word *suder,* meaning "sweat." During the medieval period, this relic was immensely popular as a destination for pilgrims who had traveled to Rome. Sebald Beham's woodcut is a powerful continuation of this tradition, as well as a potential expression of the concept of spiritual pilgrimage. Just as Veronica pressed her handkerchief onto Christ's face, so too did the printmaker for this woodcut press paper onto the inked block bearing Christ's image. Such a notion may elicit a metaphorical substitute for the religious relic of the sudarium into the hands of devoted collectors and viewers: this imposing face of Christ could serve as a tool for devotional practice, because sight—the literal act of seeing—was a real means for Christians to achieve a spiritual connection and grace in the medieval and Renaissance periods.[2]

Sebald Beham was born in Nuremberg, Germany, where he was heavily influenced by the towering presence of Albrecht Dürer. His work, along with that of his brother Barthel and fellow Nuremberg artist Georg Pencz, is associated with the term *Kleinmeister*

FIGURE 33. Albrecht Dürer, *Sudarium Held by Two Angels,* 1513. Engraving.

(Little Masters), referring to the very small and detailed engravings that were made, printed, and issued by these artists.[3] Beham is certainly known for these minute treasures, but he also was one of the most prolific printmakers of his time. He made more than a thousand woodcuts and approximately 270 etchings and engravings.[4] Beyond their artistic output, Sebald and his brother, along with Pencz, were politically active. In 1525, during the tumultuous time of the Protestant Reformation, the men were tried and banished from the city of Nuremberg on accusations of heresy, blasphemy, and failure to recognize city authority. Less than a year later, after frequent petitioning, they were allowed to return to the city.

Beham has been called Hans Sebald Beham, likely because of his monogram, HSB. Records and his own signature indicate his name was Sebald Beham; one speculation regarding the H in his monogram is that it may refer to the second syllable of his surname.[5]

■ JRL

Notes

1. Giulia Bartrum, *Albrecht Dürer and His Legacy: The Graphic Work of a Renaissance Artist* (Princeton: Princeton University Press, 2002), 82.
2. Bob Scribner, "Ways of Seeing in the Age of Dürer," in *Dürer and His Culture,* ed. Dagmar Eichberger and Charles Zika (Cambridge: Cambridge University Press, 1998), 107–9.
3. Giulia Bartrum, *German Renaissance Prints, 1490–1550* (London: British Museum Press, 1995), 100.
4. Ibid.
5. Ibid., 99.

ꟾERNA IPSE SVAE MENTIS SIMVLACHRA LVTHERꟾ

THE PROTESTANT REFORMATION

Lucas Cranach, the Elder, *Martin Luther as an Augustinian Monk* (details; see Plate 22).

PLATE 22

**Lucas Cranach,
the Elder, German,
1472–1553**

*Martin Luther as an
Augustinian Monk*

1520

Engraving

5⅝ × 3⅞ inches
143 × 98 mm

85-17

Hollstein VI 6

Watermark: Small coat
of arms, possibly Saxon

Lucas Cranach and Martin Luther were close friends: each was godfather to the other's children, and they collaborated on art during the Protestant Reformation. Their personal and professional intimacy is evident in Cranach's portraits of Luther. This engraving was the first of many images Cranach would ultimately create of his friend. Despite its apparent simplicity, its significance to the theological and cultural changes of the time was momentous. As an early, and apparently quite accurate, representation of Luther, this became a direct and indirect model for many subsequent portraits.

Humanist Petrus Mosellanus describes Martin Luther after seeing his debate with Johannes Eck in 1519:

> Martin is of middle height, emaciated from care and study, so that you can almost count his bones through his skin. He is in the vigor of manhood and has a clear, penetrating voice…He is affable and friendly, in no sense dour or arrogant…he is vivacious, jocose, always cheerful and gay no matter how hard his adversaries press him.[1]

Luther's gaunt face, Augustinian tonsure, simple garment, and intent gaze present a scholarly and ascetic young monk to viewers. Cranach's Luther is a resolved, pious, and trustworthy figure to admire and follow, and Martin Luther was indeed a devout scholar monk. This image reflects his life in the period 1512–19, when he was a biblical scholar and professor at the University of Wittenberg while the Reformation was beginning. The inscription on the engraving reads: "Luther himself gave form to an eternal likeness of his spirit; Lucas portrayed the mortal appearance." Under the inscription is the date of the print and Cranach's monogram, a crowned serpent with wings holding a ring in its mouth. The monogram

derives from the coat of arms Cranach was granted in 1508 by Duke Friedrich, the Wise, of Saxony.[2]

In 1517 Luther posted his famous Ninety-five Theses on the door of the Wittenberg Castle church, the act historically considered to mark the start of the Protestant Reformation. He did not intend to break from the church when he posted his theses but rather hoped to stimulate discussion and much needed reform. Theological debate had been ongoing among clergy, scholars, and laypersons for some time. Luther was a tremendously gifted scholar and theologian whose thoughtful call for change resonated throughout Europe.

Religious and daily life in Europe when the Reformation began was often stressful. Death and disease were ever present, reminding people of the futility of life. Popular images and songs about death, witchcraft, magic, and astrology were common, as was the fear of damnation. Luther and many others felt that the effort to attain salvation was a never-ending cycle of sin and redemption. Christians were encouraged to confess constantly and engage in pious practices such as the purchase of indulgences to offset their sinful nature. What had once been a system to relieve the fears of damnation, the doctrinal practices now related to "good works" to attain salvation and absolve sins had become misused, abused, and overwrought. Even more, the papacy was widely considered to be corrupt, there were massive problems in the church and major political instability in the Holy Roman Empire, and rapidly shifting societal changes predominated. Luther's own anxiety over attaining salvation and righteousness was shared by many Christians.

Notes

1. Christiane Andersson and Charles W. Talbot, *From a Mighty Fortress: Prints, Drawings, and Books in the Age of Luther, 1483–1546* (Detroit: Detroit Institute of Arts, 1983), 232.
2. Ibid., 215.
3. Ibid., 232.
4. Ibid.

While engaged in biblical study of Paul's Letter to the Romans, Luther famously came upon chapter 1, verse 17: "the one who is righteous will live by faith." This sparked his doctrine of *Justification by Grace through Faith* that became one of Luther's primary theological tenets and was eventually shared by many reformers. Luther concluded that Christians are justified, or attain salvation, through the freely given gift of God's grace. Humans can and need do nothing to deserve or earn salvation, which does not depend on one's goodness or righteousness: God's righteousness and love through faith save humanity. Ultimately this relatively simple concept comforted and revolutionized the religious lives of countless Christians who were reassured by Luther's reasoned writings.

When this engraving by Cranach was made in 1520 Luther's reputation and views were well established. There was a public demand for portraits of this notable, radical personage. Cranach's three famous engravings made in 1520 and 1521 (two impressions of which are in the Thrivent Financial Collection of Religious Art) absolutely met this demand and became prototypes for contemporary and later copies.

A change in state occurs when the print matrix (the plate or the block) is altered. The three states of this engraving tell an interesting story of its likely distribution and function. The first state (of which only two impressions are extant) contains one horizontal line separating Luther from the inscription. The second state adds another horizontal line above the inscription with vertical hatchings and includes a curious bearded figure in profile in the upper left, probably not added by Cranach but indeed in his lifetime; one unique impression exists of this state.[3] The

PLATE 22. Lucas Cranach, the Elder, *Martin Luther as an Augustinian Monk,* 1520. Engraving (actual size).

third state, to which this Thrivent Financial impression belongs, is fairly rare today as well, with about thirty known impressions. Traces of the bearded figure are visible still, yet most of him has been burnished out. This state was published in an edition, probably in the later sixteenth century. This print, the earliest portrait engraving of Luther by Cranach, became a prototype for subsequent portraits and a model for the second engraving Cranach made of Luther in 1520 (Hollstein 7) in which he stands in a niche, holding a book. That engraving was the editioned, circulated portrait and the direct model for Hans Baldung's 1521 woodcut (Plate 24).[4]

■ JRL

PLATE 23

**Lucas Cranach,
the Elder, German,
1472–1553**

*Martin Luther
in Profile with
Doctoral Cap*

1521

Engraving

8³⁄₁₆ × 5⅞ inches
206 × 149 mm

97-01

Hollstein 8 II/II

Watermark: Running
horse

Notes

1. Christiane Andersson
   and Charles W. Talbot,
   *From a Mighty Fortress:
   Prints, Drawings, and
   Books in the Age of
   Luther, 1483–1546*
   (Detroit: Detroit
   Institute of Arts, 1983),
   234.
2. Ibid.
3. For an excellent study
   of art during this
   period, see Joseph
   Leo Koerner, *The
   Reformation of the Image*
   (Chicago: University of
   Chicago Press, 2004).

Martin Luther wears the doctoral cap of theologians in this portrait, intended to be visual evidence of his scholarship, piety, and authority. He obtained his doctorate degree in 1512, and in 1521 a portrait that emphasized his academic background was of utmost importance to Luther and his supporters, because in this year he appeared at the Diet of Worms and was condemned for heresy and excommunicated. This commanding portrait also commemorates Luther's profile in the ancient tradition of ensuring the image of the subject for posterity.[1]

The first and second states of this engraving are both quite rare, with five known impressions of the first and eleven known impressions of the second (one of which is in the Thrivent Financial collection). The second state differs from the first in that Cranach added hatched lines to darken the background and provide a visual foil for the profile; he also added the second line with vertical hatchings just above the inscription, which reads, "Lucas's work is this picture of Luther's mortal form, but Luther himself expressed his spirit's eternal form."[2] Like other portraits of Luther by Cranach, this engraving was copied many times by artists in different prints of varying quality.

Luther's ideas initiated major changes across most aspects of early sixteenth-century European society. He inspired new artistic subject matter and influenced the reasons to create and distribute art.[3] This is especially true for prints, which were considered fundamentally different from lavish church decoration, such as the elaborate altarpieces and gilded sculpture that reformers criticized. Progressive social movements were already under way with the onset of the Renaissance and humanism across Europe, an increase in secularism throughout society and culture,

and new political and religious developments. During the Reformation, prints were appreciated for serving potential instructional roles and furthering an individual's understanding of the Bible and religious ideas. While Luther and other reformers warned against misdirected worship of images and saints (which some radical reformers interpreted as supporting iconoclasm), the Reformation also encouraged artistic innovation. Luther did not condone the destruction of religious images, and he participated in great artistic collaboration, such as that with Lucas Cranach. Many propaganda and polemical prints and broadsheets were also produced on both sides of the Reformation debate, from the fairly mild to the extremely vulgar.

Portraiture, pamphlets, and other prints were crucial to the dissemination of Reformation theology and ideas. Luther's theology was strong, but it needed distribution to take hold. Portraits of Reformation leaders made by artists like Cranach and Albrecht Dürer not only gave a face to the name of these revolutionary figures but also ensured that their ideas were widely distributed, thus discussed. Reformers' writings and both Catholic and Protestant statements were mass produced on the printing press and then publicized. Earlier reform attempts were unsuccessful in part because at that time there had not been an affordable and accessible way to communicate information, but the invention of the press allowed ideas to travel quickly and gain momentum over broad areas. Books were previously rare and expensive, requiring hand-copied pages. The widespread use of the printing press was absolutely a vital component to the success of the Protestant Reformation because it provided a relatively inexpensive means of replicating ideas and images.

■ JRL

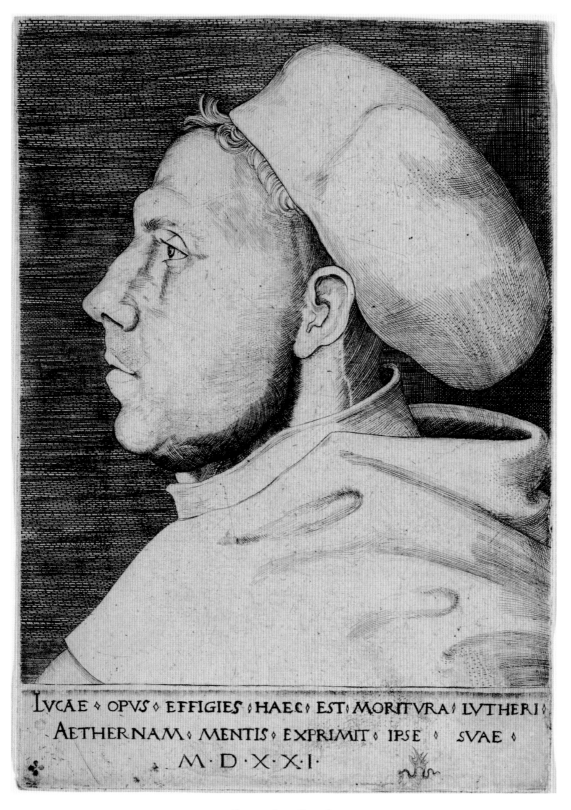

LVCAE ◆ OPVS ◆ EFFIGIES ◆ HAEC ◆ EST ◆ MORITVRA ◆ LVTHERI ◆
AETHERNAM ◆ MENTIS ◆ EXPRIMIT ◆ IPSE ◆ SVAE ◆
◆ M ◆ D ◆ X ◆ X ◆ I ◆

PLATE 23. Lucas Cranach,
the Elder, *Martin Luther in
Profile with Doctoral Cap*,
1521. Engraving (actual
size).

PLATE 24. Hans Baldung (Grien), *Martin Luther as an Augustinian Friar,* 1521. Woodcut (actual size).

Radiant light surrounds Martin Luther's head, visually likening him to a saint. This forceful portrait conveys essential aspects of his theology, cultural influence, and perception. The book in his hands represents his belief of *sola scriptura* (Scripture as the sole authority for Christians), and direct inspiration from the Holy Spirit is shown with the dove above his head. In the woodcut Luther touches the book, which is symbolically a conduit for divine inspiration: from the Holy Spirit through Luther to the book, he serves as an interpreter of God's word. Hans Baldung presents Luther's belief in *sola scriptura* as divinely inspired, and the nimbus of light over Luther's head and the dove are visual attributes historically reserved for saints in art.

This woodcut is an example showing how Reformation leaders depicted in prints were presented as a new type of saint and portrait imagery in visual culture, a practice that bolstered the Protestant cause and incited anger from Catholics (see Plate 25, *Philipp Melanchthon,* by Albrecht Dürer, as well as Dürer's engraving of Friedrich, the Wise,

Figure 34). Both sides of the Reformation debate created and distributed crude and exaggerated propagandistic and polemical imagery, but relatively simple portraits of Luther such as this one could provoke even stronger anger and response from the church. Because "saintly" Luther is here divinely inspired after he had been condemned and excommunicated from the church, this was indeed sensational material. This particular portrait of Luther was banned by papal authorities at the Diet of Worms in 1521, and many extant copies of the woodcut were defaced and even burned because opposing Catholics accused owners of the image of idolatrously kissing it.[1] This impression from the Thrivent Financial collection, in good condition, survived unscathed.

Baldung made this print after Lucas Cranach's second engraved portrait of Martin Luther made in 1520 (Hollstein 7). Baldung's version, a reverse of Cranach's, omits the niche where Luther stands but is otherwise modeled from the earlier engraving and includes the book. Baldung adds two significant elements to his woodcut: the Holy Spirit (the dove) and Luther's actual touch of the book that he holds. With this woodcut portrait we can see how Cranach's early prototype portraits of Luther (Plates 22 and 23) provide strong inspiration and models for other works that proved highly influential in their own right. Baldung's portrait was probably seen and handled even more than Cranach's first portrait of Luther, which was never published for wide distribution. Certainly the banning of this image by the church in 1521 would have increased the public's interest in and reaction to it.

This woodcut illustrated the title page of the first edition of *Acta et Res Gestae,*

Dr. Martini Lutheri (Acts and deeds of Dr. Martin Luther), published in Strasbourg in 1521; the Latin title is on the verso, with the woodcut printed on the recto. It was reissued many times by the printer Johann Schott. On the Thrivent Financial impression, ink traces remain of an addition by hand in the lower portion, which appears to be a direct copy of the inscription from Cranach's early portraits of Luther. At the end of the "inscription" is the designation "Cranach"— thus intentionally linking this impression to Cranach's portraits. This addition to the impression demonstrates the enduring function of this Reformation print, one that continued the legacy of Cranach's portraits of Luther and potentially the perception of Luther as a powerful, influential man. Perhaps a collector at some point would consider the woodcut incomplete without Cranach's inscription.

Hans Baldung was a pupil of Albrecht Dürer and worked in his studio for approximately four years starting in 1503. The two men maintained a friendship even after Baldung moved to Strasbourg, where he spent most of his life. He created a number of paintings, including an important altarpiece of the Coronation of the Virgin for the cathedral of Freiburg, which was his masterpiece. Baldung was a prolific printmaker and draftsman who made many hundreds of drawings and prints. He is often called "Hans Baldung Grien," and after 1507 a G was added to his monogram. The nickname may have been granted by Dürer and may refer to Baldung's love of the color green, or it may be related to *Grienhams,* which means devil, because of the artist's regular inclusion of demons, death, and witchcraft in his work.[2]

■ JRL

PLATE 24

Hans Baldung (Grien), German, 1484/1485–1545

Martin Luther as an Augustinian Friar

1521
Woodcut
6⅛ × 4½ inches
156 × 115 mm
90-03
Hollstein 270,
Bartsch VII.313.39

Provenance

Friedrich Quiring (born 1886), Eberswalde (Lugt 1041c); Gutekunst & Klipstein, Stuttgart, 1950, sale 57; Albert W. Blum (1882–1952), New Jersey (Lugt 79b).

Notes

1. Joseph Leo Koerner, *The Reformation of the Image* (Chicago: University of Chicago Press, 2004), 115.
2. Giulia Bartrum, *German Renaissance Prints, 1490–1550* (London: British Museum Press, 1995), 67.

PLATE 25. Albrecht Dürer,
Philipp Melanchthon, 1526.
Engraving (actual size).

Philipp Melanchthon (1497–1560) was considered one of the most brilliant men of his time and arguably the most gifted scholar of Greek in Europe, along with Erasmus of Rotterdam. Melanchthon was a prodigy as a child and became a famous humanist and theologian known throughout Europe from a very young age. The prominent forehead, slightly furrowed brow, and bulging veins featured in this engraving do not simply reveal his physical characteristics but also reinforce his reputation as a great thinker and scholar. As in many other portraits created by Albrecht Dürer, tiny window reflections can be seen in Melanchthon's eyes.

Martin Luther called on Friedrich, the Wise, who founded the University of Wittenberg in 1502, to find an expert on Greek and Hebrew for the university. Philipp Melanchthon arrived in Wittenberg in 1518 at the age of twenty-one and soon established a close friendship and intellectual rapport with Luther. The university lectures of Luther and Melanchthon were renowned throughout Europe, and together they grounded the University of Wittenberg with profound and sound teachings in biblical humanism, a return to the original languages and text of Scripture for scholarly study, and sound biblical translations and commentary. Luther's influential translations of Scripture into German became one of his chief theological and historical contributions. The year this portrait was made, Melanchthon published a Greek grammar textbook and was invited to Nuremberg by the city council to help establish the town's first public school,[1] tasks that gained him the name *Praeceptor Germaniae,* "the teacher of Germany." He contributed to the Reformation by writing a systematic theological textbook, *Loci communes rerum theologicarum* (Fundamental theological themes), in 1521 and by drafting the statement of faith known as the Augsburg

Confession in 1530, which remains a foundational tenet for Lutheran churches today. The inscription on this engraving reads, "Dürer was able to depict Philipp's features as if living, but the skilled hand could not portray his soul."[2] Of course, Dürer attempts to do just that, and ultimately the humility of the inscription is outwon by the artist's mastery of the medium and keen understanding of Melanchthon's influence.

Melanchthon's portrait was one of many by Dürer and his contemporaries of key Reformation figures. These images provided faces for the names and views that were discussed and debated in daily life. Such portraits also functioned in part as replacements for the declining imagery of saints in religious art and popular culture as the Reformation progressed. Saints had long been depicted in religious art, but most detailed legends about the lives of the saints are derived from noncanonical sources or church tradition; Luther taught that Scripture was the sole authority for Christians, thus subjects for religious art not from Scripture began to decrease as secular subject matter increased. Artists of the sixteenth century began to produce portraits of church leaders, both Protestant and Catholic, in positions traditionally held by saints in these artworks (primarily prints, but also other media, such as large, austere altarpieces). In Lucas Cranach's *Wittenberg Altarpiece,* Melanchthon is visible in the upper right panel officiating an infant baptism, a role customary for saints in altarpieces.[3] A living person performing an activity usually reserved for a historical saint could serve as a representation of complex theological issues, such as the argument against saints as intercessors for human salvation. Melanchthon substituting for John the Baptist could also become a tangible and accessible expression of the heated debate

PLATE 25

Albrecht Dürer, German, 1471–1528

Philipp Melanchthon

1526
Engraving
6¹³⁄₁₆ × 4¹⁵⁄₁₆ inches
173 × 126 mm
82-20
Bartsch 105, Meder 104a
Watermark: Small jug (Meder 158)

Provenance

For *Philipp Melanchthon,* J. C. D. Hebich (1818–1891; Lugt 1251). For *Friedrich, the Wise,* Alfred Morrison (1821–1897; Lugt 151).

Notes

1. Giulia Bartrum, *German Renaissance Prints, 1490–1550* (London: British Museum Press, 1995), 61.
2. Ibid., 60.
3. Joseph Leo Koerner, *The Reformation of the Image* (Chicago: University of Chicago Press, 2004), 199.

over the validity of infant baptism versus later baptism by choice.

Reformers' concerns over idolatry, the overt worship (as opposed to pious veneration) of saints and religious imagery, instigated debate and questions about the creation of religious art. Extreme proponents of this view even resorted to iconoclasm, the violent destruction of religious imagery—an activity that Luther and many of his supporters did not condone. Ultimately, after substantial reflection and deliberation, Luther, Dürer, and many of their contemporaries determined that religious art and music were wonderful and permissible, provided they were expressed in service to God, who created them. This would be opposed, for example, to the excessive decoration of churches and to commissions for religious art made by the wealthy attempting to practice "good works" to attain salvation.

In 1524 Dürer engraved a portrait of Friedrich III, the Wise, elector and Duke of Saxony (1463–1525) (Figure 34). Friedrich was a powerful nobleman, one of seven electors of the Holy Roman Emperor and inheritor of one of the largest collections of relics in Europe. Humanist and great patron of the arts and sciences, Friedrich also became a chief supporter of Martin Luther. Most notably, he welcomed Luther at Wartburg Castle when Luther was in physical danger after refusing to recant his beliefs at the Diet of Worms in 1521 and was condemned and excommunicated for heresy. Friedrich was also one of Dürer's earliest and most important patrons. In this portrait Friedrich is dressed richly and accompanied by two coats of arms. This engraving was made one year before his death; the duke gazes outward with a commanding presence as he undoubtedly did during his life.

Dürer, also a leading thinker and humanist, passionately wrote appeals to great leaders of Europe, including Erasmus and Friedrich, to support Luther and his Reformation cause. In Dürer's diaries we learn that he owned and valued many books and pamphlets of Luther's writings, and he was distraught while in Antwerp in 1521, worrying for Luther's safety: "[Martin Luther is] a man enlightened by the Holy Ghost, a follower of Christ and of the true Christian faith, and whether he lives yet or whether they have put him to death, I know not…if he has suffered it is for the sake of Christian truth and because he has fought with the un-Christlike papacy."[4] Dürer was undoubtedly relieved to learn that Friedrich sheltered Luther after the Diet of Worms, especially since he had earlier written to Friedrich requesting that he protect Luther.

■ JRL

FIGURE 34. Albrecht Dürer, *Friedrich, the Wise,* 1524. Engraving.

Notes

4. Albrecht Dürer, *Dürer's Record of Journeys to Venice and the Low Countries,* ed. Roger Fry (New York: Dover Publications, 1995), 83–84.

PLATE 26. Barthel Beham, *Chancellor Leonhart von Eck,* 1527. Engraving.

Deep folds and creases in thick fabric mimic the character lines on the face of this imposing figure, Leonhart von Eck (1480–1550), who was the chancellor to Duke Wilhelm IV of Bavaria. This portrait by Barthel Beham is a very rare first state impression of the engraving. In the second state, Beham added a sumptuous fur coat and wide-brimmed hat, which necessitated a change in the placement of the upper inscription. The skullcap (traditional for scholars) and less formal garments worn by the chancellor in the first state probably indicate that this initial state was intended for his friends and family, whereas the second, more formal state was an official portrait.[1] This engraving clearly declares the subject's identity with its inscription of von Eck's name and his age of forty-seven, along with Beham's initials and the date.

Although the first impression of this engraving shows von Eck in simpler attire than the second state, he still wears the clothing of a wealthy individual. His undershirt, likely made of fine lawn or linen, is constructed with an excessive (thus expensive) gathering of material, topped with an embroidered collar. The pleated wool robe over the undergarment is lined with a trimming of fur and is also constructed with abundant fabric. Certainly

with the addition of the fur coat and hat in the second state, the chancellor would appear to the sixteenth-century viewer an affluent, powerful man.

For centuries, those who commissioned portraits of themselves chose to be presented in their finest and most formal appearance. A clear contrast can be made, however, when we consider how Martin Luther is customarily depicted around this time (see Plates 22 and 28). Luther is often intentionally portrayed in simple, usually austere garments with little or no embellishment. Many Christians at the time criticized the wealth and luxury enjoyed and demanded by nobility, the church, and some clergy, and portraits of nobility and clergy in elegant and expensive dress could incite anger from average viewers and reformers. Practices such as the inappropriate sale of indulgences that contributed to papal extravagance could be underscored by the visual representation of reformers in plain and inexpensive clothing— proof of their opposition to such excess. Beham may not have intended to make this point with von Eck's fine attire in this particular engraving; most likely he dressed von Eck according to the chancellor's wishes. Yet in examining depictions of reformers and those opposed to the Reformation (such as Chancellor von Eck), we see how portraits became layered with complex meaning and function, capable of far more than just showing what someone looked like or representing an individual for posterity.

Barthel Beham, along with his brother Sebald Beham and their contemporary Georg Pencz, is known as one of the "Little Masters" for the tiny, meticulous engravings they created. Beham's command of the medium is evident in his small engravings as well as in this superb impression of *Chancellor Leonhart von Eck.* Beham was born in Nuremberg, where he was heavily influenced by Albrecht Dürer and by his brother, with whom he may have trained. Barthel Beham moved to Munich in 1527 and soon began to work in the service of the strongly Catholic dukes of Bavaria, including Duke Wilhelm IV.[2] This engraving was made shortly after he arrived at the court in Munich.[3]

■ JRL

PLATE 26

Barthel Beham, German, 1502–1540

Chancellor Leonhart von Eck

1527
Engraving
4⁵⁄₁₆ × 3¾ inches
109 × 82 mm
99-10
Bartsch 64 I/II,
Hollstein 94

Provenance

H. Nestle-John, Frankfurt/Main; C. G. Boerner, Leipzig, Versteigerung 193, June 1937, no. 29; Das Bibliographikon (Hans and Wolfgang Boerner), Berlin, Ausstellungsprospekt, November 1939, no. 4.

Notes

1. Suzanne Boorsch and Nadine M. Orenstein, "The Print in the North: The Age of Albrecht Dürer and Lucas van Leyden," *The Metropolitan Museum of Art Bulletin* 54, no. 4 (1997): 49.
2. Giulia Bartrum, *German Renaissance Prints, 1490–1550* (London: British Museum Press, 1995), 122.
3. Boorsch and Orenstein, 49.

PLATE 27

Albrecht Dürer,
German, 1471–1528

The Last Supper

1523

Woodcut

8⅜ × 11¾ inches
213 × 299 mm

96-02

Meder 184 a.b/e

Watermark: High crown,
Meder 20

In Albrecht Dürer's *Last Supper,* dated 1523 (six years after Martin Luther posted his Ninety-five Theses), a charger is prominently displayed in the foreground, curiously empty. The lamb typically included on such a plate but absent here refers to the theological doctrine of transubstantiation and the Eucharistic sacrament. Another *Last Supper* by Dürer from his *Large Passion* series, published in 1511, is a more traditional depiction of the scene: the charger on the table holds the carcass of a lamb, the representation of the sacrifice and actual body of Christ. In this 1523 woodcut, both the bread and wine are in the right foreground, likely referring to the reformers' rejection of the exclusivity of the cup for clergy only in the Eucharist—the vessel, containing the wine, is available to all at this table. As early as 1520 Luther preached that all Christians should receive the Eucharist in both forms.

Technically, this woodcut is marvelous to absorb. A sophisticated interplay of grays and ordered lines are complex, yet seem perfectly restrained, giving an effect of austerity, monumentality, and strength. There is a sense of controlled horizontality, but Dürer also includes small diagonal lines to animate the scene. He has further made the print visually interesting by introducing asymmetry and skewing compositional centrality.[1]

During the medieval period, the meaning and theology of the Eucharist was passionately debated. In the thirteenth century, at the Fourth Lateran Council, the doctrine of transubstantiation was established; based on Greek metaphysical theories, it stated that during mass the priest miraculously consecrates the bread and wine such that they remain bread and wine but contain the body and blood of Christ through God's power.[2] This was extremely significant theologically because the church had long taught that through the Eucharist Christians can become a part of Christ by consuming his body and blood, and thus attain grace and salvation through his sacrifice and God's love. Most pre-Reformation Christians believed the Eucharist to be a reenactment or repetition of the culmination of the Passion story, the Crucifixion,[3] but some felt it was rather a *remembrance* of Christ's sacrifice.

Reformers proposed and implemented important changes to the mass and the sacrament of the Eucharist: mass was said in the vernacular language of the people, not Latin; the Eucharist in both forms, bread and wine, was given to all Christians, rather than withholding wine from laity; and transubstantiation was rejected. Luther ultimately accepted the real presence of Christ in the Eucharist but many reformers did not, and the doctrine of transubstantiation continued to be challenged. The reformers no longer considered the mass and the Eucharist a "sacrifice," and in some Last Supper imagery from the time of the Reformation the sacrificial lamb has been removed. Last Supper scenes, a part of the Passion story, were historically associated with the Eucharist because Christ shares a meal with the Apostles before his sacrifice, and similarly the Eucharist can be understood as Christ sharing his body with his believers.

FIGURE 35. Sebald Beham, *Protestant Satire on the Eucharist,* c. 1520–25. Pen and ink drawing.

PLATE 27. Albrecht Dürer,
The Last Supper, 1523.
Woodcut.

This woodcut may have been intended for an oblong Passion series by Dürer that never was completed.[4] Dürer created this woodcut later in his life, during years of intense reflection prompted by reformers' debates over whether religious art was permissible. We know from his writings that he struggled with the issue, as did Luther, but by 1525 Dürer and Luther were both openly defending and upholding the value and joy inherent to religious art. They derided the notion that art caused idolatry; rather, the unthinking person did.

Eucharistic theology was discussed in various aspects of society and was evident in many examples of art. *Protestant Satire on the Eucharist,* by Sebald Beham, c. 1520–25 (Figure 35; see Plate 21 for information on Beham), is a small circular pen and ink drawing in the Thrivent Financial collection that features a goat, dressed in a monk's robe, presenting a plate of meat to three men; two appear to accept it, but the figure on the far right seems to reject it. The goat is probably meant to be Hieronymous Emser (1477–1527), a Catholic priest and chaplain to Duke George of Saxony, whose family crest was a goat's head. Initially, Emser sympathized with many of Luther's views, but gradually the two became divided by heated debates and insults. In 1519 Luther began to call him "Bock Emser" (*bock* meaning "goat") after he attacked Luther's views in a pamphlet and assisted Johannes Eck at the Leipzig debate. This drawing, which warrants further study, may have been a model for a potential illustration for one of the many propagandistic broadside woodcuts against Emser published around this time.[5] The drawing includes a collector's mark with the initials C and R in the lower center of the recto.

■ JRL

Provenance

Dr. W. A. Ackermann (1793–1865; Lugt 791).

Notes

1. Jordan Kantor, *Dürer's Passions* (Cambridge: Harvard University Art Museums, 2000), 39–40.
2. Carter Lindberg, *A Reformation Reader* (Oxford: Blackwell Publishing, 1996), 185.
3. Joseph Leo Koerner, *The Reformation of the Image* (Chicago: University of Chicago Press, 2004), 349.
4. Kantor, 38.
5. An idea proposed by William H. Schab, 1984.

PLATE 28

**Hans Brosamer,
German, 1506–1554**

*Portrait of
Martin Luther*

c. 1540

Hand-colored woodcut

14¼ × 10 inches
359 × 254 mm

01-02

Hollstein 595,
Geisberg–Strauss 425

Watermark: *Schreitender bar*
(Striding bear)

PLATE 28. Hans Brosamer,
Portrait of Martin Luther,
c. 1540. Hand-colored
woodcut.

Hans Brosamer was a painter and printmaker who closely followed Lucas Cranach, the Elder and was further influenced by the work of Albrecht Dürer and Hans Holbein.[1] Brosamer's significant contribution to Reformation imagery includes this portrait of Martin Luther; earlier pendant woodcuts of Luther and his wife, Katherine von Bora (1530); and illustrations for editions of Luther's *Bible* (1550), *Large Catechism* (1550), *Small Catechism* (1540), and *Interpretation of the Epistles and Gospels* (1544).[2]

This rare, hand-colored impression closely emulates Cranach's later portraits of Martin Luther in which the theologian wears a dark cloak and a scholar's cap with side flaps. An engraving by Heinrich Aldegrever made around the same time (Figure 36) shows Luther in similar understated attire, further demonstrating Cranach as the primary source for Luther's visual persona. Brosamer's woodcut mimics (albeit in reverse) Cranach's paintings in which Luther's deep-set eyes gaze directly at the viewer. Even the bright green background imitates Cranach's oil versions, although curiously Luther's eyes have been inaccurately tinted blue rather than brown in the woodcut. In contrast to earlier portraits of Luther as a lean and ascetic Augustinian monk, here he is a strong family man with a stout neck and full face—an ideal leader for a new church in which clergy were encouraged to marry.[3]

The Latin inscription above the portrait also offers a clue as to how Luther appeared to reformers in the mid-sixteenth century:

> *In silentio et spe erit fortitudo vestra.*
> *Martinus Luther abconterfect.*

> In quietness and in hope shall be your strength.
> Martin Luther portrayed.[4]

The first line is a phrase from Isaiah 30:15, quoted by Luther in his lecture on Romans as he explains that "One who believes in Christ does not hasten or flee; he is not frightened, because he fears nothing; he stands quiet and secure, founded upon a firm rock, according to the teaching of the Lord."[5] With this reference from Isaiah in mind, the word *abconterfect* in the second line takes on an especially interesting dual meaning.

Commonly adapted in a variety of Latin and vernacular forms during the Renaissance to describe portraiture, the Latin word *contrafactum* (literally, "counterfeit") is perhaps best interpreted as a "representation" that conveys information about the portrayed subject; it implies that the image is a true likeness.[6] The variant form in the inscription here, *abconterfect*, reinforces the idea that the portrait is derived from another source.[7] On the surface, *abconterfect* can mean that the portrait is a likeness or effigy of Martin Luther taken from life. It might also have been understood that Brosamer's woodcut was based on another picture of Luther, perhaps one of Cranach's portraits. But read within the context of the full inscription, *abconterfect* could subtly refer to the previous line and suggest that Luther's likeness here is drawn from the quiet fortitude promised through faith and hope in Christ. Luther's compelling gaze, masterfully carved into the woodblock and transferred to the page, conveys calm resolve.

The text below the portrait indicates that it was published by Hans Guldenmund of Nuremberg.[8] Active for half a century until his death in 1560, Guldenmund was a book dealer whose workshop printed pamphlets, broadsides, and single-leaf woodcuts by many German artists, including Brosamer, Dürer, and Sebald Beham.[9] Although there is no evidence that Guldenmund designed or cut woodblocks, he certainly was an illuminator, increasing the possibility that this rare impression in the Thrivent Financial collection was hand-colored in his workshop.[10]

■ JRW

FIGURE 36. Heinrich Aldegrever, *Portrait of Martin Luther*, 1540. Engraving.

Notes

1. F. W. H. Hollstein, *Hollstein's German Engravings, Etchings, and Woodcuts. Volume 4: Beischlag—Brosamer* (Amsterdam: M. Hertzberger, 1954), 208; Walter L. Strauss, ed., with Max Geisberg, *The German Single-Leaf Woodcut, 1500–1550* (New York: Hacker Art Books, 1974), xvi.
2. Hollstein, 232–33, 242–44.
3. Lyndal Roper, "Martin Luther's Body: The 'Stout Doctor' and His Biographers," *American Historical Review* 115 (April 2010): 355.
4. The translation here is consistent with that of Luther's *Bible,* in which *spe* was translated into German as *Hoffen,* meaning "hope." The New Revised Standard Version (NRSV) uses the word "trust" instead.
5. Martin Luther and Wilhelm Pauck, *Luther: Lectures on Romans* (Louisville: Westminster John Knox Press, 2006), 283.
6. Peter W. Parshall, "Imago Contrafacta: Images and Facts in the Northern Renaissance," *Art History* 14, no. 4 (December 1993): 555.
7. Ibid.
8. Roper, 357.
9. David Landau and Peter W. Parshall, *The Renaissance Print, 1470–1550* (New Haven: Yale University Press, 1994), 223.
10. Ibid.

ITALIAN PRINTS & DRAWINGS

Pellegrino Tibaldi or Giulio Clovio, *Moses and the Miracle of the Serpents* (details; see Plate 30).

PLATE 29. Attributed to
Domenico Campagnola,
Susanna and the Elders,
c. 1540–60. Pen and
brown ink, brown wash
(actual size).

PLATE 29

Attributed to
Domenico
Campagnola, Italian,
1500–1564

*Susanna and
the Elders*

c. 1540–60
Pen and brown ink,
brown wash
7¾ × 6¾ inches
197 × 172 mm
93-30

As related in the apocryphal book of Susanna, two elders, driven by lust, surprise Susanna while she bathes alone in her garden and threaten to falsely charge her with adultery unless she submits to their licentious desire. Beyond the far archway, two maidservants rush to find their mistress, who has cried out in anguish: Susanna knows that if she chooses not to sin in the eyes of the Lord, the elders will sentence her to death.

As apprentice and adopted son of Giulio Campagnola (c. 1482–after 1515), Domenico was trained in the Venetian school, and his style is indebted to Giovanni Bellini (c. 1431/36–1516), Giorgione (c. 1477/78–1510), and Titian (c. 1488/90–1576). A master in his own right, Domenico was a leading painter in the nearby city of Padua, where he produced frescoes and panel paintings for churches and palaces. Already during his lifetime, Domenico's pastoral woodcuts and drawings were collected and appreciated.[1] Today these same works capture the interest of scholars, who celebrate his role in developing the Italian landscape in the graphic arts, which influenced the landscapes of northern artists such as Hieronymus Cock (Plate 44) and Hendrik Goltzius.

Venetian artists strove to achieve *poesia,* the idea that their art should function like poetry.[2] Attributed to Domenico, *Susanna and the Elders* is distinctly Venetian for its sensuality and lyricism, qualities captured in both the composition's subject and drawing style. Susanna appears here as one of the *belle donne* of Venetian Renaissance art: an idealized female form that often represented Venus or other classical women. Lightly draped, Susanna demurely covers her breasts with one arm and turns her face away from the leering men. Her chaste reaction asserts her innocence in the encounter and also purifies her body for the external viewer, who is meant to appreciate her natural beauty. This theme is carried beyond the symmetrical architecture of Susanna's gazebo into the lush garden. Between the arches the artist has suggested a broad pastoral landscape of hills and foliage. Most prominently, two pairs of trees flank Susanna, framing her body with symbols that reiterate her beauty as innate to God's creation.

The artist's use of the pen supports the poetic treatment of the subject. His flowing lines offer a sense of shape rather than a modeling of mass, as seen in the central Italian style of *Moses and the Miracle of the Serpents* (Plate 30). Curving lines that begin in the upper right corner and sweep across the page to the left imply atmosphere and movement, perhaps a breeze. Similarly, the lines that shape the robes of the elders and the maidservants suggest dramatic motion. The overall composition is given variety and rhythm through the contrasting fluid and staccato strokes that form the tree trunks, foliage, hills, and architecture. Thoughtfully structured yet spontaneously executed, this drawing is a fine example of Italian Renaissance art in the Thrivent Financial collection.

■ JRW

Notes

1. Edgar Peters Bowron, Michael Clarke, and Andrew Butterfield, *Titian and the Golden Age of Venetian Painting: Masterpieces from the National Galleries of Scotland* (Houston: Museum of Fine Arts, Houston, 2010), 72.
2. Helen Gardner, Fred S. Kleiner, and Christin J. Mamiya, *Gardner's Art through the Ages* (Belmont: Thompson/ Wadsworth, 2005), 641.

PLATE 30. Pellegrino
Tibaldi or Giulio Clovio,
*Moses and the Miracle of
the Serpents,* c. 1540–90.
Pen, brown ink, brush,
and brown wash on laid
paper backed with tan
wove paper.

PLATE 30

Pellegrino Tibaldi,
Italian, 1527–1596,
or Giulio Clovio,
Croatian, 1498–1578

*Moses and
the Miracle
of the Serpents*

Moses and the Miracle of the Serpents presents a visual and art historical puzzle to its viewers. Several figures, soldiers or guards, in the left foreground were cut out and then pasted into the composition; this figural grouping is visually and compositionally set apart from the rest of the drawing. Close examination also reveals significant stylistic differences between various portions of the drawing. Michelangelesque style is evident in the lively, muscular soldiers on the left. Characteristic of the stippled manner typical of the late drawings of Michelangelo, the shading of the left foreground figure (whose back faces the viewer) is masterfully built up with many small dots. Many vertical and curving lines, along with delicate, sweeping lines and wash, suggest the musculature and fabric of this robust figure that dominates the composition. Parallel vertical lines are also prominent in the other figures in this grouping, as well as in additional sections that have been pasted into the composition (such as near Pharaoh's legs and the serpents on the far right) and some areas on the larger sheet. The stippling, however, is confined to the colossal figure in the left foreground. Rachel McGarry has suggested that these figures were executed by an earlier hand, different from the artist who completed the larger drawing; they may have been added as artistic inspiration or as an instructional element to the later work.[1]

Like many Old Master drawings, this work's attribution is not definitive. When *Moses and the Miracle of the Serpents* was acquired for the Thrivent Financial Collection of Religious Art in 1993, it had been considered for some time to be by the great sixteenth-century miniaturist Giulio Clovio, who worked in Italy during the High Renaissance. The attribution of Clovio was suggested around 1950 by Otto Benesch, Austrian art historian and director of the

Albertina in Vienna. The following is inscribed in graphite in modern script on the lower right verso of the drawing:

> Giulio Clovio 1498–1578
> Miracle of the Serpents
> CLOVIO ASSISTED MICHELANGELO
> on the Pauline Chapel at
> the Vatican the three cut out
> figures to the left have
> close affinities to the
> three soldiers to the lower
> left of the crucifixion of St
> Peter in the Chapel, painted
> by the Master. The stipple
> manner of this (Clovio) drawing
> is in MICHELANGELO technique.

> *Attribution by Otto Benesch, Director, Albertina, Vienna (1950). See "The Popes as Builders and Humanists," Houston, March 1966. Entry 20, pp. 68–9.

Maria Giovani-Visani agreed with Benesch's attribution of the drawing to Clovio.[2] Clovio was a friend of other notable artists of the period, such as Michelangelo, Pieter Bruegel the Elder, and El Greco. The influence of Michelangelo was significant in Clovio's work: he often studied and copied works by the master.[3]

In 1993, Peter Dreyer, then curator of Drawings and Prints at the Pierpont Morgan Library in New York, studied the drawing in person and suggested in a letter to Richard L. Hillstrom that the artist might be the Italian Mannerist painter and architect Pellegrino Tibaldi. Tibaldi studied under Perino del Vaga in Rome and worked in Bologna, Milan, and later Spain. Michelangelo influenced Tibaldi's oeuvre as well.

Dreyer wrote that "the shading of the reliefs are done primarily with a dense pattern of parallel brush lines rather than dots [characteristic of stippled manner]"; he goes on to

c. 1540–90

Pen, brown ink, brush, and brown wash on laid paper backed with tan wove paper

17 × 15⁹⁄₁₆ inches
432 × 395 mm

93-1

Exhibition

Builders and Humanists: The Renaissance Popes as Patrons of the Arts, University of St. Thomas Art Department, Houston, Texas, March–May 1966, illustrated in exhibition catalogue, 68–69.

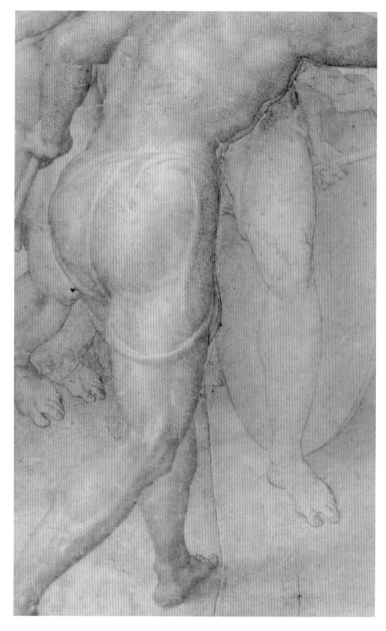

emphasize that this is typical of Tibaldi's style, especially the vertical lines.[4] Comparisons to other works by both artists that focus on formal and stylistic elements may contribute toward the determination of the attribution for *Moses and the Miracle of the Serpents.*[5]

The scene depicted in this drawing is the Miracle of the Serpents from Exodus 7: 8–12, although this sheet does not seem to show the complete composition. In the story Moses and his brother Aaron are commanded by the Lord to go to Pharaoh to ask for the release of the Israelites from slavery in Egypt. Pharaoh demands that they perform a wonder, so Aaron does as God commanded and throws down his staff, which miraculously turns into a serpent. Pharaoh calls for his magicians to do the same, but their serpents are swallowed by Aaron's. In the drawing, Pharaoh is the crowned figure on the right side pointing at serpents that can be seen in the lower right foreground, but Moses and Aaron are not apparent here. The crowds behind Pharaoh gesture and gaze at the miracle. This episode precedes the Ten Plagues and the subsequent assertion of God's omnipotence through the Passover and deliverance of the Israelites from Egypt. Despite the missing narrative figures, and regardless of its attribution, this marvelous Italian Mannerist drawing with its stylized elegance and energetic mood remains a fascinating artwork in need of further research.

■ JRL

FIGURE 37. Detail of *Moses and the Miracle of the Serpents.*

Notes

1. In a visit to the Thrivent Financial collection in 2010, Dr. Rachel McGarry, associate curator of the Print and Drawing department at the Minneapolis Institute of Arts, noted that *Moses and the Miracle of the Serpents* appeared to be created by two hands. The lower left figures in the composition may have been executed decades earlier than the rest of the sheet, perhaps by a Roman or Florentine artist in the 1540s. McGarry suggested that a later artist, maybe in the 1580s, appears to have incorporated this earlier figural group into a larger compositional study. She remarked that it was common studio practice at that time for artists to utilize Old Master drawings and even adapt or alter them for later compositions.

2. Maria Giovani-Visani, *Giulio Clovio: Miniaturist of the Renaissance* (New York: Alpine, 1980), 97.

3. In a 1577 inventory of works owned by Clovio, there is listed a copy by Clovio of a Michelangelo drawing of the same subject as this drawing, "Historia delli serpenti copiata da D. Giulio e invenzione di Michelangelo di penna," Dominique de Menil, *Builders and Humanists: The Renaissance Popes as Patrons of the Arts* (Houston: University of St. Thomas Art Department, 1966), 68–69. Comparisons to other drawings by Clovio are noted by Menil.

4. Peter Dreyer to Richard Hillstrom, Minneapolis, January 7, 1993; collection files of the Thrivent Financial Collection of Religious Art, Minneapolis, Minnesota.

5. Dealer Frederick G. Schab and Peter Dreyer both point to examples by Clovio and Tibaldi respectively in their discussions and correspondence with Richard Hillstrom. Otto Benesch, quoted in Menil, points to examples by Clovio in support of his attribution, as well as possible direct influences from both Michelangelo and Pieter Bruegel. Consideration of these examples and the overall question of attribution call for more study.

Wheels break from their chariots and soldiers cling to their horses as they struggle to stay alive in the crashing waves of the Red Sea (Exodus 14:15–31). The Israelites, safe on the high shore, seem not to notice the fray below, where churning water, overlapping lines, and thrashing figures combine to evoke a sense of pandemonium. Having escaped from Egypt, the Israelites now begin forty years of survival in the wilderness.

Orazio was the son of artist Paolo Farinati (1524–1606) and carried on the family business: all of Orazio's etchings are based on designs by his father. The original painting of this scene by Paolo emphasized a dramatic close-up of Pharaoh's drowning army, a narrative approach to the episode made popular by *Submersion of Pharaoh's Army in the Red Sea,* a monumental woodcut designed by Titian c. 1515 that measures four by seven feet and was published multiple times during the sixteenth century. This composition is not a copy after the Venetian master's woodcut but rather a fully realized original work of art. Battle-oriented scenes, with the turmoil of human figures, horses, and weaponry within a convincingly rendered landscape, required skill in composition and medium that was celebrated in Italian art since the fourteenth century and is demonstrated here by Paolo and Orazio Farinati.[1]

Thrivent Financial's *Crossing the Red Sea* is a second state impression with the printer's address "Galparo dalolio" at the bottom center. Although a later impression, it retains a clarity of line and contrast that makes it a strong example of Italian prints in the collection. ■ JRW

PLATE 31

Orazio Farinati, Italian, 1559–1616

Crossing the Red Sea

1599
Etching
14⅜ × 21⅞ inches
364 × 556 mm (sheet)
88-19
Bartsch 1
Le Blanc I, II/ii

Provenance

Earl Spencer (Lugt 2341a).

Note

1. Leon Battista Alberti, *On Painting* (London: Penguin, 2004), 74–79.

PLATE 31. Orazio Farinati, *Crossing the Red Sea,* 1599. Etching.

PLATE 32

Agostino Carracci,
Italian, 1557–1602

The Crucifixion

1589

Engraving
20 × 47¼ inches
509 × 1200 mm

98-30

Bartsch 23

Watermark: Eagle in
crowned oval in each
sheet (Heawood 87)

According to the canonical Gospels, the
Crucifixion of Jesus Christ occurred at three
o'clock on Good Friday at Mount Calvary,
or Golgotha. The Crucifixion is the most
frequently created and referenced Passion
scene in the history of art. The crucifix, or
cross, is the symbol of Christianity, and, for
Christians, Christ's suffering for humankind is
actualized and made visual in the Crucifixion,
as Christ accepts the sins of humanity—and
humanity itself—as his own. This episode is

PLATE 32. Agostino Carracci, *The Crucifixion*, 1589.
Engraving.

recounted in all of the Gospels, but each of
the Evangelists describes slightly different
circumstances. Artists or those commis-
sioning a religious work of art often choose to
combine elements from the various accounts
in the Gospels or may follow one version
closely.

Crucifixion scenes usually include many
figures: the two thieves dying alongside
Christ; the Virgin Mary and John at the foot
of the cross; Roman soldiers who helped
conduct the execution; groups of priests,
scribes, and Pharisees; another group of Mary

Magdalene, women, and friends or disciples of Christ. These scenes also brim with religious symbolism and iconography. Near the foot of the cross, pitiless soldiers throw dice for Christ's garments. Mary, in her extreme grief, often faints in the arms of those around her, while Mary Magdalene prays at the foot of the cross. Sometimes a figure raises a pole to offer Christ in his agony the meager refreshment of a vinegar-soaked sponge. Another spear is also often included, thrust by a centurion into the side of the already dead Christ. Many Crucifixion scenes, like Carracci's large depiction, are presented as a wide panorama filled with activity.

The Crucifixion is a monumental example of sixteenth-century Italian printmaking. This impressively large engraving was made after a painting by Jacopo Tintoretto (1518–1594) that was created in 1565 for the Scuola di San Rocco in Venice. The expansive horizontal nature of this piece necessitated three different plates to compose the entire scene. Large-scale prints were a trend among late sixteenth-century Italian intaglio printmakers, and Agostino Carracci made more than one oversized engraving; his oeuvre includes *Adoration of the Magi,* which measures 1116 × 1053 millimeters and is made from seven plates.[1] Such impressively large prints existed in all printmaking media. From the mid-sixteenth century on, oversized engravings began to grow in popularity concurrent with the rise of both the reproductive print and the print publishing business, which offered artist printmakers a subsidized method of producing these elaborate, large works by providing resources for the execution, production, and marketing of the prints.[2] The second state impressions comprising the Thrivent Financial collection's example of *The Crucifixion* were published by Donato Rasciotti.

The Carracci family, including brothers Agostino and Annibale and their cousin Ludovico, were major figures in sixteenth- and seventeenth-century Italian art. The Italian Baroque style emerged after late Mannerism, especially through the work of Annibale Carracci.[3] Mannerism, characterized by exaggerated and elongated forms, artificiality, and highly stylized and elegant lines, was a transitional style that developed from the Italian High Renaissance around 1520 and was gradually replaced by the Baroque from about 1580.

Agostino Carracci was one of the most skilled and prolific reproductive engravers of his time. The "reproductive" print is not a photomechanical reproduction in the contemporary sense; rather, it is an original print that reproduces or copies another original artwork, such as a painting, another print, a drawing, or a sculpture. The versatility of the line created by the burin made engraving particularly well suited to recreating painted forms, despite the lack of color in the final engraving—this is certainly true for Carracci's *Crucifixion*. Such engravings offered painters an effective way to promote themselves by recreating and distributing their designs, and they often worked with printmakers to direct the creation of reproductive prints of their paintings. The reproductive print could help establish lesser known artists within the art historical tradition, and they could practice or model their skills after better-known virtuoso artists. Artists would often make as faithful a copy as possible to the original, noting in the text portion of the print the name of the original designer or artist.[4] A reproductive print may not always be so exact, instead emulating the original's essentials or taking inspiration from it.

■ JRL

Notes

1. Larry Silver, Elizabeth Wyckoff, and Lilian Armstrong, *Grand Scale: Monumental Prints in the Age of Dürer and Titian* (Wellesley: Davis Museum and Cultural Center, Wellesley College, 2008), 47.
2. Ibid., 12.
3. Linda C. Hults, *The Print in the Western World: An Introductory History* (Madison: University of Wisconsin Press, 1996), 195.
4. Sometimes artists were involved in the reproduction of their work into prints, but often they were not. In the absence of copyright laws, and with a growing demand for popular motifs from collectors, artists were not always happy with reproductive prints from their works. For example, Albrecht Dürer famously brought a legal suit against Italian artist Marcantonio Raimondi for the latter's unauthorized and intentionally misleading reproductive prints of his work.

PLATE 33

**Giovanni Balducci,
called Il Cosci, Italian,
1560–after 1631**

*Esther Swooning
before King
Ahasuerus*

c. 1589–1600

Pen, brown ink, and wash,
over red chalk

6⁵⁄₁₆ × 9⅞ inches
160 × 252 mm (sheet)

94-02

Provenance

Chevalier de Damery
(Lugt 2862).

Notes

1. Helen Gardner, Fred S.
   Kleiner, and Christin
   J. Mamiya, *Gardner's
   Art through the Ages*
   (Belmont: Thompson/
   Wadsworth, 2005),
   648–49.
2. Ahasuerus repeats this
   promise three times in
   Esther 5:3, 5:6, and 7:2.
3. R. S. Johnson, *Old
   Master Prints and
   Drawings, 1450–1800*
   (Chicago: R. S. Johnson
   Fine Art Catalogue,
   1994), 25; Edmond de
   Goncourt, *La maison
   d'un artiste* (Paris: G.
   Charpentier, 1881), 96.

Overcome with emotion, Queen Esther sinks into the arms of an attendant after revealing her Jewish identity to King Ahasuerus and pleading with her husband to save her people from destruction (Esther 8:3). The brave efforts of this heroine of the Hebrew Bible save the Jews from massacre at a time (around 480 B.C.E.) when Jews endured great persecution. Persian King Ahasuerus's prime minister, Haman, issued an edict in the king's name to destroy Jewish people. Meanwhile, Esther's own Jewish ethnicity and faith were still secret from the king. Mordecai, Esther's cousin, became aware of Haman's plot and persuaded Esther to intervene, even though doing so could have brought about her execution. Not only was Esther's ethnicity at stake, but by law and on punishment of death she was not permitted to approach the king in his inner chamber without being called: "Only if the king holds out the golden scepter to someone, may that person live" (Esther 4:11).

Born in Florence and trained by Giovan Battista Naldini in the style of late Florentine Mannerism, Balducci's major painted work was made in Florence, Rome, and Naples. Mannerism is an art historical term derived from the sixteenth-century word *maniera,* referring not to a certain style as much as a tendency toward intricate compositions, skillful execution, and exaggerated gestures and poses.[1] Mannerism was particularly attractive to royal European courts for its intellectual capacity, and its proliferation is indebted to these noble patrons. Balducci's drawing of Esther swooning exaggerates the drama of the story through its physical gestures. Esther does not faint in the Bible, yet by including this action Balducci contributes a sophisticated set of ideas to the picture. As Esther collapses, her kneeling lady in waiting seems to continue pleading on Esther's behalf as the men of the court look on. Notably, Balducci has shown the women rushing to attend to Esther and Ahasuerus, which has a dual connotation: it reflects the subservient role of women in the Persian court, evinced by the book of Esther, yet the women's positive action, despite their socially oppressed position, reinforces Esther's bravery. Further, Balducci has pictured Ahasuerus as a young man who descends from his throne and reaches to take Esther's arm, an action that breaks the traditional protocol in which the king extends only his scepter to show favor. While the men of the court obviously react as Esther swoons, only the benevolent King Ahasuerus may appropriately step forward to assist his wife. His caring act reveals the depth of his affection for his queen and the sincerity of his promise to grant Esther's request, "even to the half of my kingdom." [2] Through Esther's bravery and the affectionate loyalty of Ahasuerus, the Jewish people are saved, and here, the agility of Balducci's pen elegantly illuminates the significance and depth of the royal couple's historic relationship.

The quality of this drawing is indicated by the blind (without ink) collector's stamp in the lower right corner that places it in the eighteenth-century collection of Chevalier de Damery, about whom Edmond de Goncourt wrote: "For collectors I should like to take note of his collector's mark, never to be found on a mediocre drawing." [3]

■ JRW

PLATE 33. Giovanni
Balducci, called Il Cosci,
*Esther Swooning before King
Ahasuerus,* c. 1589–1600.
Pen, brown ink, and wash,
over red chalk.

PLATE 34

Giovanni Benedetto
Castiglione, Italian,
c. 1609–1664

*Entry into
Noah's Ark*

c. 1650

Etching

8¼₆ × 15¹³⁄₁₆ inches
205 × 400 mm

99-22

Bartsch 1

Cattle, horses, dogs, cats, mice, and ducks gather with Noah's family, who brings barrels and packs of goods in preparation for a long journey. These are their last moments on dry land before the torrential rains promised by God flood the world. Noah, his family, and every kind of animal will live safely in the ark for twelve months (Genesis 7:11–8:19).

Giovanni Benedetto Castiglione was one of the most influential Genoese artists of the mid-seventeenth century and arguably the most technically innovative etcher of the Italian Baroque period.[1] Like Rembrandt, his Dutch contemporary, Castiglione explored printmaking as a painterly pursuit.[2] *Entry into Noah's Ark* in the Thrivent Financial collection is a rare, early, and exceptional impression with brilliant contrast. It was once owned by A. Hyatt Mayor, the late curator of Prints and Drawings at the Metropolitan Museum of Art

in New York, who wrote about Castiglione in his book *Prints and People: A Social History of Printed Pictures*: "He may have never seen a painting by Rembrandt, but he was the first artist outside the Netherlands to adopt Rembrandt's early etching manner of scribbled shadows."[3] Castiglione's strong chiaroscuro, contrasting light and dark, demonstrates his affinity for Rembrandt's etchings of the 1630s. Compare, for example, the etched lines that create deep shadow in *Entry into Noah's Ark* and in *Christ Driving the Money Changers from the Temple* (Plate 58). Both artists used the barest sketched lines to define the shapes of the lightest, most distant figures in these prints. Castiglione's active group of carefully lit animals is strikingly reminiscent of the startled herd in Rembrandt's *Angel Appearing to the Shepherds* (Figure 55).

■ JRW

PLATE 34. Giovanni Benedetto Castiglione, *Entry into Noah's Ark,* c. 1650. Etching.

Provenance

A. Hyatt Mayor
(1901–1980).

Notes

1. Linda C. Hults, *The Print in the Western World: An Introductory History* (Madison: University of Wisconsin Press, 1996), 202.
2. Ibid.
3. A. Hyatt Mayor, *Prints and People: A Social History of Printed Pictures* (New York: Metropolitan Museum of Art, 1971), nos. 526–527.

The biblical figure of Moses, called by God to lead the Israelites, is best known for bringing the stone tablets bearing the Ten Commandments down to the people from Mount Sinai and for leading them out of enslavement in Pharaoh's Egypt through the Red Sea. At the time of Moses' birth Pharaoh feared that the Israelites would continue to multiply in numbers and in strength, so he commanded that all baby boys born to the Hebrews be killed. When Moses was born his mother initially hid him for three months, then, recognizing she could do so no longer, she plastered a papyrus basket, placed the baby in it, and set it in the Nile River. His sister watched to see what would happen to the child. He was soon spotted by Pharaoh's daughter, who was bathing by the river with her maidservants. She saw the basket among the reeds and sent her attendants to collect the child (Exodus 2:5–6): this is the precise moment depicted in this etching. Pharaoh's daughter assumes the child is Hebrew and sends for a Hebrew woman (who happens to be Moses' real mother) to nurse this child on whom she has taken pity. Pharaoh's daughter ultimately raises Moses as her own child. In the etching, the female figure standing and pointing at Moses is probably Pharaoh's daughter, who first spots the baby, while the kneeling woman reaching out to Moses is one of her attendants. The delicacy of the etched line in this print enhances the tenderness of the crucial moment when the child is rescued from the river and from probable death.

The finding of Moses is presented here in a lyrical manner, typical of Bartolomeo Biscaino's style with curving lines, short strokes, and a refined sweetness. This artist worked in Genoa, Italy; he was strongly influenced by Italian Mannerism and the tradition of Giovanni Benedetto Castiglione (Plate 34) and Parmigianino (Figure 38). Biscaino died of a plague at the young age of twenty-eight. He created a number of prints, drawings, and some paintings, and the subject of the finding of Moses was presumably one of his favorites, as he repeated it in several paintings, etchings, and drawings.

■ JRL

PLATE 35

Bartolomeo Biscaino, Italian, 1629–1657

The Finding of Moses

1650–57
Etching
7¼ × 9⁷⁄₁₆ inches
184 × 240 mm
93-21
Bartsch 183.2

PLATE 35. Bartolomeo Biscaino, *The Finding of Moses,* 1650–57. Etching.

Plate 36. Guido Reni,
The Holy Family,
c. 1590–1610. Etching
(actual size).

PLATE 36

Guido Reni, Italian, 1575–1642

The Holy Family

c. 1590–1610

Etching

9 × 5¾ inches
229 × 145 mm

85-58

Bartsch 9

Guido Reni's prolific output of religious art redefined the Madonna, Christ, and the saints into Christian icons that have been copied and distributed worldwide as devotional images ever since.[1] The style of both his religious paintings and prints evokes a quality of aesthetic grace that deeply coincides with the early Christian idea that God's grace

FIGURE 38. Parmigianino, *The Entombment,* c. 1530. Etching.

literally glowed on the faces of the saints. Richard E. Spear, a scholar of Reni's works, aptly points out that "the analogy between light, the divine, and beauty, which has a very long, rich metaphysical history nourished in the Christian West by Augustine's writings, reappeared prominently in late sixteenth-century art theory, [which] defined beauty as the spiritual *grazia* radiating from the countenance of God."[2] The aesthetic *grazia* that

pervades nearly all Reni's printed devotional imagery further translates the theological concept of God's grace into a visual form.[3]

In *The Holy Family*, Reni's spare, flowing, and broken lines create a shimmering effect that contributes warmth to the already tender composition. Although trained in the dominant Carracci school by Agostino and Ludovico Carracci, Guido Reni adapted their firmer modeling into a lighter, more fluid style. This early plate by Reni is particularly indebted to Parmigianino (1503–1540), who established in the sixteenth century a distinct approach to etching that continued to influence Italian printmakers such as Reni, Giovanni Benedetto Castiglione (Plate 34), and, in the eighteenth century, the Tiepolos (Plates 39, 40, and 41).[4] Mary's elegant posture toward the Christ child and her elongated arms, as well as the turned head of Joseph, betray Reni's attraction to Parmigianino's Mannerist prints like *The Entombment* (Figure 38).

The picture above and behind the Madonna and child shows an episode when Moses strikes the rock and water miraculously springs forth for the thirsty Israelites, an act that occurs twice in the Hebrew Bible (Exodus 17:2–6; Numbers 20:2–13). This juxtaposition of pictorial schemes promotes the idea that Christ is the new Moses who will bring salvation to all humanity. For a viewer familiar with the story in Numbers, Reni's miniature narrative offers both a theological parallel and contrast: unlike Moses, who appeared to claim credit for the water God provided, Christ's selfless sacrifice identifies him as the true Messiah to Christians.

■ JRW

Notes

1. Richard E. Spear, *The "Divine" Guido: Religion, Sex, Money, and Art in the World of Guido Reni* (New Haven: Yale University Press, 1997), 128.
2. Ibid., 121.
3. Ibid., 121–22.
4. Linda C. Hults, *The Print in the Western World: An Introductory History* (Madison: University of Wisconsin Press, 1996), 184.

PLATE 37

**Circle of Giovanni
Francesco Barbieri
(Guercino), Italian,
1591–1666**

*Christ Child
with the Infant
St. John*

Mid-seventeenth century

Red chalk

6⅛ × 4⅞ inches

155 × 124 mm (sheet)

87-39

PLATE 37. Circle of
Guercino, *Christ Child
with the Infant St. John,*
mid-seventeenth century.
Red chalk (actual size).

The artist of a drawing or the reason why it was drawn are often uncertain. Drawings fulfill a variety of purposes, such as to learn and practice technique, to sketch out ideas for compositions, to study details for finished paintings or prints, and even to function as independent artworks expressly for a collectors' market. As a skill, drawing lies at the foundation of the visual arts and is the fundamental means by which an artist transforms ideas into a comprehensive work of art. Drawings have been collected and appreciated for centuries, and many fine exemplars survive to the present day—though often without clear documentation about their origins. The challenge for those who study Old Master drawings is to observe and interpret each work's history based on what appears on the page, which includes not only the image and inscriptions laid down by the artist but also notations and collectors' marks added over time.

Guercino was a natural and prolific draftsman who used drawings to carefully plan his designs. Most of his drawings were made as studies in preparation for painting or print projects. He rapidly sketched ideas for compositions in pen and ink, but red chalk was often used to explore nuance of light and shade in closer studies of faces, drapery, and the physical relationships between figures before rendering them in the final picture.[1] The page on which *Christ Child with the Infant St. John* appears includes red chalk drawings on both the recto (front, Plate 37) and verso (back, Figure 39).

Although close in style to Guercino, these drawings were likely made by one of his students or by another artist in his workshop. The recto depicts John the Baptist and Christ as toddlers; the image eloquently highlights their relationship and endows them with an endearing degree of humanity. The elegant familiarity of the figures is indebted to Guercino's style but also to the pervasive

earlier influence of Guido Reni, who transformed devotional imagery so that it reflected a sense of grace, both aesthetic and theological (Plate 36). Christ and his cousin play together sweetly and naturally. John's identifying cross, drawn with two simple lines, appears as a toy the boys share, but it is also an allusion to the mission each will undertake as a man.

The verso reveals a second figural study of two children. Less successful compositionally, it seems that the artist struggled to shade the praying figure on the right or form his head in three-quarter profile from behind. The identity of the children is not clear. Infants are frequently featured in Guercino's paintings, especially as putti, but the recto image hints that the artist may have been working on possible motifs for Christ and John the Baptist—and flipped over the page to explore another idea. A painting by Guercino from 1652, *Madonna col Bambino, San Giovanni Battista, San Giovanni Evagelista e San Bartolomeo,* now at the Palazzo Rosso in Genoa, shows the two boys in similar poses, with John wearing hides of wild animals, one of his common attributes.[2] Perhaps the lines quickly sketched over the kneeling figure on the right were made as a student imitated his master's work and contemplated clothing for the infant St. John the Baptist.

The collector's stamps of Giuseppe Vallardi and Carlo Prayer appear on both sides of the paper and are a testament to the survival and appreciation of these simple yet poignant drawings.

■ JRW

FIGURE 39. Circle of Guercino, *Study for Two Infants,* mid-seventeenth century. Red chalk.

Provenance

Giuseppe Vallardi (1784–1863; Lugt 1223); Carlo Prayer (1826–1900; Lugt 2044); Christie's, London, December 8, 1987, lot no. 241.

Notes

1. Nicholas Turner, "Guercino" in *The Dictionary of Art*, ed. Jane Turner (New York: Grove, 1998), 13: 788.
2. Guercino and Nefta Barbanti Grimaldi, *Il Guercino, Gian Francesco Barbieri, 1591–1666* (Bologna: Tamari, 1957), no. 143.

PLATE 38

**Jusepe (José) de
Ribera, Spanish,
1591–1652**

*St. Jerome
and the Angel
of Judgment*

c. 1621

Etching

12¼ × 9⅛ inches
312 × 231 mm

97-24

Bartsch 4, I/ii;
Brown 5, I/v

Notes

1. Linda C. Hults, *The Print in the Western World: An Introductory History* (Madison: University of Wisconsin Press, 1996), 197.

2. José de Ribera, Craig Felton, and William B. Jordan, *Jusepe de Ribera, Lo Spagnoletto, 1591–1652* (Fort Worth: Kimbell Art Museum, 1982), 113.

3. Ibid., 114.

Jusepe de Ribera was born the second son of a shoemaker in the Spanish region of Valencia, but he lived and worked his entire career in Italy, primarily in Rome and Naples. Ribera, like Guido Reni, became one of the most influential producers of seventeenth-century Italian art, though he had quite a different aesthetic, especially in his prints. *St. Jerome and the Angel of Judgment,* dated around 1621, reflects Ribera's earliest painting style, heavily influenced by the naturalism of Caravaggio and the Dutch and Spanish "Caravaggisti," who eschewed idealist tastes for a coarser sense of reality.[1] Jerome's slender limbs, shrunken musculature, and sagging skin portray a stark image of an aging ascetic and attest to Ribera's ability to render remarkable naturalism with his etching needle. The stone desk, the flurry of fallen books, the battered toothy skull, the bark and broken branches of Jerome's stump altar, and his silken, rumpled sheet combine to offer the viewer a composition enriched with textures. The dark, energetic lines that shade the rising outcrop of rock behind the saint delineate—or perhaps conflate—the space between Jerome's natural world and the supernatural realm from which the angel bursts forth.

Jerome was painted more frequently by Ribera than any other subject and appears in the artist's earliest as well as latest works. He painted a similar composition of the saint and the angel of judgment in 1626 for the

Trinità delle Monache in Naples. Both this print and the painting unite multiple episodes in the story of Jerome's life from c. 345–420 C.E. The legendary vision of the angel of judgment occurs soon after his conversion to Christianity, when he is still a young man in his thirties; this transformative encounter inspired Jerome to renounce his material life and spend four years as a hermit in the Syrian Desert.[2] The pen in his hand and the pile of books represent his decision to dedicate his life to Christian texts rather than classical philosophy. This led him to produce, much later, his monumental translation of the Bible into Latin during the latter decades of his life at a monastery in Bethlehem. The lion, whose very human head calmly enters from the left, alludes to an event when Jerome removed a painful thorn from its paw and the animal became his lifelong companion.

All together, these episodes and attributes express a complete image of St. Jerome that encompasses the full import of his life. Living in a time of theological upheaval during the collapse of the Roman Empire, Jerome was an outspoken reformer who advocated for the legitimacy of the papacy; this, along with his personal struggle between spirit and flesh, made him popular during the Counter Reformation and a favorite among Baroque subjects.[3]

■ JRW

PLATE 38. Jusepe (José)
de Ribera, *St. Jerome and
the Angel of Judgment,*
c. 1621. Etching.

PLATE 39. Giovanni
Domenico Tiepolo, *Led by
an Angel* (Plate 12) from
Flight into Egypt series,
c. 1750–53. Etching.

Domenico Tiepolo was the eldest surviving son and heir to the Venetian artist Giovanni Battista Tiepolo (Giambattista, 1696–1770), one of the most renowned Italian painters of the eighteenth century. Domenico was apprenticed to his father in the 1740s, and he learned primarily by copying Giambattista's compositions in drawings and etchings. By 1750, Domenico had become his father's assistant and associate, working with him on decorative fresco paintings for royal patrons like King Charles III of Spain.

From 1750 to 1753, Domenico collaborated with his father for the first time on a major commission: he was Giambattista's primary assistant on decorations for the new residence of Prince-Bishop Karl Philipp von Greiffenklau in Würzburg.[1] In his spare time while working on this job, Domenico etched the series *Flight into Egypt,* which he presented with a dedication to their German patron. A tour de force in its own right, *Flight into Egypt* represents Domenico's first artistic achievement independent of his renowned father; as such it has been called his "artistic manifesto" for its suite of inventive pictures.[2]

Canonical description of the Holy Family's urgent passage from Bethlehem to Egypt in order to spare the Christ child from Herod's deadly wrath is limited to one verse in the Bible, which offers no details of the journey: "Then Joseph got up, took the child and his mother by night, and went to Egypt" (Matthew 2:14). Yet Domenico etched twenty-four scenes for their journey, largely separate from apocryphal episodes in literary sources since the second century and in art since the Middle Ages.[3] Instead, he created picturesque variations on the theme inspired from life and his own fertile imagination.

Working with a cast of characters that centers on the Christ child, Mary, Joseph, a mule, and a coterie of angels, each scene in the series is an original composition with a new setting, action, and relationship between the figures (compare Plate 39 and Figures 40 and 41). The familial care and affection

shared among all members of the holy entourage pervade the peaceful scenery of lovely natural vistas, charming villages, and dappled light.[4]

The etching style and composition certainly reflect the printed work of his father but also seem to have been influenced by prints that Domenico collected by Rembrandt and Giovanni Benedetto Castiglione, among others.[5] His variations hint at his Venetian roots through the romantic and pastoral landscapes, in which he incorporates elements of ancient ruins, a trend made especially popular in paintings and prints by artists from his hometown such as Marco Ricci (1676–1730), Giovanni Battista Piranesi (1720–1778), and Giovanni Antonio Canal (Canaletto, 1697–1768). In the spirit of Venice, Domenico created a few scenes that depict the Holy Family and their donkey traveling in a small boat, fancifully steered by an angelic gondolier (Figure 41). Images of the Holy Family traveling by boat existed in art before Domenico's series, but his vibrant treatment of the scenes, with sparkling waters and vast skies, is particularly Venetian.[6]

Domenico's title page appropriately describes the series as "Picturesque Ideas on the Flight into Egypt of Jesus, Mary, and Joseph." A dedication and a heraldic frontispiece bring the total number of plates in the series to twenty-seven, all of which are represented in the Thrivent Financial Collection of Religious Art.

■ JRW

Above: FIGURE 40. Giovanni Domenico Tiepolo, *Joseph Adores the Child* (Plate 9) from *Flight into Egypt* series, c. 1750–53. Etching.

Below: FIGURE 41. Giovanni Domenico Tiepolo, *Crossing a River* (Plate 17) from *Flight into Egypt* series, c. 1750–53. Etching.

Notes

1. Colta Feller Ives and Giovanni Domenico Tiepolo, *Picturesque Ideas on the Flight into Egypt* (New York: G. Braziller, 1972), unpaginated.
2. Jane Martineau and Andrew Robison, *The Glory of Venice: Art in the Eighteenth Century* (New Haven: Yale University Press, 1994), 335.
3. Ives and Tiepolo.
4. Linda C. Hults, *The Print in the Western World: An Introductory History* (Madison: University of Wisconsin Press, 1996), 333.
5. Ives and Tiepolo.
6. Ibid.

PLATE 40. Giovanni
Domenico Tiepolo,
*God the Father Carried by
Angels,* c. 1790s. Pen and
brown ink, brown wash,
with traces of pencil
(actual size).

PLATE 40

**Giovanni Domenico
Tiepolo, Italian,
1727–1804**

*God the Father
Carried by Angels*

c. 1790s

Pen and brown ink,
brown wash, with traces
of pencil

9⅛ × 6¹¹⁄₁₆ inches
231 × 169 mm

86-55

Signed in ink, lower right;
inscribed "45" in the
upper left corner

Domenico Tiepolo returned to Venice from Spain after the death of his renowned father, Giovanni Battista Tiepolo (Giambattista), in 1770. Late in his career he made many works of art for his close circle of friends and for enthusiastic collectors, including numerous drawings often conceived in series. The most famous of these today are large, thoroughly planned drawings that imagine the life and adventures of Punchinello, a traditional clown-like character in the Italian commedia dell'arte. *God the Father Carried by Angels* is likely from another ink and wash drawing series that explores thematic variations of God in the clouds with angels and cherubs. The figure of God in this particular drawing is highly foreshortened, as though God is held aloft directly overhead the viewer, a popular perspective employed by the Tiepolos in their famous heavenly ceiling decorations. The artist's usual signature, "Domo. Tiepolo f" in the lower right, and the old numeral in the upper left corner are consistent with other drawings linked to this series.[1] The majority of the series remains together at Museo Correr in Venice, while other individual drawings are in the collections of the Louvre (*La Création,* REC 152); the Albertina in Vienna (*Die Apotheose des Kreuzes,* 24075); and

the National Gallery of Art in Washington, D.C. (*Creation of the Universe,* 1943.3.8110). This list, by no means exhaustive, represents only a few of the approximately sixty variations that survive in public and private collections.[2]

James Byam Shaw noted that some of the compositions in Domenico's *God the Father* series share resemblance to a figural group in an altarpiece painted by Giambattista for the Chiesa della Grazie in Este, Italy.[3] The steeply foreshortened figure of God in Thrivent Financial's drawing is very similar to one of Pope Leo IX in a study painted with oil on canvas by Domenico for his ceiling of the church of San Lio in Venice; this oil sketch at the Victoria and Albert Museum in London (CAI.95) includes a figural group with God the father and a cross similar to *Die Apotheose des Kreuzes* at the Albertina.[4]

God the Father Carried by Angels is a fine, notable example of the Tiepolo family's dominant presence in eighteenth-century Italian art. As a sister leaf to others in world-class collections, it is also a testament to the quality and historical significance of the religious art conserved in the Thrivent Financial collection.

■ JRW

Notes

1. The "f" following the artist's signature is an abbreviation for *fecit,* meaning "made."
2. James Byam Shaw, *The Drawings of Domenico Tiepolo* (Boston: Boston Book and Art Shop, 1962), 32.
3. Ibid. A painted sketch for the altarpiece is in the collection of the Metropolitan Museum of Art in New York (*St. Thecla Praying for the Plague-Stricken,* 37.165.2).
4. James Byam Shaw, "A Sketch for a Ceiling by Domenico Tiepolo," *Burlington Magazine* 101, no. 681 (December 1959): 448.

PLATE 41

Lorenzo Baldissera Tiepolo, Italian, 1736–1776

Beheading of John the Baptist

c. 1760

Red chalk, pen and brown ink, brown and gray wash, heightened with white

14⁹⁄₁₆ × 10⁵⁄₁₆ inches
370 × 263 mm

92-02

Lorenzo Baldissera Tiepolo grew up in the shadow of his brother, Domenico, but developed his own niche in portraits of wealthy eighteenth-century patrons produced in chalk and pastel.[1] As part of the Tiepolo workshop, he traveled with his father to Würzburg and Spain, and, like his brother, he learned basic draftsmanship by copying his father's designs into drawings and prints.

Lorenzo's *Beheading of John the Baptist* is a splendid example of the Tiepolo workshop's process of reworking motifs into an array of compositions appropriate for many different stories or scenarios. This practice must have aided the rapid proliferation of their art across Europe, giving their patrons unique works in the fashionable Tiepolo style that were efficient to produce. Like a variation on a musical theme, this drawing is similar—though not an exact copy—to several from the Tiepolo workshop that depict the decapitation of Christian martyrs. It has much in common with a drawing by his father, Giambattista, circa 1732–33 and now at the Metropolitan Museum of Art in New York (37.165.15), of the beheading of a male and a female saint. The executioner's platform over the grated prison window, the stairs to the right, and the deep archway that frames the dramatic action are structurally the same, though not a direct copy from Giambattista's tableau. Within this setting, Lorenzo has drawn a new cast of characters with poses and actions designed to narrate John the Baptist's death.

Iconologically, the treatment of this subject is somewhat peculiar. The executioner

heroically stands over the contorted, headless corpse as he leans on his broadsword and holds up John's head. His cape billowing in the breeze, the figure seems more appropriate for a scene of David and Goliath than for the martyrdom of a saint. Yet perhaps his bravado aptly contributes horror when paired with the demeanor of Salome, who barely seems to notice the murder as she waits apathetically with her platter. Together these two figures highlight the selfishness and misguided circumstances that led Herod to command the execution of John the Baptist (Matthew 14:1–12; Mark 6:17–29).

The extent to which Lorenzo was overtly concerned with these iconological details cannot be known. This drawing was probably intended to practice his compositional skill, and we can glimpse the artist's mind as he exercised the link between imagination and page. A ghostly head and shoulders to the left of the executioner, for example, are all that remain of an idea that Lorenzo abandoned. Close examination of the area around John's extended arm reveals that it was originally sketched on a diagonal; when working over the preliminary red chalk sketch with ink, Lorenzo must have reconsidered and decided that the arm should hang downward instead.

Lorenzo's drawing, typical of the Tiepolo style, may also be appreciated for its Venetian elements. The Palladian arches and stone rail; the bright, soft light; and Salome's sophisticated coif, bare neck, and high-collared dress give the biblical story an air of eighteenth-century Venice.

■ JRW

Provenance

Christie's New York, January 15, 1992, lot no. 42.

Note

1. Jane Martineau and Andrew Robison, *The Glory of Venice: Art in the Eighteenth Century* (New Haven: Yale University Press, 1994), 344.

PLATE 41. Lorenzo
Baldissera Tiepolo,
*Beheading of John the
Baptist,* c. 1760. Red chalk,
pen and brown ink, brown
and gray wash, heightened
with white.

PLATE 42. Ubaldo
Gandolfi, *The Flagellation,*
c. 1748–81. Pen and
brown ink, brown wash.

PLATE 42

Ubaldo Gandolfi,
Italian, 1728–1781

The Flagellation

c. 1748–81
Pen and brown ink,
brown wash
9½ × 7⅞ inches
240 × 200 mm
88-10

Ubaldo Gandolfi, along with his brother, Gaetano, and nephew Mauro, was among the most successful artists in a family that produced frescoes, paintings, drawings, prints, and sculptures. Working while Italian art transitioned from late Baroque to Neoclassical style, Ubaldo primarily made frescoes and paintings of religious and mythological subjects. He produced a vast number of drawings and, as an exceptional draftsman, continued the Bolognese graphic arts tradition that had been founded by the Carraccis in the sixteenth century.[1]

In this excellent ink and wash drawing, thick diagonal beams of light pass behind solid classical columns as Christ is bound and beaten by a group of men during an episode from his Passion. The artist's spontaneous, rapid pen energizes the scene, infusing a natural grace into the men's intense physicality, which is heightened further by the accuracy of the male anatomy for which Ubaldo is known.[2] His drawing style is distinguished by its highly fluid, calligraphic lines, most apparent in the musculature of the helmeted man on the right, who leans away from Christ with whip overhead as he prepares to strike. Pale wash, applied with equal speed and acuity, is expertly placed to enhance the composition with contrasts of light shadow. The wet brush naturally blurred the penned lines, which brings unity to Ubaldo's strokes with the pen and the brush and lends variety and depth to the composition.

One subtle kinetic element is found in the switches held in the hand of the man standing at left. While his body is physically still, the quickly rendered cluster of lines that form the switches in his right hand makes them appear to vibrate, as if he is subconsciously brandishing his whip as he contemplates his next strike on Christ's slumping body.

The verso of this sheet is a testament to the generally transient role of a piece of paper in the artist's workshop and its nature as a forum to express the artist's active mind. On the back of the page is part of a letter, along with studies of a woman's face. A tracing of the standing soldier at left was made with the same degree of virtuosity as appears on the recto (Figure 42). With no wash to blur his lines, the true calligraphic quality of Ubaldo's hand becomes apparent, especially in the diamond-shaped ornamental flourish integrated across the figure's chest. This delightful, whimsical sketch has certainly survived because of the outstanding drawing on the other side.

■ JRW

Provenance

Christie's, London,
April 19, 1988, lot no. 58.

Notes

1. Mimi Cazort,
"Gandolfi," in *The
Dictionary of Art*, ed.
Jane Turner (New York:
Grove, 1996), 12: 37–38.
2. Ibid.

FIGURE 42. Ubaldo Gandolfi, verso of *The Flagellation* (detail), date unknown. Pen and ink.

PRINTS & DRAWINGS
OF THE NETHERLANDS
& FRANCE

Rembrandt van Rijn, *Christ Preaching* (details; see Plate 60).

Rembrandt van Rijn, *Christ Preaching* (details; see Plate 60).

PLATE 43

Philips Galle, Dutch,
1537–1612

*Samson Fighting
with the Lion*

c. 1560

Engraving

10¼ inches
260 mm (diameter)

95-14

Hollstein 34, I/ii;
New Hollstein 13, I/iii
(Philips Galle, Part 1);
New Hollstein 86
(Maarten van
Heemskerck, Part 1), I/iii

Notes

1. Christine van Mulders,
"Galle," in *The
Dictionary of Art*, ed.
Jane Turner (New York:
Grove, 1998), 12: 15.
2. Ibid.
3. Manfred Sellink and
Marjolein Leesberg,
Philips Galle, Part 1
of the *New Hollstein
Dutch and Flemish
Etchings, Engravings, and
Woodcuts, 1450–1700*
(Rotterdam: Sound
and Vision Publishers,
2001), 24.

Samson's powerful limbs grapple with the legs and jaws of a snarling lion. To the right, thick vines, laden with grapes, mark the vineyards of Timnah, where the Israelite encountered the beast and, empowered by God, ripped it apart with his bare hands (Judges 14:5–10). The couple to the left of Samson, walking toward the city, is his parents, with whom he was traveling to Timnah before this episode. This round-format engraving by Philips Galle is one of six that depict scenes from Samson's life (Judges 13–16). Samson was miraculously born to a barren mother, who was commanded by the angel of the Lord to drink no alcohol and let no razor touch her son's head, and upon this lifelong vow Samson drew his uncommon strength.

Filled with heroic acts of Herculean might tempered by a weakness for beguiling women, the chronicle of Samson became popular subject matter for prints in the largely Protestant Netherlands. Prior to the Reformation, saints and other noncanonical subjects were copiously produced in all forms of art, but reformers Martin Luther and John Calvin believed that Christians must look to Scripture for spiritual authority. Thus, in a culture wrestling with the politics of iconoclasm, pious icons waned in favor of secular imagery, while narratives taken directly from Scripture were accepted for their authoritative source. Because one of Calvin's primary concerns was lavish decoration in churches, prints provided an ideal platform for religious subjects, as they were small in format and could be enjoyed apart from worship in church. On the printed page, biblical figures like Samson found a place among the time-honored heroes of ancient Greek and Roman legends, and artists enthusiastically applied classical ideals to their biblical protagonists, apparent here in the attention paid to Samson's proportioned musculature and sculpture-perfect curly hair.

Haarlem native Philips Galle was an enterprising printmaker and publisher, much like his mentor, Hieronymus Cock (Plate 44), who gave Galle work in Antwerp for several years and published his first prints in 1557. Soon after, Galle began his own print business and toured the Netherlands, France, Germany, and Italy before settling in Antwerp and establishing a workshop. His extensive engraved oeuvre includes original compositions as well as prints after the designs of others. Painter Maarten van Heemskerck (1498–1574) designed *Samson Fighting with the Lion* and the other five images in the series. The inscription at lower right of the engraving in the Thrivent Financial collection indicates it is a first state impression and attributes the depiction to van Heemskerck, the burin work to Galle, and the printed edition to Cock, thus highlighting the collaboration of these artists. The six round plates for the series were listed in an inventory of Cock's widow, but they must have been acquired later by the Galle family; Philips Galle's son, Theodore, and grandson, Johannes, published two later editions.

■ JRW

PLATE 43. Philips Galle,
*Samson Fighting with the
Lion,* c. 1560. Engraving.

PLATE 44

**Hieronymus Cock,
Flemish, c. 1510–1570**

*Abraham and
Isaac Going to
the Sacrifice*

1558
Etching
8⅞ × 12⅛ inches
226 × 309 mm
83-05
Hollstein 8; Riggs II.A.38
Watermark: Crowned
hand (close to Briquet
10981)

Country towns, fields, and farmhouses sprawl among the rolling hills of a flourishing river valley. Water spills from a wooden aqueduct and turns the mill wheel beside the river where swans swim and cows graze on the banks. A trio of travelers gathers to rest and chat at a bend in a road. One leans casually on his hungry mule as it finds a grassy bite to eat. Further along, a man and boy make their way up a path that winds through a tunnel, past a church, and around to the far side of the rocky mountain.

Only a close study of the print offers a clue as to the narrative subject veiled within this idyllic pastoral landscape. In the upper

holds his knife and Isaac, unaware of his pending destruction, carries a bundle of wood for the sacrificial fire. The long road seems an appropriate metaphor for Abraham's arduous journey of faith, knowing he must surrender his beloved son to honor the will of God.

Born in Antwerp, both Hieronymus and his brother, Matthijs, traveled to Italy to study art. Matthijs was best known for his landscape paintings; he was among the first to effectively apply perspective to the genre. Hieronymus was never a painter, but he was an excellent draftsman and an enterprising print and painting dealer who recreated a number of works by his brother. *Abraham and Isaac Going*

PLATE 44. Hieronymus Cock, *Abraham and Isaac Going to the Sacrifice,* 1558. Etching.

Note

1. F. W. H. Hollstein, *Dutch and Flemish Etchings, Engravings, and Woodcuts* (Amsterdam: M. Hertzberger, 1949), 4: 179.

right corner, an angel sweeps down from billowing clouds over the high plateau where Isaac kneels on an altar and Abraham raises a long knife to sacrifice his only son. Upon discovering this dramatic scene, the identities of the man and boy on the road become clear, and their possessions are heavy reminders of the dreadful test that lies ahead. Abraham

to the Sacrifice is probably based on a drawing by Matthijs.[1] As one etching from a set of fourteen landscapes with biblical and mythological subjects, it is an excellent example of the continuing conflation of secular and sacred subject matter in Netherlandish art of the sixteenth century.

■ JRW

Jnmitis Pharao monstris non territus ullis   At Moyses, fratersq· manent quae damna tyrannum,
Neglepit inuicti iussa minasq· dej   Verbaq· Signaq· per tristia multa monent.
                                A. Statie.

Fabricius Zucharus de S. Angelo inuen.   Rome ex Typis Haed.
                                                D. Salamonis.

PLATE 45. Cornelis Cort, *Moses and Aaron before Pharaoh*, 1567. Engraving.

In the Book of Exodus two seminal occur-
rences, the exodus from Egypt and the
revelation on Mount Sinai establishing God's
covenant and law, form Israel's religious
tradition through the prophetic interpretation
of Moses. There are also two episodes in
Exodus that describe Moses and Aaron
before the Egyptian Pharaoh. This engraving
likely depicts the brothers' first appearance
(Exodus 5:1–9), in which Moses asks Pharaoh
to allow the enslaved Hebrews to journey
into the wilderness to make a sacrifice to
and celebrate the Lord. Pharaoh denies
their request and increases the work of the
enslaved people. In this image, the enthroned
Pharaoh points out his doorway at the
Hebrews, presumably speaking the words
"Moses and Aaron, why are you taking the
people away from their work? Get to your

labors!" (Exodus 5:4).
Pharaoh's resistance
brings about the
destructive Ten
Plagues, followed
by the first Passover
and Israel's departure
from Egypt.

Moses is a
central figure repre-
sented in Western
religious art. *Moses
and Aaron before
Pharaoh* shows him
with his traditional
"horns" on the top
of his head. This
symbolism stems
from early transla-
tions of the Hebrew
verb *qāran* to relate
to the Hebrew noun
qeren (horn) in the
biblical passage
about Moses' descent
from Mount Sinai;
later translations,
including the New
Revised Standard
Version, recognize
the meaning of *qāran*
as "to shine."[1] In
artistic representa-
tions, the horns
eventually morph into horn-like rays of light,
as seen here, melding the traditional depiction
with continuing scholarship about the
mistranslation. This iconography for Moses
endures and may be seen in Marc Chagall's
print suite *Songes* (Plate 91).

Cornelis Cort was active as an engraver
and draftsman in Flanders and Italy. He is
associated with Hieronymus Cock's publishing
establishment (see Plate 44). Cort left
Antwerp in 1565 and traveled to Italy, where
he spent many years. He met the painter
Titian, moved into his home, and subsequently produced many sculptural engravings
after the painter's monumental works.[2] The
reproductive engraving *Moses and Aaron before
Pharaoh* is after a Vatican fresco created in 1563
by Italian artist Federico Zuccaro (1542–1609).

■ JRL

PLATE 45

**Cornelis Cort,
Netherlandish,
1533–1578**

*Moses and Aaron
before Pharaoh*

1567
Engraving
15¾ × 10¼ inches
400 × 261 mm
00-09
New Hollstein 17.IV

Notes

1. John H. Hayes,
   "Moses," in *The Oxford
   Companion to the Bible,*
   ed. Bruce M. Metzger
   and Michael D. Coogan
   (Oxford: Oxford
   University Press, 1993);
   Oxford Reference
   Online, http://www.
   oxfordreference.com,
   accessed August 18,
   2010. The mistranslation
   also occurred in Latin,
   as explained for Plate 91:
   cornuto means "shining
   with rays of light" and
   also "horned."
2. Timothy A. Riggs
   and Larry Silver, eds.,
   *Graven Images: The Rise
   of Professional Printmakers
   in Antwerp and
   Haarlem, 1540–1640*
   (Evanston: Mary and
   Leigh Block Gallery
   and Northwestern
   University Press, 1993),
   111.

Plate 46

**Hendrik Goltzius,
Dutch, 1558–1617**

*The Adoration
of the Shepherds*

1598–1600

Engraving

8⅜ × 6¹⁄₁₆ inches
213 × 154 mm (sheet)

88-01

Bartsch 21, Strauss 362,
Hollstein 15

Watermark:
Crown and shield

Provenance

Max Egon Fürstenberg
(1863–1941; Lugt 995).

Note

1. Timothy A. Riggs
   and Larry Silver, eds.,
   *Graven Images: The Rise
   of Professional Printmakers
   in Antwerp and
   Haarlem, 1540–1640*
   (Evanston: Mary and
   Leigh Block Gallery
   and Northwestern
   University Press, 1993),
   89.

Gentle, illuminated faces gaze on the Christ child, spanning the width of this unfinished print. The tender expressions, stunningly executed, are remarkably realistic and animated. Mary's quiet pride and the shepherds' joyful delight are vividly portrayed. Multiple swelling, curving engraved lines and crosshatching skillfully build the tonal areas and character of the men's faces, with expert tapering and blank space to suggest the suffused glow of the candlelight. Mary's more refined visage is made by incorporating dot and lozenge areas, small flicks or dots within crosshatching, thereby further enlivening her loving gaze. We cannot see the Christ child admired by this group, but we have no doubt that he is the object of attention below the onlookers. The unfinished nature of this print allows for an intriguing glimpse into the pure devotion and joy directed at the infant, as well as revealing the printmaker's task and gift of creating meticulous line and form from blank space.

This engraving is a first state, unfinished proof and shows how artists work on prints through various states. In printmaking, a change in state happens whenever the print matrix is altered. Artists may work on a print matrix over time, revising it for aesthetic or thematic reasons or to make it more marketable, or they may simply abandon a plate or block for other projects or because of their circumstances. This engraving may be unfinished because around 1598 Hendrik Goltzius began to lose interest in engraving and gave all of his printmaking and publishing duties to his stepson and pupil, publisher and engraver Jacob Matham (1571–1631); Goltzius then pursued other media until his death.[1] Though engraved around 1598–1600, *The Adoration of the Shepherds* was published by Matham in 1615 and probably distributed after Goltzius's death in 1617.

Hendrik Goltzius's artistic virtuosity is demonstrated by his exceptional technical talents in both reproductive and original printmaking; he is a significant master of Dutch printmaking. He overcame crippling childhood burns on his right hand and apprenticed in the studio of engraver Dirck Volkertsz Coornhert. Goltzius became a superb draftsman and established a very successful business in Haarlem in 1582 that published original and reproductive works by many contemporary artists. During his lifetime the art market changed, and prints were sought by collectors as original examples of fine art as much as for the subject matter that had attracted earlier collectors and owners. Reproductive prints were increasingly created and sold by professional engravers as copies or records of other artists' work in various media, some intending to faithfully copy the original work while others emulated it and included original features. Goltzius trained a number of artists who became the next generation of Netherlandish reproductive printmakers, including his stepson Jacob Matham, Jan Saenredam, and Jan Muller.

Along with many northern European artists of the late sixteenth century, Goltzius visited Italy and was heavily influenced by Italian motifs and ideals, which were evident in Italian Mannerist prints that were widely available in the north. His rich, meticulous designs epitomize and surpass the Mannerist style and were sold throughout Europe. Goltzius achieved remarkable technical brilliance and originality in his many prints, even those that were "reproductive" and copied or emulated other masters' works. The vast majority of Goltzius's prints were in fact his own designs. The period of 1590 to 1598, after he returned from Italy, was his most important artistic period, when he created some of his finest, most innovative engravings.

■ JRL

Cum privil. Sa. Cæ. M.^tis
HGoltzius Fecit
I. Matham excud.

PLATE 46. Hendrik
Goltzius, *The Adoration of
the Shepherds*, 1598–1600.
Engraving (actual size).

PLATE 47

**Hendrik Goltzius,
Dutch, 1558–1617**

The Circumcision

1594

Engraving

18¾ × 14⅛ inches
476 × 357 mm

94-08

Bartsch 18, Strauss 322

Watermark:
Large coat of arms
and Strasburg lily

FIGURE 43. Albrecht Dürer, *The Circumcision,* from *The Life of the Virgin* series, 1503–5. Woodcut.

The infant Jesus was circumcised and named in the temple eight days after his birth, in accordance with Jewish tradition (Luke 2:21). Circumcision was a symbol of God's covenant with God's people, as told to Abraham (Genesis 17: 9-14).

Behind the robed priest who holds the child, a piercing self-portrait of Goltzius peers out at the viewer. Goltzius has placed this scene inside the Church of St. Bavo in Haarlem.

The Circumcision is one of six large engravings that Goltzius made detailing the *Life of the Virgin* known as his *Meesterstukje* or master engravings, which emulated or paid homage to works by other artists: Raphael, Parmigianino, Jacopo Bassano, Barocci, Lucas van Leyden, and Albrecht Dürer. Not to be considered in the same category as the strictly reproductive print, these original works were made in the style and manner of other artists. *The Circumcision* was made after Dürer's woodcut version, 1503–05 (Figure 43).

Goltzius's emulation of other artists' work is taken to the highest level in this engraving. His ability to capture Dürer's style and manner was so well executed that Karel van Mander (1548–1606), the famous biographer of Netherlandish artists, notes that a joking attempt by Goltzius to pass off the print as a Dürer original by removing his own monogram and portrait, and aging an impression with smoke, was successful in fetching a very inflated price before the artist owned up to the trick.[1] Van Mander relates this story in order to make the point that Goltzius is so supremely skilled in his imitation of other artists that he creates a new kind of original "reproductive" print, one

that, as Walter S. Melion writes, "subsumes invention itself into the process of imitation, inventing in the manner of Dürer and Lucas."[2] These are indeed original prints, not ones intended to copy the work of another artist for commercial reasons. As Goltzius creates something new in his imitation he incorporates elements from Dürer's version. Similar clothing and gestures on both versions' figures can be noted; the mohel sits on the same type of cushioned stool; and a large braided candle is held up near the child in both prints. Goltzius also inserts unique details perfectly in the manner of Dürer, but not present in the German artist's woodcut; a large crown glass window, used famously by Dürer in his 1514 engraving *St. Jerome in His Study* (Plate 13), illuminates the scene. Dürer's pre-Reformation version includes an ornate interior wall decoration, while Goltzius's later engraving set in the austere interior of the Church of St. Bavo reflects contemporary religious views against lavish church decoration in the predominantly Calvinist Dutch Republic.

■ JRL

Notes

1. Walter S. Melion, "Theory and Practice: Reproductive Engraving in the Sixteenth-Century Netherlands," in Timothy A. Riggs and Larry Silver, eds., *Graven Images: The Rise of Professional Printmakers in Antwerp and Haarlem, 1540–1640* (Evanston: Mary and Leigh Block Gallery and Northwestern University Press, 1993), 57.
2. Ibid.

Plate 47. Hendrik
Goltzius, *The Circumcision,*
1594. Engraving.

PLATE 48

Hendrik Goltzius,
Dutch, 1558–1617

Pietà

1596

Engraving

6⅞ × 4⅞ inches
174 × 124 mm

88-18

Bartsch 41, Strauss 331,
Hollstein 50

The Pietà devotional motif is a variation on the Lamentation theme that originated in German convents as early as the fourteenth century. Mary individually mourns Christ as her own son in this intimate moment of grief. The Gospels mention little of Mary after Christ's childhood. In medieval religious tradition, just prior to his entry into Jerusalem during the Passion, Christ meets with his mother to "take leave" of her, saying farewell. We recall this meeting as we reflect in Pietà scenes on Mary's sacrifice in giving up her son as the savior, and we are also reminded of depictions of Mary holding her infant son, such as the Nativity.

The Pietà differs from traditional Lamentation scenes in that Mary is usually alone with Christ and, rather than remaining bound by grief, she achieves a sublime peace, understanding that Christ's death has saved humankind. Pietà scenes are often situated at the foot of or near the cross. In this stunning second state impression of Hendrik Goltzius's *Pietà,* Christ's crown of thorns is discarded near the feet of Mary and Christ, and Mary, in heavily draped garments that mimic the limp body of Christ, grieves acutely but quietly in this solitary and private event; her thick tears glisten and mirror the blood seeping from Christ's wounds. Goltzius highlights the mother-son connection and the power of the occasion with many engraved lines surrounding their heads as divine light. He successfully conveys the beauty and divinity of this specific human grief. Goltzius was strongly influenced by Michelangelo's famous large *Pietà* sculpture at St. Peter's Basilica at the Vatican; Michelangelo's interpretation of the motif inspired numerous Pietà images in subsequent centuries. Christ's limp arm hanging across Mary's knee is devastatingly realistic in both Michelangelo's and Goltzius's renderings.

Hendrik Goltzius's *Pietà* splendidly captures the style and manner of Albrecht Dürer, though the earlier artist never created such an engraving. This is an original engraving by Goltzius, but the technique, composition, and style evince his marvelous incorporation of Dürer's spirit in his own work.

■ JRL

PLATE 48. Hendrik Goltzius, *Pietà,* 1596. Engraving (actual size).

Provenance

Max Egon Fürstenberg
(1863–1941; Lugt 995).

PLATE 49

Hendrik Goudt,
Dutch, 1583–1648
after Adam Elsheimer,
German, 1578–1610

*Tobias and
the Angel*

1613
Etching and engraving
9¾ × 10⅟₁₆ inches
247 × 255 mm
93-20
Hollstein 2

PLATE 49. Hendrik Goudt (after Adam Elsheimer), *Tobias
and the Angel,* 1613. Etching and engraving.

Verdant foliage fills this scene with a lush
mood as nature's details seep through the quiet
darkness. Tobias walks alongside the angel
Raphael, dragging the large fish he caught that
will miraculously cure his father's blindness.
The sumptuous nocturnal lighting is typical
of northern Baroque artists, and Dutch artists
(including Rembrandt, who created remarkable
nocturne etchings) were strongly influenced
by Hendrik Goudt's prints. Glimmers of
light flick the edges of leaves and illuminate
Tobias and the angel, who appear as alabaster
emerging from the darkness with gorgeous,
sophisticated texture to their forms. The
chiaroscuro effect anticipates the printmaking
technique of mezzotint. Goudt's characteristic
elaborate calligraphic inscription perfectly
suits the splendid, rich look of the print.

In the Old Testament and Hebrew Bible
book of Tobit, Tobias, the devoted son of
Tobit, embarks on a journey at his father's
request with the disguised angel Raphael as his
companion. With Raphael's assistance, Tobias
captures a fish and is instructed by Raphael
to save the gall, heart, and liver (Tobit 6:1–9).
Tobias later uses the gall to perform cataract
surgery on his blinded father. The restoration
of Tobit's sight is just one miraculous result
of this journey; another sign of God's favor is
the return of Tobit's fortune through riches
obtained by Tobias on the trip. *Angel Departing
from the Family of Tobias,* by Rembrandt
(Plate 59), depicts another scene from this story.

Tobias and the Angel is created after a
painting by the German artist Adam Elsheimer.
Hendrik Goudt is primarily known for seven
engravings he made after Elsheimer's work.
Born in The Hague, Goudt traveled to Rome
in 1604, where he met Elsheimer; census
records state that he lived in Elsheimer's home
from 1607 to 1609.[1] By the time this etching
and engraving was completed in 1613, Goudt
had returned to the Netherlands.

■ JRL

Note

1. Keith Andrews, "Goudt,
   Hendrik," in Grove Art
   Online. Oxford Art
   Online, http://www.
   oxfordartonline.com,
   accessed August 18,
   2010.

Cum reverteretur percusso Philisthao David, et ferret caput eius in Ierusalem, egressa sunt mulieres de universis urbibus
Israel et praecinebant ludentes atq; dicentes. Percussit Saul mille, et David decem millia . 1 . Regum . 18 .

N. de Clerck ex

I. Saenredam sculp.

1600

PLATE 50. Jan Saenredam,
David Returning in Triumph
with the Head of Goliath,
1600. Engraving.

PLATE 50

**Jan Saenredam,
Dutch, c. 1565–1607**

*David Returning
in Triumph with the
Head of Goliath*

1600
Engraving
10¹⁵⁄₁₆ × 7⅜ inches
278 × 187 mm
93-26
Hollstein 11, III/v
Watermark: Eagle
(close to Briquet 155)

David brings Goliath's massive head—impaled on the giant Philistine's own sword—from the battlefield to Jerusalem. A group of well-dressed women greets him at the city gate and heralds his victory in song. To the left of the blade, a pair reads from a sheet of music with large notes, while across from them another holds a lute. On the far left, a young woman with hair dressed in a mass of leaves holds a wreath of small flowers, waiting to crown the hero. The composition is based on a painting by Lucas van Leyden, now lost, dated to between 1510 and 1515.[1] The earliest mention of this work, painted on glass, is in the biography of van Leyden written by the Dutch artist Karel van Mander in 1604. Van Mander places the painting in the collection of Hendrik Goltzius and mentions a print made after it, "very well engraved by Jan Saenredam."[2]

King Saul, who in the biblical text returns to Jerusalem with David, seems strangely absent from the scene. 1 Samuel 18:6–9 explains that the women were "singing and dancing to meet King Saul," but the words to their merry song were "Saul has killed his thousands, and David his ten thousands." Angered, Saul worried whether David would usurp his kingdom. Could the lone man on the far left edge of the engraving, outside the attention of the group and barely included in the scene, be the king of Israel? This figure's furrowed brow and intense gaze seem to express concern rather than awe or joy, which might be a subtle allusion to the conclusion of the biblical episode: "So Saul eyed David from that day on." The furcated cloth hat may seem unlikely on a king, but this choice for royalty by van Leyden is not unprecedented. Similar hats can be seen on Mordecai, who is dressed in the king's clothing in van Leyden's *Triumph of Mordecai* (1515), and, most convincingly, in his circa 1515–16 woodcut illustration of Emperor Charles V as a youth.[3]

After finding some success in mapmaking, Jan Saenredam became a pupil of Hendrik Goltzius and engraved his first prints in 1589. He quickly learned Goltzius's characteristic method of swelling and tapering the lines, as shown in *Annunciation to the Shepherds* (Figures 44 a and b), where the style is quite different from the lines in *David Returning in Triumph with the Head of Goliath*. Made around the time Goltzius stopped engraving at the end of the sixteenth century, the latter print is a clear continuation of his teacher's revivalist work in the 1590s, when Goltzius strove to emulate early sixteenth-century masters like Albrecht Dürer (see Plate 47) and Lucas van Leyden.[4] Saenredam was not as successful as his former teacher at mimicking van Leyden's handling of the burin, but he obviously attempted to lighten and evenly weight the lines to suggest the style of the old master.[5] Published with van Leyden's monogram "L" on the rock in the lower right, this print must have appealed to collectors seeking examples of the older master's work, even if copied.

■ JRW

Above: FIGURE 44a. Jan Saenredam, *Annunciation to the Shepherds,* 1599. Engraving.

Left: FIGURE 44b. Detail from *Annunciation to the Shepherds.*

Notes

1. Elise Lawton Smith, *The Paintings of Lucas van Leyden: A New Appraisal, with Catalogue Raisonné* (Columbia: University of Missouri Press, 1992), 98.
2. Rik Vos and Karel van Mander, "The Life of Lucas van Leyden by Karl van Mander," *Nederlands Kunsthistorish Jaarboek* 29 (1978): 475.
3. Ellen S. Jacobowitz and Stephanie Loeb Stepanek, *The Prints of Lucas van Leyden and His Contemporaries* (Washington, D.C.: National Gallery of Art, 1983), 158.
4. Timothy A. Riggs and Larry Silver, eds., *Graven Images: The Rise of Professional Printmakers in Antwerp and Haarlem, 1540–1640* (Evanston: Mary and Leigh Block Gallery and Northwestern University Press, 1993), 88.
5. Ibid., 112.

PLATE 51

Jacques Callot,
French, 1592–1635

Superbia from
The Seven
Deadly Sins

1621
Seven etchings
3 × 2¼ inches
77 × 58 mm (each plate)
99-04
Lieure 354-360

PLATE 51. Jacques Callot, *Superbia* (Pride), from
The Seven Deadly Sins, 1621. Etching (actual size).

Jacques Callot was one of the first artists to work exclusively in the graphic arts; he did not paint at all. He was born in the region of Lorraine, France, and his father was a designer of court pageants.[1] Jacques resisted his family's plans to make him a cleric, and he began his artistic career by training and working in Italy—first in Rome among the followers of Cornelis Cort and then, around 1612, in Florence. There he was employed by Cosimo II de Medici to create visual records of the *feste,* or festivals, sponsored by the powerful Florentine family. This work taught Callot to construct theatrical compositions filled with many small-scale figures. His highly Mannerist art is characterized by animated scenes and often fueled by an imaginative use of grotesques, inspired in part by his close association with court pageantry in both France and Italy. When the Grand Duke died in 1621 (the year Callot etched *The Seven Deadly Sins*), the artist returned to his hometown of Nancy, France.

This series of miniature allegorical figures impersonates the seven deadly sins, labeled in Latin text on each print: *Avaritia* (Greed; Figure 45), *Superbia* (Pride; Plate 51), *Invidia* (Envy; Figure 46), *Luxuria* (Lust; Figure 47), *Gula* (Gluttony; Figure 48), *Ira* (Wrath; Figure 49), and *Pigritia* (Sloth; Figure 50). These sins, also called cardinal sins or capital vices, were designated during the Middle Ages. Evagrius Ponticus (c. 345–399) created a list of eight evils that was later adapted into the seven sins as they are known today.[2] In Callot's illustrative interpretation, a characteristic animal accompanies each figure, like a peacock for Pride and a goat for Lust. At least one winged demon is also present in each etching, encouraging the sinful behavior.

Artists often depicted the deadly sins with a variety of female figures, a misogynistic tactic akin to "the power of women" theme (see Plate 15), which linked original sin to Eve. There is one male in Callot's series: *Ira* is a young man armed with a sword and paired with a lion. The demon appears to provoke this soldier, whose eyes look up, following the demon as if to strike it down. Callot's allegory of wrath, then, is something of a paradox, suggesting that this capital vice can be redirected, ideally against the sin itself. Anger might be appropriate for men inspired to fight against evil with the fury of righteous indignation.

Callot's etching style imitates engraving, made possible in part by his use of the sharpened, oval end of an échoppe. By twisting the échoppe, he varied the width of the lines drawn in the ground, most noticeable here in the dress of *Pigritia,* where the lines swell and taper as if made with a burin.[3] Callot's etching technique had a lasting effect on French printmaking. His student Abraham Bosse (Plate 52) published an illustrated treatise on etching that featured many of Callot's methods.

■ JRW

Provenance

Émile Galichon
(1829–1875; Lugt 1059).

Notes

1. Linda C. Hults, *The Print in the Western World: An Introductory History* (Madison: University of Wisconsin Press, 1996), 205.
2. F. Refoule, "Evagrius Ponticus," in *New Catholic Encyclopedia* (New York: McGraw-Hill, 1967), 5: 644–45.
3. Hults, 206.

Auaritia.

Inuidia.

Luxuria.

Gula.

Ira.

Pigritia.

Left to right, by row:

FIGURE 45. *Avaritia (Greed)*.

FIGURE 46. *Invidia (Envy)*.

FIGURE 47. *Luxuria (Lust)*.

FIGURE 48. *Gula (Gluttony)*.

FIGURE 49. *Ira (Wrath)*.

FIGURE 50. *Pigritia (Sloth)*.

PLATE 52. Abraham Bosse,
L'istoire de l'enfant prodigue
(The Prodigal Son, Plate 1:
The Prodigal Son Saying
Farewell to His Family),
c. 1636. Etching and
engraving.

PLATE 52

Abraham Bosse,
French, 1602–1676

*L'istoire de l'enfant
prodigue
(The Prodigal Son,
Plate 1: The
Prodigal Son
Saying Farewell
to His Family)*

c. 1636
Etching and engraving
10¼ × 12⅞ inches
264 × 330 mm
83-04
Blum 1184

Seventeenth-century costume is highlighted in *The Prodigal Son Saying Farewell to His Family,* one of six etching/engravings by Abraham Bosse depicting the story of the Prodigal Son. Bosse created scenes with meticulously executed, accurate examples of popular seventeenth-century fashion in many of his prints, thus providing historians records of contemporary clothing and modes.[1] He also created a relevant moralizing genre scene—a slice of daily life of the bourgeois class that directly comments on the standards of French society at the time.

The Prodigal Son is dressed in elegant finery. He wears beautifully rendered fashions of mid–seventeenth-century France, including a plumed beaver hat, the ultimate luxury accessory for men in Europe then. These hats, worn both indoors and out, varied in height and were usually made of taffeta, velvet, or hair of a fine quality. The styling of these valuable hats might indicate one's religious beliefs and social status; for instance, feathers would not be added or worn by Puritans.[2] His loosely fitted doublet has fanciful, puffy, slashed sleeves that may have been lined with brocade or satin extending to the wrist. At the neck of his doublet is a large square-shaped falling collar, composed of lace or linen. His breeches, called grègues, were short pants that puffed out and extended to the thigh, with hose underneath. As the son says goodbye to his saddened family, we can see a horse being prepared for his departure on the far left side of the print; the horse strains against the reins, eluding to the son's desire to break free.

Abraham Bosse's interest in theoretical aspects of printmaking was realized through his significant writings and teachings. He lectured and published studies on perspective in art, influenced by his friendship with geometer Gérard Desargues. Bosse was also a contemporary of the French etcher and engraver Jacques Callot, from whom he learned the Italian method of hard-ground etching on linseed oil and resin, which helps create a precision and fineness of line in the final etching.[3] In 1645, Bosse wrote the first treatise on engraving and etching, essentially a manual for printmakers, in which he advocated that etching should attempt to imitate engraved lines.[4]

In the seventeenth century, the technique of etching was increasingly used by artists and printmakers. The medium was attractive and less time consuming for printmakers when acid was used to bite the lines in the plate, rather than applying physical strength to engrave lines. Many artists followed Bosse's example, considering etching a less labor intensive method for producing lines that looked engraved. Other seventeenth-century artists, the most notable being Rembrandt van Rijn, employed the medium of etching to achieve a more painterly and spontaneous style. Rembrandt's innovations in printmaking relied in large part on technical experimentation inherent to the mediums of etching and drypoint (see Plate 60, *Christ Preaching,* by Rembrandt). Artists making reproductive prints commonly favored the method proposed by Bosse, whereas artists who wanted to emulate the more spontaneous look of a drawing would prefer etching in its natural state.

■ JRL

Notes

1. James Laver, *Costume and Fashion: A Concise History* (New York: Thames and Hudson, 2006), 104.
2. Gratitude to Dr. Shelley Nordtorp-Madson for this observation.
3. Colin Harrison, "Bosse, Abraham," in *The Dictionary of Art,* ed. Jane Turner (New York: Grove, 1998), 2: 468.
4. Linda C. Hults, *The Print in the Western World: An Introductory History* (Madison: University of Wisconsin Press, 1996), 212.

PLATE 53

**Nicolaes de Bruyn,
Dutch, 1571–1656**

Road to Calvary,
from *The Passion*
series

1635
Engraving
26 × 19⅛ inches
660 × 485 mm
98-33.8
Hollstein 98

Nicolaes de Bruyn made many religious prints during his career, first with small narrative scenes tucked into broad landscapes and, after 1610, with larger works, as in this Passion series. The Thrivent Financial Collection of Religious Art holds eleven of the twelve prints from *The Passion*, lacking only an impression from de Bruyn's first plate (speculated to be a title page without pictorial representation, it is also missing from the set at the Rijksmuseum in Amsterdam).[1] These engravings are among the largest single-leaf impressions in the Thrivent Financial collection.

Largely undocumented by historians, the compositions in these enormous prints draw on the work of a few sixteenth-century print masters. Most conspicuously, de Bruyn took inspiration from motifs in Hendrik Goltzius's Passion series, engraved about forty years earlier. In *Arrest of Christ* (Figure 51), for example, the details of Peter cutting the servant's ear and Judas betraying Christ with a kiss beneath a lantern are adapted from Goltzius's version of the same scene (Figure 52). But unlike Goltzius, who limits his characters to those active in the scriptural narrative, de Bruyn consistently incorporates generic people in much the same way that Lucas van Leyden did more than a century earlier in his *Ecce Homo* (Plate 16) and *Baptism of Christ* (Figure 23). Both Goltzius and de Bruyn mix elements of Middle Eastern and northern European clothing derived from contemporary attire, as did van Leyden. Like the older master, de Bruyn seems to explore the juxtaposition between historical narrative and the experiential reception of those biblical stories in contemporary Dutch life in a way that Goltzius does not. With the exception of *Last Supper* and *Agony in the Garden*, there are

groups of people in each of de Bruyn's prints who are not engaged directly in the action. They seem instead to have gathered simply to watch the proceedings, recalling perhaps the Netherlandish tradition of staging Passion plays.[2] Occasionally in these scenes, figures are altogether separate from the central narrative, further emphasizing that these portentous events are happening in the midst of a broader history—and for some will go unnoticed.

The boundary between historic and genre narratives is blurred most in the ninth scene of the series, *Road to Calvary* (Plate 53). Veronica dominates the foreground, while just beyond her kerchief Christ is led toward

FIGURE 51. Nicolaes de Bruyn, *Arrest of Christ,* from *The Passion* series, 1632. Engraving.

FIGURE 52. Hendrik Goltzius, *Arrest of Christ,* 1598. Engraving.

the clearing where one thief is already nailed to a cross. With her extra long, high-collared cloak, pinned coiffure, and large drop earrings, Veronica seems more like a wealthy Dutch woman performing a role in a drama than one in ancient Jerusalem. Meanwhile, Simon of Cyrene (to the left, wearing a farmer's hat) appears distracted. In no hurry to finish his task, Simon nonchalantly stands with Christ's cross, marked "INRI," leaning against his right shoulder while he chats with a group of men wearing a mélange of headwear: decorated turbans, a helmet, and a loopy-brimmed cap.

Notes

1. C. G. Boerner, *Kleine Szenen in großer Landschaft* (Düsseldorf: C. G. Boerner, 1998), 16.
2. J. van Herwaarden, *Between Saint James and Erasmus. Studies in Late-Medieval Religious Life: Devotions and Pilgrimages in the Netherlands,* Studies in Medieval and Reformation Thought 97 (Leiden: Brill, 2003), 76.

PLATE 53. Nicolaes
de Bruyn, *Road to Calvary,*
from *The Passion* series,
1635. Engraving.

Left: FIGURE 53. Nicolaes de Bruyn, *Christ before the High Priest,* from *The Passion* series, 1632. Engraving.

Right: FIGURE 54. Nicolaes de Bruyn, *Flagellation,* from *The Passion* series, 1634. Engraving.

Notes

3. Giulia Bartrum, *German Renaissance Prints, 1490–1550* (London: British Museum Press, 1995), 188–89; Christiane Andersson and Charles W. Talbot, *From a Mighty Fortress: Prints, Drawings, and Books in the Age of Luther, 1483–1546* (Detroit: Detroit Institute of Arts, 1983), 180.

Probably intended for wall display, de Bruyn's giant prints are engraved boldly to emphasize atmosphere over narrative detail. Set in a monumental, vaulted hall that dominates the top half of the picture, *Christ before the High Priest* (Figure 53) is filled with statuary of personages from the Old Testament, firmly suggesting the space of the Hebrew temple. On the platform in the upper left stand Moses and Aaron, and near them Abraham is about to sacrifice Isaac. On the opposite side, David holds Goliath's severed head, while in the niches below on either side of the hall are the Jewish heroines Judith, with the head of Holofernes (apocryphal book of Judith 13:1–20), and Jael, with her hammer and peg (Judges 5:24–27). Several scenes of de Bruyn's *Passion* are placed in lush woods or feature profuse vegetation, as in *Flagellation* (Figure 54), where the gateway framing the courtyard is abundantly dressed with tree leaves. Attention to lighting prevails throughout the series, heightening the sense of drama; in *Road to Calvary,* the people and trees are bathed in an ethereal light that streams divinely through the clouds. Coincidentally, this focus on environment likens de Bruyn's colossal Passion series to the woodcuts of German print master Albrecht Altdorfer, who, working at the opposite end of the scale, explored effects of mood in his miniature *Fall and Redemption of Man* (Plate 20).[3]

■ JRW

PLATE 54

**Claude Mellan,
French, 1598–1688**

*Moses and the
Burning Bush*

1663
Engraving
9⁷⁄₁₆ × 13⅛ inches
239 × 334 mm
90-15
A. de Montaiglon 4

_____

Provenance

Emanuel Levy (Lugt 876).

_____

Note

1. Lisa Dickinson
   Michaux, *Herschel V.
   Jones: The Imprint
   of a Great Collector*
   (Minneapolis:
   Minneapolis Institute
   of Arts, 2006), 134.

God blazes from the fiery branches of a bush that will not burn. On hands and knees, Moses lowers his eyes from God's face. Claude Mellan captured several elements from this famous story in which the Lord commands Moses to lead the Israelites out of Egypt (Exodus 3:1–20). Nearby on the left is the flock of sheep Moses has been tending. His empty shoes lie behind him, a reminder that God told him to remove his shoes as he approached this holy ground.

This engraving is characteristic of Mellan's boldest work, which developed after he returned to Paris from Italy around 1637.[1] His innovative and much admired technique virtually eliminates outline and instead uses swelling and tapering parallel lines to create shape and shadow. His most famous religious print, *The Holy Face* (1649), highlights this virtuosity by using a single line, spiraling from the center of the print, to emulate the impression of Christ's face on a cloth. In *Moses and the Burning Bush,* all the forms are modeled using parallel lines that follow the contours of each object. Appropriate to the supernatural subject, Mellan's mesmerizing effect offers the viewer a unique visual experience, and the entire scene appears to shimmer.

■ JRW

PLATE 54. Claude Mellan,
*Moses and the Burning
Bush,* 1663. Engraving.

PLATE 55

Jan [Johann] Sadeler I,
Flemish, 1550–c. 1600

*Jonah Thrown
into the Whale*

after 1582
Engraving
9⁷⁄₁₆ × 7¹¹⁄₁₆ inches
240 × 195 mm
01-07
Hollstein 128

Note

1. Jacques Foucart and
Pierre Rosenberg,
"Some 'Modelli' of
Religious Scenes by
Dirck Barendsz," *The
Burlington Magazine* 120,
no. 901 (April 1978):
201, note 7.

Waves crash, winds howl, and a giant sea creature writhes on the surface of the ocean. Jonah, an Old Testament prophet, is being thrown into stormy waters after confessing to his shipmates that the tempest is God's punishment for his own actions. The story, told in the short book of Jonah, begins when the Lord tells Jonah to "go at once to Nineveh" and preach to the people there. Instead, he tries to hide from God and boards a ship heading for Tarshish. Swallowed alive by the whale, Jonah lives for three days in its belly, then, after praying to God for forgiveness, is cast safely from the whale onto a beach.

Jan Sadeler, along with his brothers, Aegidius and Raphael, played a major role in the making, producing, and selling of European prints in the late sixteenth century, and he collaborated with many artists across Germany and Italy. *Jonah Thrown into the Whale* is the first in a numbered set of three prints engraved by Sadeler after the designs of Dirck

Barendsz (1534–1592), a Dutch painter and draftsman. The second print (Hollstein 128) depicts the moment when Jonah is spat out by the whale. The third image (Hollstein 251) is an exemplary demonstration of parallelism between the Old and New Testaments in sixteenth-century Christian theology: it is a traditional rendering of Christ's entombment, summarizing Jonah's time in the whale as a foretoken of Christ's interment.[1] With a Latin inscription describing the whale as a "living sepulcher," this dramatic engraving here initiates a deeper message as expressed by Christ in Matthew 12:40: "For just as Jonah was three days and three nights in the belly of the sea monster, so for three days and three nights the Son of Man will be in the heart of the earth." Sadeler's brief cycle suggests a market in which collectable print series were published not only to narrate biblical stories but also to illustrate theological themes.

■ JRW

Ionas puppe cadens, Ceto sorbente voratus,
In pelago non sensit aquas, vitale sepulcrum.

Ne moreretur habens, tandemq; e ventre ferino
Venit ad ignotas tutus sine remige terras.

PLATE 55. Jan [Johann] Sadeler I, *Jonah Thrown into the Whale,* after 1582. Engraving.

In his hometown of Amsterdam, Jacob de Wit was the leading decorative painter during the first half of the eighteenth century.[1] He specialized in Rococo ceiling and room adornment, often featuring grisaille, monochromatic shades of gray that he used to imitate relief sculpture.[2] His preparatory drawings for these ornamental works were highly sought by collectors, and he also made finished drawings for that market, including *Susanna and the Elders,* which must have been appealing for its luxurious, classical bath decorated with the bust of a Roman satyr and a dolphin and putto fountain, rendered in de Wit's specialty of grisaille.

The story of *Susanna and the Elders* is considered by Protestants to be an apocryphal addition to the book of Daniel. Two elders of Babylon spy on the married Hebrew woman Susanna while she bathes alone in her garden. Consumed with desire, the elders accost Susanna, threatening to falsely accuse her of adultery unless she submits to them. Refusing to be blackmailed and also adamant against sinning in the eyes of the Lord, Susanna is arrested and sentenced to death. God stirs the heart of the young prophet Daniel, who exposes the licentious elders' scheme.

While studying in Antwerp with Jacob van Hal (1672–1750), de Wit was exposed to the paintings of the Flemish master Peter Paul Rubens, whose work remained a source of inspiration throughout his career. In Antwerp he made drawn copies of thirty-six ceiling paintings designed by Rubens in the Jesuit church (now Saint Carlo Borromeo). After those paintings were destroyed by fire in 1718, de Wit reproduced the scenes in a print series.

The voluptuous Susanna who demurely resists the elders' lusty clutches is a tribute to Rubens's fleshy female nudes, and the composition shares an affinity with the painting *Susanna and the Elders* by Rubens circa 1611, now at the Hermitage Museum in St. Petersburg. De Wit's decorative emphasis betrays the pious theme of the biblical narrative that is evident in Rubens's version through Susanna's fearful and horrified expression. Here her innocence seems more shy than chaste, and the story has been secularized into a celebration of feminine beauty in art.

■ JRW

PLATE 56

Jacob de Wit, Dutch, c. 1695–1754

Susanna and the Elders

c. 1725
Red and black chalk, watercolor
7¹⁵⁄₁₆ × 8¹⁄₁₆ inches
221 × 225 mm

86-54

Notes

1. J.E.P. Leistra, "Wit, Jacob de," in *The Dictionary of Art,* ed. Jane Turner (New York: Grove, 1998), 33: 261.
2. Ibid.

PLATE 56. Jacob de Wit, *Susanna and the Elders,* c. 1725. Red and black chalk, watercolor.

PLATE 57. Rembrandt
van Rijn, *The Angel
Appearing to the Shepherds,*
1634. Original etched
copperplate.

Rembrandt van Rijn

Figure 55. Rembrandt van Rijn, *The Angel Appearing to the Shepherds,* 1634. Etching, engraving, and drypoint.

PLATE 57
(pages 132, 133)

**Rembrandt van Rijn,
Dutch, 1606–1669**

*The Angel
Appearing to
the Shepherds*

1634

Original etched
copperplate

10⅜ × 8¾ inches
265 × 222 mm

(thickness 1.02 mm;
weight 540 g)

00-10

Bartsch 44

The original copperplate for this dramatic nocturne etching by Rembrandt is one of eighty-one surviving plates by the artist. This plate has been reworked and rebitten.[1] Some surviving plates have not been retouched since Rembrandt's lifetime, but the reworking of his plates is prevalent, largely because many were used to print restrikes in the centuries following his death. Such repeated reprinting causes the lines to break down and become weaker over time. In the seventeenth century, publishers often retouched a plate in order to extend its printing life, thereby allowing more impressions to be pulled and thus more money to be made, despite the potential sacrifice to the artist's original vision and work.[2] After Rembrandt's death, at least 150 of his plates were printed in other hands before the end of the seventeenth century.[3]

The impression of *The Angel Appearing to the Shepherds* (Figure 55) in the Thrivent Financial Collection of Religious Art is a very fine lifetime impression (i.e., created during the artist's life). Good impressions from this plate exhibit the stunning virtuosity possible in Rembrandt's technical mastery of etching. In combining etching, engraving, and drypoint in this plate he achieves an extraordinarily tonal effect, with radiantly lit areas of compositional focus on the celestial angel and cherubs and the scattered shepherds

below. Thomas E. Rassieur aptly describes the complexity involved in the creation of this plate, including the artist's skillful composition of extremely fine yet brilliant lines and delicate, tonal passages of granular etching.[4]

Rembrandt's plates were rather thin and were made from cold hammered copper, which yielded harder plates capable of producing a larger number of good impressions with burr when drypoint was also used.[5] This plate, along with most of the surviving plates, was inked and varnished by owner Alvin-Beaumont around 1916, effectively preventing the printing of any potential restrikes afterward.[6]

Holding a copperplate along with an impression from it within the Thrivent Financial collection is educationally and historically noteworthy. While an original copperplate certainly has historical and technical significance within Rembrandt's oeuvre, the individual impressions hold more art historical value. This was true in Rembrandt's time as well as in subsequent centuries. The print is the final desired result of the artist's expression, and each impression is an original work of art with its own function and unique details. This was especially the case with the art of Rembrandt, whose impressions varied greatly as he experimented with intaglio techniques, inks, and papers.

Access to the original copperplates allows direct study of the artist's technique. Rembrandt, widely considered the greatest etcher in the history of the medium, achieved a number of technical innovations, and scholars remain unsure of some of their details and methods. With surviving plates that remain relatively untouched, scholars can potentially deduce certain techniques from his work on the plate itself, rather than from variations in paper, printing, or ink.[7] Such findings cannot always be determined by examining impressions. Perceptions of the plates' value and function have shifted from viewing them as commodities able to generate valuable restrikes, to appreciating them as art historical relics in the late nineteenth century, to the contemporary consideration of the plates as both study tools and works of art in their own right. Many questions about the plates encourage further study.

The provenance of the surviving Rembrandt plates is largely en bloc, meaning that most of the eighty-one plates were passed to owners as a group. There are gaps in the provenance, but Erik Hinterding created a useful appendix in his significant study that outlines the provenance of the various plates based on his reexamination of all known published sources.

■ JRL

Provenance

Clement de Jonghe (1624–1677), The Dutch Republic; Pieter de Hahn (1723–1766), Amsterdam, passed in his estate sale in 1767 to Pieter de Fouquet (1729–1800); Claude-Henri Watelet (1718–1786), Paris, passed in his estate sale in 1786 to Pierre-François Basan (1723–1797), Paris, then passed to son Henri-Louis Basan (1786), Paris; Auguste Jean, purchased 1810, Paris; Auguste Bernard, purchased 1846, Paris, then passed to son Michel Bernard, Paris; Alvin-Beaumont, purchased 1906, Paris; Robert Lee Humber, purchased 1938, Raleigh, North Carolina; on loan to the Museum at Raleigh, North Carolina, until 1992; private collection, Japan; Pace Prints, New York City; purchased 2000 for Thrivent Financial Collection of Religious Art.

Notes

1. In *The History of Rembrandt's Copperplates, with a Catalogue of Those That Survive* (Zwolle: Waanders Uitgevers, 1995), Erik Hinterding defines "reworked": "changes have been made to the image, such as reinforcing shaded passages with new lines, or even adding lines where there were none before…there are also cases where only existing lines have been reinforced" (40). He explains "rebitten" as "when a new etching ground is applied to the copperplate with a roller, existing etched lines are not covered, and can be deepened by immersion in an acid bath" (40). Hinterding emphasizes that both or either method can be found in retouched plates.
2. Clifford S. Ackley, *Rembrandt's Journey: Painter, Draftsman, Etcher* (Boston: MFA Publications, 2003), 70.
3. Hinterding, 8. Limiting a print run is a modern idea and was not recognized until the late nineteenth century. The reprinting of these plates did not cease until approximately the early twentieth century, when it was acknowledged to be damaging to Rembrandt's reputation and the value of his lifetime impressions (9). The abundance of restrikes from Rembrandt's plates also brings up the question of perceived value through history of impressions taken after his death. It is not always clear exactly what collectors thought over time, but many examples in Hinterding's study show that early, rare, superb, and proof impressions were valued monetarily and by contemporary connoisseurs over later impressions from reworked plates.
4. For a discussion of the "granular pitted passages" or "etched granular tone," see Thomas E. Rassieur's contribution on *The Angel Appearing to the Shepherds* in Ackley, 105.
5. Hinterding, 10.
6. Ibid., 35.
7. Ibid., 38.

PLATE 58

**Rembrandt van Rijn,
Dutch, 1606–1669**

*Christ Driving the
Money Changers
from the Temple*

1635

Etching and engraving

5¼ × 6⅝ inches
133 × 168 mm

86-17

Bartsch, Hollstein 69

Watermark: Strasbourg,
bend and lily

Provenance

Pierre Mariette II
(1634–1716; Lugt 1789).

Notes

1. Gratitude to Thomas E.
Rassieur for sharing
this observation in a
discussion at Thrivent
Financial on April 19,
2010.
2. Clifford S. Ackley,
*Rembrandt's Journey:
Painter, Draftsman,
Etcher* (Boston: MFA
Publications, 2003),
228, note 2; Shelley
Perlove and Larry
Silver, *Rembrandt's
Faith: Church and Temple
in the Dutch Golden
Age* (University Park:
Pennsylvania State
University Press, 2009),
251.
3. Perlove and Silver, 253.
4. Ibid., 254.

Coins spill from a toppling, makeshift table as Christ threatens with a scourge the bankers and vendors hawking in the temple: mayhem ensues. *Christ Driving the Money Changers from the Temple* was made during Rembrandt's earliest years as an established artist in Amsterdam, about a year after his marriage to Saskia van Uylenburgh (1612–1642), niece of his art dealer at the time. He was in his late twenties, newly wed, with a budding career in a lively commercial center; ebullient and amusing physicality are characteristic of his art during this period.[1] Rembrandt's dramatic etching is filled with physical movement, which also adds humor to the scene. Christ's outrage has sent the sacrificial livestock into an entertaining uproar. One cowhand is being dragged—kicking and yelping on his back—by the tether of a bucking young bull. In the lower right corner, another man tackles a flapping bird near the little dog that barks excitedly at Christ.

Despite Rembrandt's comedic diversion, *Christ Driving the Money Changers from the Temple* is deeply laden with a serious theological and moral message. The figure of Christ is a reverse copy of Christ in the same scene from Albrecht Dürer's *Small Passion* series. In Rembrandt's etching, the light that illuminates Christ and the people around him radiates from his raised hand, rather than from a nearby candle as in Dürer's woodcut. This innovative adaptation emphasizes the divine authority of Christ's action as he restores

the sanctity of the temple, decrying that his father's house has been corrupted from its original written purpose for prayer and worship.[2]

The Jewish priests and Pharisees gathered in the upper right evoke the Sanhedrin, or high Jewish court, and are emblematic of the traditional laws to which Christ refers. At the center of the group, a kneeling man appeals these judges. He faces a priest holding a staff, which Shelley Perlove and Larry Silver describe as representative of Moses' brazen serpent and an episode in which the Israelites who looked at it were saved from God's plague of poisonous snakes (Numbers 21:6–9). The staff in Rembrandt's print is thus a symbol of the law, but also of faith and healing.[3] With Christ in the central foreground, the composition proclaims him the new authority for judgment and redemption. Like the Israelites who died when they failed to look at the bronze serpent, the doomed money changers here turn away from Christ. The one about to be stricken glances back audaciously as he cowers, greedily embracing his sack of money.

From an ecclesial perspective, Rembrandt's particularly layered representation would have resonated with church leaders at that time, who used this story in the seventeenth century as a metaphor of their own calls for reform and purity within the Dutch Reformed Church.[4]

■ JRW

PLATE 58. Rembrandt
van Rijn, *Christ Driving
the Money Changers from
the Temple,* 1635. Etching
and engraving (actual
size).

PLATE 59. Rembrandt van
Rijn, *Angel Departing from
the Family of Tobias,* 1641.
Etching and drypoint
(actual size).

PLATE 59

Rembrandt van Rijn, Dutch, 1606–1669

Angel Departing from the Family of Tobias

1641
Etching and drypoint
4 × 6 inches
103 × 154 mm
95-26
Bartsch, Hollstein 43

The story of Tobit and his son Tobias derives from the apocryphal book of Tobit. Blinded and made poor as a result of a good deed, Tobit asks his son to travel with the disguised angel Raphael to regain the wealth Tobit has lost. Tobias shows great bravery and devotion to his father in his adventurous quest. With Raphael's assistance, Tobias soon captures a fish and is instructed by Raphael to save the magical innards, which he later uses to perform cataract surgery on his father. On his journey Tobias recovers the family's fortune and marries his wife, Sarah, through further miraculous means.[1] Sarah and Tobias return home to much celebration, and Raphael announces his true identity and God's great favor and blessing on the family.

The dramatic moment when Raphael departs from the family is shown in this plate. Tobias bows his head, eyes closed, in deep veneration for God's favor, while Tobit's hands are clasped reverently as he gazes toward the angel. Tobias's wife, Sarah, raises her hands in apparent shock and turns her head away into shadows. Rembrandt also portrayed Anna, Tobit's wife, with perfectly human gesture as her hands hover upward during the prodigious event; her eyes, however, linger on the restored fortune in the chest at lower right, perhaps suggesting her overwhelming gratitude.

Whimsy and humor are included in some of Rembrandt's etchings. In *Angel Departing from the Family of Tobias,* Raphael's feet dangle in the upper right corner as he leaves the family. Rembrandt chose to infuse the sacred scene with a lighthearted mood. The family would see the feet dangling from above, but so too does the viewer, and we can be sure Rembrandt thought of that, creating an additional connection between the viewer,

artist, and print—almost as if he is sharing a joke with us by depicting Raphael in terms of our common human experience. We also see the backside of the little family dog next to Tobias, a simple reality of family life but also perhaps an extension of the "joke" of seeing only the angel's backside as he exits. This playful nature of many of Rembrandt's prints also reveals his commitment to realism and genre—sometimes humorous or gritty, but also fresh presentations of historical and biblical subjects as genre scenes. By secularizing components of these subjects, Rembrandt makes the daily life of biblical figures as accessible as our own family life.

Technically, this etching displays Rembrandt's mastery of etched granular tone. Rembrandt and his contemporaries experimented with adding areas of tone successfully to a plate, and many technical approaches endeavored to achieve tone. Rembrandt developed a unique method, some details of which remain unknown: he probably carefully brushed a corrosive agent or paste onto specific areas on the copperplate that would bite or pit the surface of the plate with numerous tiny specks, creating defined, deliberate areas of tone.[2] The second state impression in the Thrivent Financial collection exhibits this granular tone especially in the cloak that the central figure, Anna, wears. The outer cloak is made tonally rich and darker by many small specks, and Rembrandt leaves the lining of the cloak lighter and brighter by a presumed exact placement of the corrosive agent.[3] Rembrandt's use of this technique contributes to his stature as one of the most innovative and inventive printmakers of all time.

■ JRL

Provenance

The Albertina, Vienna.

Notes

1. Sarah, a pious woman, had been married seven times previously, but on each wedding night the demon Asmodeus had slain each groom. Raphael instructs Tobias on how to exorcise the demon and survive his own wedding night. He is then blessed further and able to restore his family's fortune through the generosity of his new father-in-law (Tobit 7, 8).

2. Tom Rassieur, "Chapters in Rembrandt's Life as a Printmaker," in *Pursuit of Faith: Etchings by Rembrandt from the Thrivent Financial Collection of Religious Art,* ed. Shelley Perlove (Dearborn: University of Michigan, Dearborn, 2010), 39.

3. Ibid., 39–41.

PLATE 60. Rembrandt
van Rijn, *Christ Preaching
(La Petite Tombe),* c. 1652.
Etching, engraving, and
drypoint.

PLATE 60

Rembrandt van Rijn, Dutch, 1606–1669

Christ Preaching (La Petite Tombe)

c. 1652
Etching, engraving, and drypoint
8⅛ × 6 inches
154 × 206 mm
84-22
Bartsch, Hollstein 67
Watermark: Foolscap

Listeners tightly surround Christ, whose upraised hands and serene countenance emanate toward the crowd. A simple halo sits atop his head, and his lips are parted in speech as his onlookers sit or stand around him, several pensively holding their head with a hand. Such details, as well as a distracted boy in the central foreground who discarded a toy top in favor of drawing in the dirt with his finger and a sleepy elderly man on the far right, build on Rembrandt's brilliant incorporation of genre and human gesture into his religious prints. Rembrandt employs shadow and light masterfully here: each element of the crowd and its surroundings contributes to a mixture of tone and shadow, while Christ is accentuated by his lighter clothing and open space beneath him, and the divine light radiating from the halo is emphasized by a pillar immediately behind.

Christ Preaching, along with another etching known as *The Hundred Guilder Print* (Figure 11), presents a universal picture of Christ's ministry. These are not only two of Rembrandt's most celebrated prints but also two of the most recognized images in the history of art. Not meant to represent one single biblical episode, the scenes instead portray the theme of Christ's teachings and time on earth. The inclusion of children, elderly, and ill members of society in both prints signals a reference to the Gospel of Matthew, specifically the parables in chapters 18 and 19, in which Christ praises and blesses the humility of children and the poor.

The more prominent, velvety black areas in this impression are a consequence of drypoint and its resulting burr; Rembrandt experimented with this technique to great effect in his prints. When applying drypoint, the artist scratches the surface of the plate directly with a needle, often after other intaglio techniques have been used to principally make up the drawing. The scratches cause tiny metal shavings, called burr, to rise on the sides of each line. When the plate is inked and wiped, the burr captures and holds onto ink, creating varying degrees of rich, velvety, dense areas (also called burr) on the printed sheet where the superfluous ink has spread. Many factors influence the amount and effect of burr in individual impressions, such as the paper, the pressure with which the drypoint is applied, and how early in the life of the plate an impression is pulled. Drypoint can produce a softer line and overall look, or dramatic areas of inky density (as with this impression of *Christ Preaching*). Although not the first artist to use drypoint, Rembrandt was the first to understand and exploit its visual potential, and it became a chief way for him to create accent and highlight shadow in his prints.[1]

The alternate title of this work, *La Petite Tombe,* derives from a note in print dealer Clement de Jonghe's inventory that lists it as *Latombisch plaatjen* (La Tombe's little plate), a reference to the La Tombe family, who may have commissioned this print.[2]

■ JRL

Provenance

Theodore De Witt
(Lugt 2428).

Notes

1. Tom Rassieur, "Chapters in Rembrandt's Life as a Printmaker," in *Pursuit of Faith: Etchings by Rembrandt from the Thrivent Financial Collection of Religious Art,* ed. Shelley Perlove (Dearborn: University of Michigan, Dearborn, 2010), 35.
2. Clifford S. Ackley, *Rembrandt's Journey: Painter, Draftsman, Etcher* (Boston: MFA Publications, 2003), 208, note 6.

PLATE 61

Rembrandt van Rijn,
Dutch, 1606–1669

Flight into Egypt:
Crossing a Brook

1654

Etching and drypoint

3⅝ × 5⅝ inches
92 × 143 mm

92-28

Bartsch, Hollstein 55

Note

1. Tom Rassieur, "Chapters in Rembrandt's Life as a Printmaker," in *Pursuit of Faith: Etchings by Rembrandt from the Thrivent Financial Collection of Religious Art,* ed. Shelley Perlove (Dearborn: University of Michigan, Dearborn, 2010), 41. Rassieur points out that the effect may have occurred from the etching ground failing late in the biting stage, or, alternatively, Rembrandt could have intentionally distressed the ground and then reintroduced the plate into the acid.

Mary and the Christ child softly emerge from dense shadow of night. Mary's body is slightly hunched from exhaustion, yet she firmly enfolds the infant in her cloaked embrace. She curls around Christ, her eyelids falling in a resigned but protective gaze while she grips a fur pack behind the donkey's head for stability. Joseph wearily but steadily leads the donkey ahead, his walking stick helping to guide the family through the water and on to rest. Rembrandt's rendering is fully aware of familial intimacy: this pair is as much mother and child as Savior and Virgin Mother.

Abundant cross-hatching surrounding Mary suggests dark shadows of the nocturnal wilderness. Less densely etched lines and tone seem to illuminate the mother and son. Abstractions of nature appear throughout this scene; rocky areas, grasses, the gentle flow of water, and rustling trees and foliage overhead are all masterfully suggested but never perfectly defined. Rembrandt employs a multitude of varying lines and areas of tone to build this small scene into a visually complex, dense woodland background.

Further technical experimentation enriches this print. At the very bottom irregular acid-biting can be seen, which creates the look of the moving water through which the family traverses. This effect may have been intentional: a quick acid rinse on the copper-plate makes surface texture through a gentle roughening of the plate; along with small

areas of gray tone between the parallel etched lines in the background, this contributes a unique effect that Rembrandt must have liked, regardless of his intentions, because he printed many impressions of this plate.[1]

The Gospel of Matthew is the scriptural source for this scene. After the birth of Jesus, Joseph is warned by an angel in a dream to flee with his family to Egypt to avoid King Herod's decree to destroy the child, proclaimed in fear that Jesus, foretold to be the Messiah, would eventually overtake his power; "then Joseph got up, took the child and his mother by night, and went to Egypt" (Matthew 2:14). They remained there until King Herod's death.

Tender, familial depictions of the Holy Family occur frequently in Rembrandt's oeuvre. This print is one of several that he produced in the 1650s that feature Christ's infancy. Rembrandt's renderings of such scenes teem with the intimacy felt within one's own home. Flight into Egypt scenes were ideal compositions for artists to explore the domes-ticity of Christ's family. The Holy Family traveling together naturally offered opportunity to interpret the daily life of Mary, Joseph, and Jesus, and the scriptural text from Matthew encouraged artists to develop the popular nocturnal imagery that was emerging in paintings and prints of the time (see Plate 49, *Tobias and the Angel,* by Hendrik Goudt).

■ JRL

PLATE 61. Rembrandt
van Rijn, *Flight into Egypt:
Crossing a Brook,* 1654.
Etching and drypoint
(actual size).

PLATE 62. Rembrandt van
Rijn, *Descent from the Cross
by Torchlight,* 1654. Etching
and drypoint (actual size).

PLATE 62

Rembrandt van Rijn,
Dutch, 1606–1669

*Descent from the
Cross by Torchlight*

1654
Etching and drypoint
8¼ × 6⅜ inches
209 × 162 mm

88-13

Bartsch, Hollstein 83

Provenance

Alexander Beugo
(Lugt 81).

Notes

1. Shelley Perlove and
   Larry Silver, *Rembrandt's
   Faith: Church and Temple
   in the Dutch Golden
   Age* (University Park:
   Pennsylvania State
   University Press, 2009),
   303.
2. Tom Rassieur,
   "Chapters in
   Rembrandt's Life as a
   Printmaker," in *Pursuit
   of Faith: Etchings by
   Rembrandt from the
   Thrivent Financial
   Collection of Religious
   Art,* ed. Shelley Perlove
   (Dearborn: University
   of Michigan, Dearborn,
   2010), 41.
3. Ibid.
4. Perlove and Silver, 301.

Plunged into the black of night and lit with a single flame, Christ's descent from the cross has been transformed by Rembrandt into an intimate yet dramatic play of light and dark. Neither Christ nor the cross is entirely visible, which places an emphasis on the actions and gestures of the disciples and makes them the true subject of the scene.[1] Rembrandt's composition narrates in detail the practical tasks of their solemn undertaking. One man simply holds the torch as several others manage the long cloth used to lower Christ's body, the weight of which seems to lie entirely in the arms of the man with his back turned to the viewer. Standing precariously on the rocky ledge, he waits for the man with a hammer behind the post to tap out the nail that still attaches Christ's foot to the cross. In the shadows of the lower right corner, a bier is prepared with a second white cloth that reflects the flickering torchlight. Behind the bier, more of Christ's followers are mourning and praying, their ghostly faces barely visible in the inky blackness of Rembrandt's thick lines.

From this void a single hand reaches toward Christ and into a blaze of light, creating what is perhaps the most striking element in the scene. The hand, ready to help lower Christ's body, is whiter than almost every other area in the etching—even those closest to the torch. Curiously, the clothing of the man standing to the far right, furthest from the flame, is also lighter. It is not known how Rembrandt created this slight difference in tone, although possibilities for his technique have been proposed. Perhaps by quickly washing acid over all other areas of "white" on the plate, microscopic pits were bitten into the metal surface, which in turn transferred just the slightest tint of gray to the paper.[2] Or, Rembrandt may have polished the copper at the hand and the man's clothing especially well to ensure they would be the brightest on the page.[3] Regardless of his method, the visual effect suggests that these elements—particularly the hand that rises out of the darkness in the center of the image—are lit by Christ rather than the torch, stressing that, even in death, true light and the promise of life come from Christ. The form of the temple in the distance reiterates this glimmer of hope. Placed diagonally just to the right of Christ in the composition, its solid but shadowed presence contrasts the New Testament with the Old, and alludes theologically to Christ's promise in John 2:19: "tear down this temple, and in three days I will raise it up."[4]

■ JRW

PLATE 63

Rembrandt van Rijn, Dutch, 1606–1669

Abraham's Sacrifice

1655

Etching and drypoint

6 × 5⅛ inches

150 × 130 mm

96-06

Bartsch, Hollstein 35

_____

Notes

1. Christopher White, *Rembrandt as an Etcher: A Study of the Artist at Work* (New Haven: Yale University Press, 1999), 105.
2. Clifford S. Ackley, *Rembrandt's Journey: Painter, Draftsman, Etcher* (Boston: MFA Publications, 2003), 134. The question whether Abraham actually sees the angel or only hears his voice calling from heaven in this rendering was also discussed in Jakob Rosenberg, *Rembrandt: Life and Work* (London: Phaidon Press, 1964), 176.
3. In *Rembrandt's Faith: Church and Temple in the Dutch Golden Age* (University Park: Pennsylvania State University Press, 2009), Shelley Perlove and Larry Silver discuss this print and offer an alternative reading of Rembrandt's interpretation that asserts that he may have closely followed a literal reading of the scriptural text and annotations as found in the *Statenbijbel,* the Dutch translation of the Bible available in the seventeenth century. They note that the annotation for this passage in the *Statenbijbel* reads: "The angel came from behind, so that in turning about he [Abraham] did spy the ram, instantly apprehending that he was to offer the same in his son's stead" (91).
4. Ackley, 135.

One hand shields Isaac's eyes from the dreadfulness of the imminent sacrificial moment. In the book of Genesis, Abraham's faith is tested by God, who tells him to take his only beloved son to a mountain and sacrifice him (Genesis 22). This command and its outcome represent God's renewal of God's promise and blessing to Abraham and his descendants: God ultimately provides for Abraham, sending an angel who intervenes and a ram to give up in offering rather than Isaac. In the Christian tradition, this story has long been considered a precursor to God's sacrifice of God's own son; God provides the ram as Isaac's substitution just as Christ is provided for humankind. Abraham's story was reexamined by Rembrandt multiple times in various media.

In the biblical text, Isaac is saved when the angel calls down to Abraham from heaven, stopping him; Abraham then looks up and sees the ram (Genesis 22:10–13). Rembrandt pushes the biblical interpretation further by bringing the angel down to physically prevent Abraham from carrying out the act. The angel's outstretched wings hover around the father and son, enveloping them in his merciful errand from God. Molded together as if carved from one block of marble,[1] the three figures seem suspended in time. Isaac's eyes are shielded from the horror of the moment by his father's hand, while Rembrandt makes Abraham's own eyes black sockets, his face confused, bewildered by the angel's interruption. Perhaps the moment is more than this loving father can bear—does he truly see the angel who in the scriptural text only calls down from heaven? Has Rembrandt made visually literal a symbolic intervention that is suggested through Abraham's distraught face and darkened eyes?[2] The artist successfully conveyed the torment and anguish of the moment and Abraham's decision to follow the will of God through sacrificing his child. Rembrandt's ability to rearticulate and explore complex religious traditions and subjects is one of his remarkable gifts and underscores the pivotal role of religious subject matter in his oeuvre (see "The Religious Print" essay).

Although slightly departing from the scriptural text with the physical presence of the angel,[3] closeness to the text is also indicated by including other elements in the etching. The small pile of wood in the middle foreground is ready to complete the burnt offering that God commanded (Genesis 22:2), and the donkey and two young companions Abraham brought along on the journey (Genesis 22:3) are huddled against a rock wall in the lower right side of the etching.

Rembrandt employs shafts of heavenly light as compositional and thematic devices. Two diagonal lines on the right side of the print highlight the angel's left hand firmly restraining Abraham's left arm (and his hand that holds the knife). These shafts of light also divide the scene into sections: the knife, and sacrificial act, is separated from the three central figures. The sacrificial ram can be seen in a dark shadow directly to the left of the angel. *Abraham's Sacrifice* is typical of Rembrandt's etching style in the mid-1650s: etched with clean, clearly delineated lines and solidity of form, then made softer and more densely shadowed in areas with drypoint.[4]

■ JRL

PLATE 63. Rembrandt
van Rijn, *Abraham's
Sacrifice,* 1655. Etching
and drypoint (actual size).

PLATE 64. Rembrandt
van Rijn, *The Agony in the
Garden*, c. 1657. Etching
and drypoint (actual size).

The episode of Christ's Agony in the Garden takes place during the Passion, when Christ goes with his disciples to pray in the garden of Gethsemane, at the foot of the Mount of Olives, directly before he is betrayed by Judas and arrested. The artistic tradition of an angel being present at the scene is derived from the Gospel of Luke, in which an angel appears to comfort Christ and offer him strength as he prayerfully prepares for his impending sacrifice.[1] Surrounded by the darkness of night and apart from the sleeping apostles, Christ is utterly alone in this trying moment until the angel arrives to support him, both physically and psychologically. As with much religious imagery of the Passion, the artist here combines elements from several Gospels: Matthew 26:37 and Mark 14:33 relate that Christ brings three companions (Peter, James, and John), but Luke includes the angel and explores more fully Christ's deep agony, describing how he prayed so fervently that his sweat fell like great drops of blood (Luke 22:43–44).

The Agony in the Garden exemplifies Rembrandt's ability to portray religious scenes rich with human emotion and expressive drama. He often presented traditional subject matter in new ways, finding nuanced moments of a story to exploit both visually and emotionally. His rendering of this event focuses on Christ and the angel. Beams of divine light stream diagonally behind the angel, who has descended on this path directly from heaven to embrace and uplift an anguished Christ. The drama of this arrival is intensified by the nocturnal setting (emphasized by the full moon behind dark clouds) and the surface tone and drypoint burr, which create a darkened mood. Rembrandt humanizes the moment by bringing the angel physically down to earth, his foot firmly planted on the ground, and he marks Christ's solitude by placing him on a raised outcropping. True to the biblical text, the disciples slumber in the left foreground, and a crowd in the background behind the angel's wings, led by Judas, is ready to descend on Christ and arrest him. Through instinctively

constructed gesture in the angel's outstretched arms, gently tilted head, and concerned face, and Christ's sorrowful but resigned visage, Rembrandt conveys a restrained but highly expressive interpretation of this moment in which Christ must bolster his resolve and accept God's will and his own fulfillment of Scripture. Rembrandt also uses artistic technique to highlight the drama: crosshatched portions are darkened by inky areas of tone and drypoint burr surrounding Christ and the underside of the rock outcropping, allowing them to emerge from soft, hazy darkness.

This impression of *The Agony in the Garden* is printed on Japanese paper. Rembrandt began to use Japanese paper for some of his prints around 1647; this exotic and new type of imported paper differed in texture, body, and look from the common European white papers.[2] A suffused warmth and softness typically characterize impressions on Japanese paper. During printing, this paper takes the ink differently; the smooth, less absorbent surface allows a slight bleeding and receptivity of the ink that gathers in the drypoint burr, which results in a blending of closely placed lines into washlike areas of tone.[3] Impressions on Japanese paper were highly sought by contemporary collectors of Rembrandt's prints, and today they remain valued and desirable for their rarity, because Rembrandt used the paper in moderation. Like most impressions on Japanese paper, this work in the Thrivent Financial collection displays clarity of line as well as several areas of soft, velvety drypoint burr that contribute to an evocative, atmospheric effect.[4]

This plate evinces Rembrandt's innovative experimentation with individual impressions of his prints. After careful execution of the plate, he meticulously addressed the specific printing processes for each sheet, varying, for example, papers and how he wiped the ink from the plate before printing in order to achieve his intended result for each impression. Each print was a unique work of original art.[5]

■ JRL

PLATE 64

Rembrandt van Rijn, Dutch, 1606–1669

The Agony in the Garden

c. 1657
Etching and drypoint
4¼ × 3¼ inches
108 × 83 mm
97-4
Bartsch, Hollstein 75

Notes

1. These verses about the angel at Gethsemane were likely not original to the scriptural text, but they have been known to Christian writers since the second century and hold an established tradition in relating the Passion as told in the Gospel of Luke (Bruce M. Metzger and Roland E. Murphy, eds., *The New Oxford Annotated Bible, with the Apocryphal/ Deuterocanonical Books* [New York: Oxford University Press, 1994], 118 NT, notes 43–44). The tradition of an angel appearing to "strengthen" Christ during his self-doubt is equally established in the history of art.
2. Tom Rassieur, "Chapters in Rembrandt's Life as a Printmaker," in *Pursuit of Faith: Etchings by Rembrandt from the Thrivent Financial Collection of Religious Art,* ed. Shelley Perlove (Dearborn: University of Michigan, Dearborn, 2010), 42.
3. Clifford S. Ackley, *Rembrandt's Journey: Painter, Draftsman, Etcher* (Boston: MFA Publications, 2003), 208.
4. Rassieur, 43.
5. Christopher White, *Rembrandt as an Etcher: A Study of the Artist at Work* (New Haven: Yale University Press, 1999), 111. White notes that at least six impressions from this plate were printed on Japanese paper, presumably including the one in the Thrivent Financial collection.

PLATE 65. Jan Lievens,
Resurrection of Lazarus,
c. 1630–31. Etching.

PLATE 65

Jan Lievens, Dutch,
1607–1674

*Resurrection
of Lazarus*

c. 1630–31
Etching
13⅞ × 12⅜ inches
353 × 309 mm
85-29
Hollstein 7, I/iii
Watermark: Coat of arms
with a post horn

Great beams of light radiate from Christ, who with folded hands raises his eyes and voice to God. Astonished onlookers marvel to see the hands of Lazarus—already dead four days—rise out of his open grave (John 11:1–44). This rendering of Lazarus's resurrection by Jan Lievens differs from most others, which depict Christ lifting his hand in a commanding gesture to stress the moment when he cries, "Lazarus, come out!" Instead, Lievens chose to emphasize the verses just prior in the text, when Christ thanks God for hearing his prayer. This version, which Lievens also completed as a painting in 1631, would certainly have been favored by Protestants, who taught that God alone could offer new life through Christ.[1]

Although today Jan Lievens's name is not nearly as well known as Rembrandt's, his early career was just as bright. One year younger than Rembrandt and born in the same city of Leiden, Lievens was studying painting in his hometown by age eight and in Amsterdam with history painter Pieter Lastman by about the age of ten. When Rembrandt finished his six-month apprenticeship with Lastman in 1625, Lievens was already operating his own successful studio. Starting around 1626, the two young artists became friendly rivals in Leiden and heavily influenced each other's work for the next several years. Both painters developed their etching skills during this period, largely ignoring prescribed techniques and instead using the copperplate like a

sketch pad.[2] *Resurrection of Lazarus* was created near the end of their close association, and Lievens's etching has much in common with Rembrandt's free and spontaneous lines and intense contrast of light with deep shadow.[3] Each figure has a distinct countenance as Lievens, like Rembrandt, strives to establish individual human characters.

Rembrandt left Leiden for Amsterdam in 1631; Lievens went to London in 1632. As his career unfolded, Lievens was notably influenced by Flemish and Italian painting. He moved frequently and continued to explore and adapt his style. He realized international renown in his lifetime and won prominent painting commissions in major cities such as London, Antwerp, Berlin, and Amsterdam. His etching style also evolved, and late in his career he made etchings of patrons, who cherished these highly finished, honorific portraits.[4]

In later centuries, Lievens did not achieve the same sensational reputation as his hometown contemporary. By the 1900s, he was almost entirely ignored by connoisseurs, who favored Rembrandt's distinctly Dutch qualities over Lievens's international style.[5] Still, this rare, first state impression of *Resurrection of Lazarus* represents a critical point in the development of both artists' careers, and it is an important complement to the strong selection of Rembrandt prints in the Thrivent Financial Collection of Religious Art.

■ JRW

Notes

1. Lloyd DeWitt, "The Raising of Lazarus," in *Jan Lievens: A Dutch Master Rediscovered*, ed. Arthur K. Wheelock Jr. (Washington, D.C.: National Gallery of Art, 2008), 142.
2. Stephanie Dickey, "Jan Lievens and Printmaking," in Wheelock, 56.
3. Linda C. Hults, *The Print in the Western World: An Introductory History* (Madison: University of Wisconsin Press, 1996), 224.
4 Dickey, 66.
5. Wheelock, 3.

PLATE 66

Nicolaes Maes,
Dutch, 1634–1693

Temptation
of Christ

c. 1680

Pen, brown ink, and wash

7⅞ × 9¼ inches
197 × 232 mm

02-04

Sumowski 1939

Provenance

P. de Boer; J. Theodor Cremer; Mak Van Waay, Amsterdam, November 1980.

Notes

1. William W. Robinson, "Nicolaes Maes as a Draughtsman," *Master Drawings* 27, no. 2 (1989): 146.
2. Ibid.
3. Ibid., 159.
4. Ibid., 154.
5. R. S. Johnson, *Old Master Prints and Drawings, 1450–1800* (Chicago: R. S. Johnson Fine Art Catalogue, 1994), 34. The Rembrandt drawing, c. 1632–33, can be seen in Benesch 1, no. 65 recto and illustration 64, and Benesch 1973 with illustration 75.

Nicolaes Maes studied with Rembrandt in his studio from about 1650 until 1653, learning from the brilliant Dutch master during the formative years of his career.[1] Although Maes was primarily a portraitist, a small number of his subject pieces, including biblical subjects, survive, and he is regarded as one of the most innovative and important genre painters in the Netherlands.

Like many drawings by pupils of Rembrandt, *Temptation of Christ* was once attributed to the Dutch master. A handwritten graphite inscription on its verso reads "Rembrandt van Rijn," undoubtedly added by a collector or dealer at some point in the drawing's history. The study of drawings by Rembrandt's pupils is valuable not only for the insight they offer to that particular artist's oeuvre but also for what they may tell us about how Rembrandt's skill, methods, and influence resonated with the next generation of Dutch artists. With Maes, we know that his practices as a draftsman aided in his artistic creativity, self-discipline, exploration of motifs, and preparation for his paintings; he was one of only a handful of important Dutch genre painters who were also strong draftsman.[2] His ability to render acutely human gesture and emotion in his figures and his strongly narrative, sophisticated compositions exhibit Rembrandt's monumental influence as much as they reveal Maes's own gifts. The drawings of Rembrandt and his students brim with material for further rich study.

Drawings produced by painters have long served mainly as preparatory sketches for paintings. For Rembrandt, as well as some pupils such as Maes, drawings could have various functions. Drawings by both artists were produced principally as independent sketches and finished compositions, especially for historical and biblical subjects.[3] Biblical subjects number few in Maes's painting oeuvre, but they constitute more than a third of his 160 known drawings.[4] A companion drawing to this one, another *Temptation of Christ* (Sumowski 1938), shares the figure, type, and gesture of the devil, also reminiscent of an early Rembrandt drawing in Frankfurt.[5]

The curious little tempter here is drawn in the same lively manner as Christ and their surroundings. The small, weak-looking devil appears to plead with Christ more than to challenge him, perhaps emphasizing this moment as a true temptation by an intentionally cunning and less threatening creature than we might imagine the devil to be. A smoothness and ease to the compositional arrangement in the drawing is led by the flow of dynamic gestures Maes gives both figures, as well as the active, organic rendering of the rocks, trees, and landscape lines around them. Like many of Maes's biblical drawings, the figures seem a natural part of their environment while simultaneously emerging out of it.

While this drawing has both a spontaneity and a finished feel, signs of the artist's process remain visible. Pentimenti around the right foot and leg of Christ along with small traces of a moving fingerprint in the upper right corner, above the tree, allow a glimpse into Maes's actual work; we can imagine his thumb holding the sheet as he sketched in other areas and his thought process as he experimented with Christ's stance and gesture. The story of the temptation of Christ derives from the Gospel of Matthew, in which Christ endures forty days and forty nights of fasting in the wilderness after which a devil challenges him to turn stones into bread if he truly be the Son of God. The precise scene in this drawing is Christ's response to the tempter, as he points toward the heavens uttering the words, "One does not live by bread alone, but by every word that comes from the mouth of God" (Matthew 4:4).

■ JRL

PLATE 66. Nicolaes Maes,
Temptation of Christ,
c. 1680. Pen, brown ink,
and wash.

THE NINETEENTH CENTURY

13
Who is this that darkeneth counsel by words without knowledge
Then the Lord answered Job out of the Whirlwind
Who maketh the Clouds his Chariot & walketh on the Wings of the Wind
the Drops of the Dew
Hath the Rain
a Father & who hath begotten
W Blake invenit & sculp
London Published as the Act directs March 8:1823 by William Blake N:3 Fountain Court Strand
Proof

PLATE 67. William Blake, Plate 13 in *The Book of Job* series ("Then the Lord answered Job out of the Whirlwind"), 1823–25. Engraving (actual size).

WILLIAM BLAKE

PLATE 67

William Blake, English, 1757–1827

Plate 13 in *The Book of Job* series ("Then the Lord answered Job out of the Whirlwind")

1823–25

Engraving

15¾ × 10⅝ inches
400 × 269 mm (sheet)

8⅜ × 6⁷⁄₁₆ inches
213 × 164 mm (plate/image)

86-58 through 86-79 (series)

Bindman 625-46

William Blake, the most innovative printmaker of the late eighteenth century in England, inspired the ideas and formal qualities behind many European avant-garde styles and movements of the nineteenth century. Uniquely gifted as both poet and visual artist, he incorporated various artistic media and literature in his work. Epically imaginative with balanced compositions, his *Book of Job* series is technically impressive and reflects the rich history of literary and visual arts. Not since Albrecht Dürer had an artist committed to and achieved with the original engraved line what Blake does with this series.[1] Blake frequently combined several visual and literary media in one work, composing poetry to be illustrated by his original designs—which might also be executed in more than one medium, such as relief and intaglio methods with direct application of paint onto a print matrix or hand coloring after printing. With the pictorial narrative established from the outset, through both the original biblical text and his earlier interpretation of it in other media, in *The Book of Job* Blake turns to the purity of the engraved line with marvelous visual and symbolic results.

The Book of Job series comprises twenty-two plates (twenty-one illustrative plates and a title page) and is considered one of Blake's—and graphic art's—greatest achievements. The set derives from a series of twenty-one watercolors painted by Blake in 1810 to illustrate the Book of Job for Thomas Butts. Blake's friend and publisher John Linnell asked him to engrave the designs on copperplates in 1823.[2] The engraved set was complete in 1825 and published in 1826. The set in the Thrivent

Financial Collection of Religious Art is from the first published edition, one of sixty-five sets printed on French paper, and bears the word "Proof" in the lower right of each plate, along with the publication inscription, "London. Published as the Act directs March 8: 1825. by Willam Blake No 3 Fountain Court Strand."

One of Blake's hallmark contributions is his integration of text and image. This concept was a precursor to the visually sophisticated prints and illustrated books, including children's books by artists such as Walter Crane (1845–1915), that emerged in the nineteenth century as well as the contemporary revival of medieval arts, especially renewed interest in medieval manuscript illumination. *The Book of Job* exemplifies this melding of word and image on one page. The decorative margins demonstrate the influence of medieval manuscript illumination, especially in Plate 20 (Figure 56, "There were not found Women fair as the Daughters of Job") with delicately undulating foliage and vines, small angels, and musical instruments. The text in the series is mainly derived from the Book of Job but also includes Scripture from other books, including Genesis. The margins of Plate 14 (Figure 57, "When the morning Stars sang together, & all the Sons of God shouted for joy") feature ovals visually and textually outlining the stages of creation from Genesis while the central illustration shows a flank of idealized angelic figures singing in the heavens above God, who is surrounded by allegorical creatures that hover above Job. Such plentiful detail and layered symbolism is typical of the series and of Blake's work.

Notes

1. Laurence Binyon, *The Engraved Designs of William Blake* (New York: Da Capo Press, 1967), 7–8.
2. Ibid., 65.

Left: FIGURE 56. William
Blake, Plate 20 in *The
Book of Job* series ("There
were not found Women
fair as the Daughters
of Job"), 1823–25.
Engraving.

Right: FIGURE 57. William
Blake, Plate 14 in *The
Book of Job* series ("When
the morning Stars sang
together, & all the Sons
of God shouted for joy"),
1823–25. Engraving.

The marginalia, with different text and
subjects, are harmoniously incorporated into
the overall composition, often reflecting the
individual design aesthetic for each plate. In
Plate 13 (Plate 67, "Then the Lord answered
Job out of the Whirlwind") Blake's signature
organic, flowing lines surround God and Job;
these lines are perfectly continued in the
margin drawings of clouds, wind, and tree
roots that enclose the scene.

Abundant, complex symbolism and
spiritualism abound in Blake's artistic and
literary oeuvre. Through his highly symbolic,
often philosophical work he led many

nineteenth-century artists to aspire toward
spiritual and societal reawakenings and reform.
He was a strong proponent of the literary and
artistic movement known as Romanticism,
which can be understood in part as a reaction
against heightened rationalism during the
eighteenth-century Enlightenment. Blake's
intense interest in the strength and character
of the human spirit and the individual's place
within religion and history coexisted with a
constant examination of the dualities of life
and humanity, i.e., good and evil, darkness
and light, all made visually and theoreti-
cally clear in works that expressed his own

personal mythology. Plate 11 (Figure 58, "With Dreams upon my bed thou scarest me & affrightest me with Visions") with its highly angular, graphic forms amid the flowing lines typical of the series effectively illustrates the tension and drama of Job's and Blake's internal struggles. Blake dealt with the character and scriptural book of Job numerous times, and many scholars agree
that Job represented for him a culmination of his philosophical and spiritual inquiries—specifically, the triumph of spirit over reason seen through Job's eventual acceptance of faith during great adversity.

Blake's influence on artists of the nineteenth and twentieth centuries is immense. His dedicated attention to the individual and manual creation of much of his work anticipates the deep commitment of the emerging Aesthetic and Arts and Crafts movements to the integrity of handmade objects, and his aesthetics inform myriad aspects of modern and progressive design, from the detailed, richly patterned medievalist style of the Pre-Raphaelites (see Figure 56) to the undulating whiplash of Art Nouveau (see Plate 67).

■ JRL

Left: FIGURE 58. William Blake, Plate 11 in *The Book of Job* series ("With Dreams upon my bed thou scarest me & affrightest me with Visions"), 1823–25. Engraving.

Right: FIGURE 59. William Blake, Plate 1 in *The Book of Job* series ("Thus did Job continually"), 1823–25. Engraving.

PLATE 68

**Eugène Delacroix,
French, 1798–1863**

*Étude pour le
Groupe des Anges
(Study for a Group
of Angels)*

c. 1824–27

Graphite and sepia wash

6 ¹³⁄₁₆ × 6 ⁹⁄₁₆ inches
173 × 167 mm

91-14

Watermark: partial,
Napoleonic, man's head
in profile with circular
inscription "Le Grand
Empereur"

Provenance

A. Vacquerie before 1895;
passed to Mme E. Lefevre
upon his death in 1895;
passed to her son
P. Lefevre-Vacquerie
upon her death in 1899;
passed to his daughter
Mme A. Gaveau upon his
death in 1933; passed to
her son M. P. Gaveau.

Exhibition

*Centennaire du Romantisme
E. Delacroix,* Musée du
Louvre, Paris, 1930 (no.
264).

Notes

1. M. Pierre Georgel,
   "Bulletin: Item 21,"
   *Société de l'Histoire d'Art
   Français* (1968): 188.
2. Ibid.

This drawing is a study of two angels for Eugène Delacroix's painting *Le Christ au jardin des Oliviers (Christ in the Olive Garden),* created and shown at the Salon in 1827 and now at the Church of St. Paul and St. Louis in Paris.[1] The finished painting includes three ethereal angels hovering in a cloud above and to the right of Christ; this study focuses on the middle and right angels in the final group. The weeping angel on the right with wings outstretched, legs tucked under, and head in hands is relatively unchanged in the final composition. The left angel, whose face in this study shows such compelling emotion, is ultimately altered by Delacroix in the painting; the angel there, while still depicted with windswept hair and gazing at Christ, lacks the emotional intensity felt in the study and instead seems quietly sad and somber rather than acutely distraught or in pain.[2] The angels in the drawing convey startlingly moving emotion and overwhelming sadness in their weeping and expression.

The final painting and its study reveal a poignant interpretation of Christ at Gethsemane, or the Garden of Olives (Matthew 26:36–54 and Luke 22:39–52). In the painting a large crowd with swords and clubs, led by Judas and coming to arrest Christ, can be seen in the far left distance; Christ, head bowed, eyes closed in resignation, sits on a rock in the central foreground and raises his hand to the group of angels, as though holding them back, while his disciples sleep next to him. The tradition in religious art of an angel present at this scene stems from the Agony in the Garden motif, derived from Luke 22:43, in which an angel from heaven comes to comfort Christ and offer him strength as he prays in anguish. A group of angels, however, is unusual. Could Delacroix be referring to a passage in Matthew in which

Christ instructs one of his followers to put down his sword after the man attempts to fight off the arresting crowd: "Do you think that I cannot appeal to my Father, and he will at once send me more than twelve legions of angels? But how then would the Scriptures be fulfilled, which say it must happen this way?" (Matthew 26:53–54)? Does Delacroix imagine the angels attempting to aid Christ, but he bravely stops them with his halting hand in order to fulfill Scripture?

Delacroix was one of the most influential artists of nineteenth-century France. He embodied Romanticism, a European artistic movement and style that emerged in the late eighteenth century as a literary movement and eventually spread to the visual arts. Dominant in the early nineteenth century, it gradually became eclipsed by Realism by midcentury. Strong proponents of Romanticism opposed the classical or academic tradition, placing artists such as Delacroix against ones like Jean-Auguste-Dominique Ingres (see Plate 69). Stylistically, Romanticism was articulated in various ways. Many artists were keen to study and implement new scientific ideas on color theory and its effects on optic nerves. This largely theoretical movement was visually expressed by Delacroix and other artists in an expansive painterly manner with grand historical subjects. The Romantics often treated history subjects sensually, with elements of exoticism and Orientalism, differing from history paintings by the Neoclassicists. Romanticists, sharing a desire to elicit spiritual reawakenings and sensory human experiences, hoped to evoke emotional responses to their work. As evidenced by this drawing, Delacroix's highly personal art consistently conveys not only expressive emotion but also great visual drama.

◼ JRL

PLATE 68. Eugène
Delacroix, *Étude pour le
Groupe des Anges (Study
for a Group of Angels)*,
c. 1824–27. Graphite and
sepia wash (actual size).

PLATE 69.
Jean-Auguste-Dominique
Ingres, *The Virgin at Prayer,*
c. 1840. Pencil.

PLATE 69

Jean-Auguste-
Dominique Ingres,
French, 1780–1867

The Virgin at Prayer

c. 1840

Pencil

9⁹⁄₁₆ × 7¾ inches
242 × 192 mm

86-24

Signed in pencil, lower
right

This study of Marian devotion is rendered in a close manner, focusing on the Virgin's face, covered head, and clasped hands. The delicate, heavenward gaze of Mary is perfectly balanced by her strong gesture of prayer, both combining to create a somber, powerful reflection. Though softly executed, this drawing expresses a simplicity and ideal of academic formal qualities. Ingres's use of line is confident and deliberate down to each fold in Mary's clothing, typical of his style and the high degree of finish in his work. His process for the execution of Mary's left arm can be seen directly to the right of it in an alternate rendering of the fabric folds. Ingres was a major force on the creation of religious art in nineteenth-century France and produced large quantities of religious drawings (in particular, many images of the Virgin Mary) influenced by his careful research of earlier masters such as Raphael.[1] Ingres was living in Rome during the period when this drawing was likely created.

After the death of Jacques-Louis David in 1825, with whom Ingres had studied early on, Ingres emerged as the leading (and last significant) proponent of French classical painting. Working in the Neoclassicist tradition, he painted grand historical and allegorical subjects, nudes, stylized decorative works, and important portrait commissions. He was prolific and perfectionistic, often reworking compositions multiple times. His paintings display a high degree of finish, balanced composition, and rich color and texture, yet line and form preceded all other technical components. Conservative in his art and life, Ingres lived and is remembered as a major Neoclassicist opposed to the divergent style of Romanticism in French art of the nineteenth century.

In a letter dated November 2, 1986, Dr. Hans Naef, author of the catalogue raisonné on Ingres's drawings, provided provenance and exhibition information on *The Virgin at Prayer.* Dr. Naef notes that the signature and inscription above Mary's left shoulder, "demi-teinte," are consistent with Ingres's handwriting.[2] In the lower right corner of the drawing is the collector stamp of previous owner Étienne-François Haro (1827–1897). Haro was a distinguished nineteenth-century collector and dealer, whose important private collection included many fine examples by prominent contemporary artists, such as Ingres and Delacroix, whom he also counted as friends (see Lugt 1241).

■ JRL

Provenance

Anonymous sale, Hotel Drouot, Paris, May 6–7, 1867, no. 36; Étienne-François Haro (1827–1897; Lugt 1241); Walter Paul Sutter, Basel and Chicago; by descent to his son-in-law, Gerald K. Bergman, 1985; sale, Christie's, New York, February 2, 1986, sale no. 6068, lot no. 173.

Exhibitions

J. A. D. Ingres, Palais de l'École Imperiale des Beaux-Arts, Paris, 1867 (cat. no. 110).

Notes

1. Robert J. F. Kashey and Martin L. H. Reymert, *Christian Imagery in French Nineteenth-Century Art, 1789–1906* (New York: Shepherd Gallery, 1980), 116.
2. Dr. Hans Naef to Jill Newhouse, New York, November 2, 1986, collection files of the Thrivent Financial Collection of Religious Art, Minneapolis, Minnesota. Also mentioned in the letter is a solo exhibition of Ingres's drawings in Paris in 1861, with a catalogue published by Émile Galichon, "Des Dessins de M. Ingres," *Gazette des Beaux-Arts,* Paris (May 15, 1861): 344–61. A drawing by Ingres is described there as a sketch of the Virgin with joined hands, with the body covered by a robe and the head covered by a veil; the height given in millimeters in the catalogue corresponds with the drawing in the Thrivent Financial collection.

PLATE 70

**Léon-Joseph-Florentin Bonnat,
French, 1833–1922**

La Douleur (Grief)

c. 1860

Pen and brown ink
over pencil

6⁹⁄₁₆ × 9¹⁵⁄₁₆ inches
167 × 251 mm

92-39

Bénézit 159

Signed, lower right

This intensely expressive study of the depth of human grief allows a glimpse into the moment that Adam finds the lifeless form of his son, Abel, killed by his own brother, Cain. Poignantly expressed by L.-J.-F. Bonnat in this drawing, Adam's anguish is palpable. Father holds son tightly to his own body, head bowed, lips touching his son's head, with one hand firmly clasped against his other arm in a close embrace, as though he would never let his child go: their bodies are so joined they seem as one. Bonnat shows the still face of Abel clearly, but Adam's entire head is darkened, contributing a visual force and shadow to the depiction of his living grief. The chiaroscuro effect of Adam's face and other areas of shadow may reflect the influence on Bonnat from a young age of painters whose work he viewed in Madrid, including José de Ribera (Plate 38) and Diego Velázquez. Bonnat's line and form here is bold and confident, clearly delineated and starkly realistic, typical of French Realist artists such as Édouard Manet (Plate 73) and Gustave Courbet, and revealing the growing influence of photography on nineteenth-century arts.

In 1860 Bonnat completed a painting of a similar subject, in which both Adam and Eve grieve at their discovery of their son's body. Submitted to the 1861 Salon, this painting is now in the collection of the Palais des Beaux-Arts de Lille. The drawing in the Thrivent Financial collection may have been an alternate design for the painting, which features the limp, motionless body of Abel lying on the lap of his mother, with Adam in an agonized stance above them.

Bonnat's oeuvre within the French Realist tradition has a wide, consistently expressive range. His early work was primarily historical and biblical subjects; later he found great success painting portraits of American and European society. Because of his studio and classes at the École des Beaux-Arts in Paris, he is also remembered as an important teacher of emerging artists in the mid- to late nineteenth century.

■ JRL

PLATE 70. Léon-Joseph-Florentin Bonnat, *La Douleur (Grief)*, c. 1860. Pen and brown ink over pencil.

This pencil drawing bears this inscription on the bottom recto: "This drawing was made by John S. Sargent about 1876 describing to me a monument for a Pietà—Carroll Beckwith." The monument depicted strongly resembles Michelangelo's famous Vatican Pietà. Carroll Beckwith, the original owner of this drawing, was an American expatriate artist in Paris who enjoyed a long and close friendship with Sargent; they even shared studio space in Paris. They met while both men studied in the progressive atelier of French artist Carolus-Duran. In the mid-nineteenth century, Beckwith was a recognized landscape and genre artist and portraitist. Although John Singer Sargent was initially drawn to landscapes, he is best known for the marvelous, remarkably expressive portraits that promoted his career and sealed his reputation as one of the greatest portrait painters in the history of art. His works express instinctive qualities of Realism and visual sensuality. Sargent lived and traveled throughout the world, and wealthy clients often traveled to him for a portrait.

The Pietà devotional motif is a variation on the Lamentation of Christ theme that originated in German convents as early as the fourteenth century. Mary privately mourns Christ as her own son in this moment of grief. A strong tradition for Pietà sculptures exists in the history of art, but Pietà scenes are found in all artistic media.

Sargent's rendering of the traditional Pietà motif in an empty space emphasizes the singular intimacy for mother and son, Savior and Virgin Mother, with a marked reduction of line and background. The solitary nature of this moment is made clearer by such austere surroundings and simple fluid lines of the drawing. The artist created this drawing merely as an illustrative sketch for a friend, yet viewing it among other examples of Pietà scenes highlights its appropriate, powerful simplicity (see Hendrik Goltzius's *Pietà*, Plate 48). The way that Mary holds the dead Christ is not described in the Gospels, but this posture has developed over time in religious art. The Pietà was born from devotional ideas and practices; as with much religious subject matter, this specific visual motif reflects more the tradition in religious art than of Scripture.

■ JRL

PLATE 71

John Singer Sargent, American, 1850–1925

Pietà

c. 1876
Pencil
9⅝ × 11¾ inches
245 × 300 mm
85-20

Provenance

James Carroll Beckwith (1852–1917); Paul J. Sachs (1878–1965); Bernhard Gutmann (1869–1936).

PLATE 71. John Singer Sargent, *Pietà*, c. 1876. Pencil.

PLATE 72

Rodolphe Bresdin,
French, 1822–1885

Le Bon Samaritain
(The Good
Samaritan)

1861

Lithograph

24¾ × 18⅞ inches
629 × 479 mm (sheet)

22⅛ × 17⅜ inches
562 × 444 mm (image)

84-41

Van Gelder 100

Out of the remarkably dense wilderness, tiny creatures and compact foliage emerge. Each of the careful details contributes to a visually cohesive whole that almost seems woven within a luxurious and rich tapestry of nature. Even the fluffy clouds become a natural element of the composition, which is made up of pattern upon pattern. Thistles and water birds, monkeys and gnarled tree stumps meld with ferns and palm fronds, an iguana and abundant grasses: this lithograph is a veritable kaleidoscope of minutiae, allowing the viewer to seek and find new particulars at each encounter with the work. Such profuse detail, better suited and more easily achieved with engraving or etching, is astonishing and unusual for the medium of lithography, and the influence of Albrecht Dürer, Hieronymus Bosch, and Rembrandt is notable in Rodolphe Bresdin's art.[1] Far in the distance, between the break in the trees, the city of Jerusalem is visible above the camel. The central figures are also organic to the scene though Bresdin sets them apart from the meticulous surroundings in a lightened clearing. Their presence, along with the city behind them, elicits the suggestion of humanity amid the wilds of nature, an appropriate sentiment for this subject matter.

The story of the Good Samaritan emphasizes the morality and righteousness of kindness to strangers and outcasts. A Samaritan, a foreigner not expected at that time to show compassion to Jews, is the only person who stops to aid a robbed and wounded Jewish man who had been traveling from Jerusalem to Jericho (Luke 10:30–37). The wounded man had been ignored by a priest and a Levite, both representative of the highest religious leadership for Jews, and then was empathetically cared for by the Samaritan. Bresdin's Samaritan cradles the wounded man's head on his knee as he seems to prepare a bandage, gazing over the man with concern.

Rodolphe Bresdin was largely self-taught and lived a rather Bohemian, eccentric lifestyle around France, associated with several artistic and literary circles. The French symbolist artist Odilon Redon (1840–1916) became Bresdin's pupil and close friend. Although he received commissions and critical praise during his lifetime, Bresdin never enjoyed wide success or recognition until after his death, and he struggled throughout his life with bouts of poverty and illness. The extremely large and critically praised *Le Bon Samaritain* is considered his masterpiece of lithography; it was reprinted multiple times during and after his life, offering him and his family a source of income. The Thrivent Financial impression is from an edition printed in 1867 on cream chine collé affixed to gray paper and bears the publisher's inscription "Imp Lemercier Paris." Renewed interest in nineteenth-century printmaking since the second half of the twentieth century has brought more attention to Bresdin's prints, and impressions of his spectacularly complex *Le Bon Samaritain* remain desirable for collectors.

■ JRL

Note

1. Linda C. Hults, *The Print in the Western World: An Introductory History* (Madison: University of Wisconsin Press, 1996), 499.

PLATE 72. Rodolphe
Bresdin, *Le Bon Samaritain*
(The Good Samaritan),
1861. Lithograph.

PLATE 73. Édouard Manet,
Le Christ aux Anges
(Dead Christ with Angels),
1866–67. Etching and
aquatint.

PLATE 73

Édouard Manet,
French, 1832–1883

*Le Christ aux
Anges (Dead Christ
with Angels)*

1866–67

Etching and aquatint

17¾ × 14⅜ inches
450 × 367 mm (sheet)

15⅜ × 12⅞ inches
392 × 327 mm (plate)

12⅞ × 11 inches
328 × 280 mm (image)

95-12

Guérin 34

Grieving the dead Christ in religious art is expressed in part through Lamentation scenes, which take several visual forms. In the motif known as Christ Supported by Angels, Christ's body often rests against angels or is carried and held up by them. In *Dead Christ with Angels,* with its effective use of flattened planes, Édouard Manet forces the viewer to face the certainty of the dead Christ. One angel tenderly looks on, head pressed against Christ's, while holding up his body and cradling his head, and the other angel weeps into her hand, overcome by grief.

Manet was a truly pivotal modern artist who articulated the transition from Realism to Impressionism in his boldly executed works that explored daily contemporary life, including café culture as well as social concerns and events (see "The Religious Print" essay). *Dead Christ with Angels* is his largest print, created after his painting of this subject, which was controversially shown at the Salon in 1864 and is now in the collection of the Metropolitan Museum of Art in New York City. The inscription on the painting indicates the artist's scriptural source for both images was John 20:12. Critics of the painting offered scathing remarks about Manet's Christ resembling an unwashed human cadaver.[1] Indeed, Manet's Christ appears starkly realistic and confronts the viewer with a stirring, emotionally charged encounter with a frequently depicted religious subject. Despite being a practicing Catholic and working in a time and place that supported the creation of religious art, Manet's religious works were few; the religious imagery he produced in 1864 and 1865 would become isolated within his oeuvre.[2]

Dead Christ with Angels is one of the most compelling and significant religious prints of the nineteenth century. This print is very rare, with fewer than ten known impressions of the final third state; one of these is the Thrivent Financial impression. The first state exists in only two known impressions, and the second state is known only by description.[3] In executing this etching, Manet created a watercolor in reverse, probably from tracing a photograph, in order to achieve the proper orientation that would be faithful to the painting; he then transferred the watercolor outlines to the etching plate.[4] He used aquatint to great effect, mimicking a look of watercolor wash. The final state is more refined and visually articulated than the much lighter first state. Using selective wiping and areas of tone, more fully modeled forms for the drapery and for Christ's body with strong contrasts of light and dark, Manet created in the third state an etching that closely represented the painting.[5] Because this print was never published or editioned (perhaps because of its large size), each of the impressions can be considered trial proofs.

◾ JRL

Provenance

Baron Henri Petiet, Paris, (b. 1894; Lugt 2021a).

Notes

1. Jay McKean Fisher, *The Prints of Édouard Manet* (Washington, D.C.: International Exhibitions Foundations, 1985), 73.
2. Robert J. F. Kashey and Martin L. H. Reymert, *Christian Imagery in French Nineteenth-Century Art, 1789–1906* (New York: Shepherd Gallery, 1980), 336.
3. Fisher, 74.
4. Ibid., 73–74.
5. Ibid., 74.

PLATE 74. Sir Edward
Coley Burne-Jones,
St. Matthew, 1873. Black
and colored chalks, pencil.

PLATE 74

Sir Edward Coley
Burne-Jones, English,
1833–1898

St. Matthew

1873
Black and colored chalks,
pencil
47 × 23¼ inches
1191 × 590 mm
93-28

St. Matthew is a cartoon, a preparatory drawing for a stained glass window in the south transept of Jesus College Chapel at Cambridge University in England. Sir Edward Coley Burne-Jones received this commission in 1873 for a set of windows depicting the four Evangelists. Burne-Jones designed copious amounts of stained and art glass windows, many of which were produced by Morris & Company, the decorative arts firm founded in 1861 by the towering leader of the Arts and Crafts movement, William Morris. Many designers and artists, including Burne-Jones, were employed by Morris & Co.,[1] and their collaboration on stained glass windows is monumentally important to the revival of the medium. Jesus College Chapel is the oldest college chapel in Cambridge, with its original structure dating from the twelfth century, and Morris & Co. undertook several decorative commissions for the chapel from 1867 until 1877, including the *Four Evangelists* windows.[2] The chapel's history makes the medium and design of the resulting window from this cartoon very appropriate, especially considering the medievalist style and working methods favored by Burne-Jones and his contemporaries.

The angular, elongated forms and lines in this design, as well as the classical and medieval influences and the distinctive languid face of St. Matthew, are characteristic of the Pre-Raphaelite style, made famous by one of the founders of the movement, Dante Gabriel Rossetti. Inscriptions made by Burne-Jones on the cartoon include notes in pencil on color choices for the final execution: "full ruby" is written to the left of the midsection of Matthew and "grey blue" on the Evangelist's right knee. These colors indeed appear in the finished window at Jesus College, and the overall design for the window remained quite faithful to this cartoon. Contemporary artist and art historian Aymer Vallance wrote that

the final window scheme in the south transept designed by Burne-Jones was the finest in the chapel: "no reproduction can convey the glorious effect of colour."[3] As indicated by additional notes on the cartoon, this design was reused for other churches, including St. Mary the Virgin, Speldhurst, Dent (1875), and St. Paul's Morton, Lincolnshire (1891), as well as for at least one painting by Burne-Jones.

Many avant-garde styles of the nineteenth and early twentieth centuries, including the Aesthetic, Pre-Raphaelite, and Arts and Crafts movements, encouraged strong revivals of arts associated with the medieval period, including stained glass and decorative arts. In looking to the arts and culture of the past to pursue their progressive artistic and social aims, advocates of these movements truly believed they could elicit real change in society through their art. Medievalism was idealized by many artists who attempted to duplicate the simpler, handmade integrity of the medieval craftsman over the pervasive industrialism and machine-made objects prevalent in the Victorian era. The Pre-Raphaelite Brotherhood, an artistic and literary movement founded in England in 1848, sought to reawaken the past through artistic and spiritual inspiration from the medieval and Renaissance periods. By rejecting what they considered the staid approach adopted after Michelangelo and perpetuated by the Academy, the Brotherhood (of which Sir Edward Coley Burne-Jones was an important member) hoped to reform art in part through a stylistic return to the rich color, detail, and complex compositions of earlier Flemish and Italian art. In addition to his numerous paintings and designs for stained glass, Burne-Jones also made many other decorative arts and medievalist prints, including illustrations for the well-known volume *The Works of Geoffrey Chaucer,* published by William Morris's Kelmscott Press in 1896.

■ JRL

Provenance

Private collection, London.

Notes

1. Wendy Kaplan, ed., *Encyclopedia of Arts and Crafts* (London: Quantum Publishing, 1998), 92.
2. Alex Perkins, "History of Jesus College Chapel," http://chapel.jesus.cam.ac.uk/chapel/history.html, accessed October 21, 2010.
3. Aymer Vallance, *William Morris, His Art, His Writings, and His Public Life: A Record* (London: George Bell and Sons, 1897), 74.

PLATE 75

Félix Bracquemond,
French, 1833–1914

David

1884

Etching

31¼ × 21⅝ inches
795 × 550 mm (sheet)

27⅞ × 17⅝ inches
710 × 449 mm (plate)

23⅝ × 14½ inches
600 × 370 mm (image)

96-15

Béraldi 348

Signed in pencil,
lower right

_____

Note

1. Lisa Dickinson Michaux, *Herschel V. Jones: The Imprint of a Great Collector* (Minneapolis: Minneapolis Institute of Arts, 2006), 160; Colta Feller Ives, *The Great Wave: The Influence of Japanese Woodcuts on French Prints* (New York: Metropolitan Museum of Art, 1974), 12.

King David sits pensively on his majestic throne, surrounded by ornate decoration. An angel at David's feet holds the king's lyre, a harplike instrument that David played to soothe King Saul according to the Hebrew Bible and Old Testament. Multiple patterns make up dense accents of foliage, architectural columns, and richly detailed urns and fixtures. Bracquemond made this extremely large etching after a painting by the French symbolist Gustave Moreau, whose name is inscribed in the lower right corner of the plate. The impression in the Thrivent Financial collection is from the edition of 250 on simili-Japan paper, before the added letters, and includes the publisher's address and blindstamp in the lower left corner, within the platemark. It was published in Paris by Georges Petit.

Bracquemond was a central figure of the etching revival in nineteenth-century France. His images of wildlife, nature, and portraiture show outstanding technical skill, great linear range, and meticulous attention to and passion for the printed line. One of his most important contributions to the print aesthetic of the nineteenth century was his discovery of and subsequent passion for the Katsushika Hokusai *Manga* (sketches) Japanese woodblock prints; these had been used as packing material for a porcelain shipment to the studio shop of his printer Auguste Delâtre in 1856.[1] Japanese prints, and other aspects of Japanese arts and culture, would have an enormous influence on many stylistic and aesthetic components of nineteenth-century European graphic arts. *David* does not exemplify Japonisme specifically, but instead highlights Bracquemond's technical virtuosity.

■ JRL

PLATE 75. Félix Bracquemond, *David*, 1884. Etching.

PLATE 76. James J. Tissot,
*The Prodigal Son in Modern
Life: The Departure,* 1881.
Etching.

PLATE 76

**James J. Tissot,
French, 1836–1902**

*The Prodigal Son
in Modern Life:
The Departure*

1881
Etching
17¼ × 24⅜ inches
435 × 622 mm (sheet)
12⅛ × 14⅝ inches
308 × 371 mm
(plate/image)
84-32
Wentworth 58

The parable of the prodigal son is found in the Gospel of Luke, where Christ tells of a man with two sons, the younger of whom wished to leave his family to travel. James J. Tissot's *The Departure* in his series *The Prodigal Son in Modern Life* depicts the moment the son says farewell to his family: "Father, give me the share of the property that will belong to me" (Luke 15:12). Listening to advice from his father, the son sits atop a luminous wood table that reflects the light that streams in from richly textured shaded windows; the more dependable son sits next to one of these windows and dreams of what his brother will imminently experience. Under the table one kitten strays from its mother, and one flower bud has dropped from the vase on the table—visual allegories inserted by Tissot. The subtle religious allusion of crosses made by the window frame bars showing through the shades is noted as well.[1] A sense of sharp realism in many details and textures demonstrates the growing influence of photography on nineteenth-century art.

After collecting his fortune, the son travels to distant lands, where he squanders his money and lives dissolutely (*In Foreign Climes,* Figure 60). Tissot's treatment of this part of the story is contemporarily apt: placing the son in a Japanese teahouse obviously departs from the biblical text but marks the prevalence of Japonisme, a central stylistic and thematic influence in nineteenth-century European arts and culture. Surrounded by swirling Japanese fan dancers (who certainly would have looked "exotic" to nineteenth-century Europeans), sitting among inebriated or drugged companions, and lit by dimly glowing rice paper lanterns, the prodigal son is in a scene redolent of loose living. Japanese teahouses then frequently functioned as brothels by night.[2] Many of Tissot's works display the sumptuous aesthetic interiors of affluent and fashionable homes of the time, most of which included expressions of Japonisme and the marvelous layering of pattern on pattern seen in this etching's checkered floor, soft robes, and interplay of vertical and horizontal lines. Japanese woodblock prints and objets d'art were extremely popular among the artistic and societal elite of nineteenth-century Europe. Tissot himself had an extensive collection of Japanese objects.[3] The reflection of Tissot's (and much of Europe's) fascination with Japanese arts and culture is one element that makes this series "modern."

FIGURE 60. James J. Tissot, *The Prodigal Son in Modern Life: In Foreign Climes,* 1881. Etching.

FIGURE 61. James J. Tissot, *The Prodigal Son in Modern Life: Frontispiece,* 1881. Etching.

Notes

1. Nancy Rose Marshall and Malcolm Warner, *James Tissot: Victorian Life/Modern Love* (New Haven: Yale University Press, 1999), 166.
2. Ibid.
3. Ibid., 9.
4. Ibid., 11.
5. Ibid., 9.
6. Ibid.

Born Jacques-Joseph Tissot but later called James for his ardent Anglophilia, this artist took the religious print in a fresh direction with *The Prodigal Son in Modern Life.* The series includes four illustrative plates and a frontispiece and is created after a series of paintings by Tissot of the same subjects. Tissot is best known for sumptuous, skillful etchings that depict London society in all its luxury and loveliness. Yet moralizing commentary abounds in his work: the materialism central to affluent urban life, as well as sophisticated observations on the sexual mores of Victorian England, are prevalent in Tissot's oeuvre. The artist moved from France to London in 1871. In Britain he and his contemporaries found artistic freedom, feeling less constrained by the traditional conventions of the French academy; generous patronage from wealthy industrialists and personal friendships (such as with James Abbott McNeill Whistler) also awaited Tissot in London.[4]

Tissot's stunning etchings are fine examples of the period's revival of this medium and exhibit his command of this artform with their gorgeous conveyance of texture and light. In this set Tissot balances striking visual components such as gleaming wood and filtered shadow and light with elegantly dressed figures in contemporary fashionable clothing. Tissot did not endeavor to present historically accurate renderings of the biblical text but instead placed the story in a modern setting, personalizing centuries-old religious subject matter to make it accessible to nineteenth-century viewers and applying his own penchant and talent for depicting contemporary society. He was truly an artist of modern life. Many European and American artists were influenced by the writings of French literary giant Charles Baudelaire, particularly his essay from 1863 on the aesthetics of modernity, "Le Peintre de la vie moderne," in which artists are called to treat the routine details of daily life as equal to the narrative subjects of art's history.[5] The stylish and lavish clothing of society, so marvelously depicted by Tissot, was central to the illustration of modern life in art of this time.[6]

This series may have held personal significance for the artist. Tissot's lover and most frequent model, an Irish divorcée named Kathleen Newton, was slowly dying of tuberculosis while Tissot created this series. Her death in 1882 devastated him, and he moved back to France shortly thereafter. A period of professional and personal difficulty, then religious conversion, followed. *The Prodigal Son in Modern Life* marks the beginning of a dedication to religious subject matter in Tissot's oeuvre, which, along with his personal life, became devoted to spiritualism.

The impressions of this series in the Thrivent Financial Collection of Religious Art are trial proofs, impressions that are pulled by an artist or printer before the final state and often used to visually compare changes to the print matrix. This set precedes the addition of the scriptural text (biblical passages added to accompany the images) and instead shows little notations and sketches, mathematical calculations, and needle scratches, signed and dated in the plate.

■ JRL

Above: FIGURE 62. James J. Tissot, *The Prodigal Son in Modern Life: The Return,* 1881. Etching.

Below: FIGURE 63. James J. Tissot, *The Prodigal Son in Modern Life: The Fatted Calf,* 1881. Etching.

PLATE 77

**James J. Tissot,
French, 1836–1902**

*The Prodigal
Son: Study for
the Return of the
Prodigal Son*

1863
Reddish brown chalk
with whitening on
blue paper
10½ × 9⁹⁄₁₆ inches
267 × 253 mm

93-27

The prodigal son, tender faced, kneels before his father, pleading to be welcomed back into his family: the familiar biblical story illustrates God's acceptance and forgiveness of those who return after straying. This drawing is a study for the painting *Return of the Prodigal Son* by James J. Tissot that was exhibited at the Salon in 1863. Now lost, the painting and its studies were executed in Tissot's early style, which was heavily influenced by the Flemish Germanic medievalist aesthetic of Baron Hendrick Leys (1815–1869).[1] Almost twenty years later, Tissot's series of paintings and prints titled *The Prodigal Son in Modern Life* (Plate 76) presented a much different rendering of this subject. The son's simple clothing in this drawing, in great contrast to the luxurious finery worn in Tissot's later series, invokes the historical, medievalist style of the original painting.

Despite the secular emphasis of many aspects of life and culture in nineteenth-century Europe, an abundance of artists were turning to religious subjects, due in large part to spiritual and religious revivals that personalized the religious experience for many. Tissot did not focus on religious art in earnest until after his lover, Kathleen Newton, died from tuberculosis in 1882; he then returned to Paris from London, and had a profound religious reawakening around 1886. From this point on, his art became dominated by religious subject matter. Although this change in his work and life ultimately alienated many of his close artist friends, such as Edgar Degas, it did afford Tissot a renewal of his career and financial success toward the end of his life.[2]

■ JRL

Provenance

H. Shickman Gallery,
New York; David Daniels,
New York.

Exhibitions

*Drawings from the David
Daniels Collection,* 1968,
Minneapolis, Chicago,
Kansas City, Cambridge
(cat. no. 58, illustrated
catalogue edited by Mary
Lee Bennet and Agnes
Mongan); *James Jacques
Joseph Tissot, 1836–1902:
A Retrospective Exhibition,*
1968, Providence and
Toronto (cat. no. 40,
plate 40, illustrated);
*Christian Imagery in French
Nineteenth-Century Art,
1789–1906,* Spring
1980, Shepherd Gallery,
New York (cat. no. 138,
illustrated); Fogg Museum,
Harvard University,
Cambridge, Massachusetts,
1985 and 1994.

Notes

1. Robert J. F. Kashey and
Martin L. H. Reymert,
*Christian Imagery in
French Nineteenth-
Century Art, 1789–1906*
(New York: Shepherd
Gallery, 1980), 350.
2. Ibid., 354.

PLATE 77. James J. Tissot, *The Prodigal Son: Study for the Return of the Prodigal Son,* 1863. Reddish brown chalk with whitening on blue paper.

PLATE 78. Pierre Roche (Pierre-Henry-Ferdinand Massignon), *Le Christ marchant sur la mer (Christ Walking on the Sea)*, c. 1900. Pencil and watercolor.

PLATE 78

Pierre Roche (Pierre-Henry-Ferdinand Massignon), French, 1855–1922

Le Christ marchant sur la mer (Christ Walking on the Sea)

c. 1900
Pencil and watercolor
9⁹⁄₁₆ × 12¹¹⁄₁₆ inches
243 × 322 mm (sheet)
6½ × 10⅜ inches
262 × 138 mm
(image with signature)
91-25

Dedicated and signed
in crayon

A rising sun breaks through a night storm's billowing clouds and warms them with vibrant colors of yellow, violet, and pink. Cool and solid, the tall figure of Christ hovers over rippling waves of white and aquamarine. His long robe pulled close, he presses ahead into the breeze.

The story of Christ walking on water is told in every Gospel except Luke. In all three variations (Matthew 14:22–33, Mark 6:45–52, and John 6:16–21), Christ's Apostles begin to cross the Sea of Galilee in a boat ahead of their teacher. After a stormy night, the disciples see Christ walking on the water's surface.[1] Rather than traditionally representing Christ's encounter with the Apostles in this scene, Pierre Roche has imagined a moment earlier in Christ's miraculous journey. The only indication of a boat is a tiny sketch on the horizon to the right. Roche has approached the subject symbolically, emphasizing the solitary figure of Christ, the sun, the sky, and the water to create a dreamlike vision of the miracle. Symbolism was a late nineteenth-century literary and artistic movement centered in Paris that focused on feeling through poetic suggestion. Symbolists employed a variety of approaches to evoke emotional response, including colors, shapes, and lines. Warm or cool colors, or lines moving up or down, could play a fundamental role in a picture's spiritual effect.

Roche's pensive figure of Christ appears to be modeled after one of the men in Auguste Rodin's sculpture *The Monument to the Burghers of Calais*, conceived and created between 1884 and 1889. As a developing painter and sculptor in Paris at that time, Roche would certainly have been familiar with Rodin's major commission, and this choice of model would form an appropriate symbol for Christ. The six legendary burghers of Calais chose to sacrifice themselves to save the people of their city in 1347. In *Le Christ marchant sur la mer,* Christ seems to meditate on his solemn mission while the warm colors of the sun on turbulent clouds offer a sense of hope.

The original purpose and subsequent provenance of *Le Christ marchant sur la mer* is uncertain. It is dedicated and signed "à grand homme, affectueusement, Pierre Roche" ("to a great man, affectionately, Pierre Roche"), but it is not clear to whom the artist was referring. Roche's exploration of shapes in pencil before adding watercolor suggests this is a preliminary study. Notations in the margins describe effects and coloration for the clouds, water, and figure, further indicating that the drawing may have been a study for another work of art. In Roche's oeuvre the symbol of a lone, cloaked traveler is not unique to this drawing but also appears in a gypsograph print from 1909, *The Palace of Dreams,* which depicts a similar figure in reverse, walking on a path of clouds that zigzags toward a castle floating in the center of a sun.[2] Regardless of the intent behind *Le Christ marchant sur la mer,* it stands on its own as a lovely and thought-provoking example of Parisian symbolist art.

■ JRW

Notes

1. In the accounts in Matthew and Mark, the disciples see Christ walking on the water early in the morning after a difficult night at sea. No specific time of day is mentioned in the passage in John.
2. Elizabeth Prelinger, "Pierre Roche and the 'belle gypsographie,'" *Print Quarterly* X, vol. 2 (March 1993): 146–48. The gypsograph *Palace of Dreams* has also been called *The Castle of Dreams* or *The Lunar Pilgrim.*

PLATE 79. James
Ensor, *La Cathédrale*
(The Cathedral), 1886.
Etching.

PLATE 79

James Ensor, Belgian, 1860–1949

La Cathédrale (The Cathedral)

1886

Etching

18¹¹⁄₁₆ × 14¹⁄₁₆ inches
475 × 357 mm

87-01

Tavernier 7

James Ensor © 2011 Artists Rights Society (ARS), New York / SABAM, Brussels

FIGURE 64. Detail of *La Cathédrale*.

La Cathédrale was one of the earliest attempts at etching by painter James Ensor, yet among his estimated 142 prints it is commonly singled out as his "quintessential" image.[1] It was already celebrated during the artist's life, appearing in several avant-garde periodicals during the 1890s and serving as the frontispiece for the literary journal *La Jeune Belgique* in 1891.

Ensor created his medieval shrine by piecing together architectural elements from three churches as they were illustrated in *La Magasin Pittoresque*.[2] The nave is based on the cathedral in Aachen, built by Charlemagne (Charles the Great, c. 742–814) and consecrated in the year 805; the right tower is from Antwerp's Cathedral of Our Lady; and the left tower is from the midsection of the tall spire of St. Stephen's Cathedral in Vienna.[3] Closely following the illustrations, Ensor drew the buildings onto the etching plate as they were displayed in the periodical; each was seen from a different perspective, so the towers and nave appear skewed rather than square relative to each other in his final print. Through his architectural patchwork and the image reversal inherent in the plate printing process, he translated three real cathedrals into an abstract imaginary one. *La Cathédrale* is at once familiar and unfamiliar, creating what Ensor's literary contemporary Eugène Demolder described as "the symbol of all Gothic cathedrals."[4] It is no one's church and at the same time it is everyone's, an idea evinced by the unending crush of people around the foundation of its ancient, crumbling stones.

Crowds are a repeated theme in Ensor's work. A symbol of humanity and society, these groups often hoist political signs that suggest a complex message about administrative corruption and bourgeois existence. This is not so in *La Cathédrale*, where the multitude carries tall standards with banners and seems gathered for a festival. In the foreground, a cluster of people with carnival masklike faces and costume hats peer out of the picture toward the viewer. Behind them a regiment of soldiers wears sashes, epaulets, and tall caps called *shakos*. This mass of bodies recedes into the distance, giving a sense of depth equal to the monumental height of the cathedral. With obsessive repetition, Ensor meticulously rendered row after row of figures, each diminishing in size until their forms evaporate into a mist of lines and points. Similarly, behind the main cathedral, spire after spire rises from this haze of humanity. The blur of lines between the crowd and the cathedral links them inextricably into a unified legacy of spirituality and hope passed on for generations. A very close inspection of the horizon line to the left of the cathedral reveals the barest impression of the sun (Figure 64). Simply drawn with dashed lines, its long rays reiterate this concept of timeless regularity in the physical world.

As a founding member of the Belgian avant-garde group Les XX, James Ensor was entrenched in the diverse and rapidly changing world of modern art in Europe at the end of the nineteenth century. Although his work is difficult to categorize, his style of abstraction and his political tone were important to the development of twentieth-century art movements, most notably expressionism. His masklike faces inspired Emil Nolde, who visited Ensor in 1911, the same year Nolde made the print *Schriftgelehrte* (*Scribes*, Figure 68). ■ JRW

Notes

1. Jane Block and Stephen H. Goddard, *Les XX and the Belgian Avant-Garde: Prints, Drawings, and Books ca. 1890* (Lawrence: Spencer Museum of Art, University of Kansas, 1992), 187.
2. Eric Gillis and Patrick Florizoone, *James Ensor* (New York: C. G. Boerner, Inc., 2003), 29–30.
3. *La Magasin Pittoresque* 1833 (Paris: Aux Bureaux d'Abonnement et de Vente): 65, 113; *La Magasin Pittoresque* 1834 (Paris: Aux Bureaux d'Abonnement et de Vente): 153.
4. Block and Goddard, 187.

THE TWENTIETH CENTURY

Sybil Andrews, *Station III: Jesus Falls for the First Time* (details; see Figure 73).

PLATE 80. Karl Schmidt-Rottluff, *Peter Fishing,* 1918. Woodcut.

During the first decades of the twentieth century, artists responded to the accelerated pace of modern life and challenged past ideals of style and representation. Small groups of charismatic artists rapidly defined new sets of principles regarding shape, color, media, subject matter, and the function of art in modern society. *Expressionism* is a term that characterizes the art of several groups during the early twentieth century.

Karl Schmidt-Rottluff was a leading member of the German expressionist group Die Brücke, founded in 1905. He suggested this name for the group, which means "the bridge," because he believed their work could join people of the past, present, and future to transcend ordinary human existence.[1] Concerned about the effects of materialism and industrial alienation on society, Die Brücke was attracted to printmaking for its traditional ties to hands-on craftwork and German cultural heritage. These artists revived the powerful Gothic aesthetic of the woodcut, finding inspiration in early devotional prints of fifteenth-century German printmakers.

Schmidt-Rottluff turned to religious themes after serving in World War I. *Peter Fishing* is one of nine woodcuts narrating scenes from the life of Christ. In this particular work, he portrays the moment from Luke 5:1–11 when Christ called Simon Peter to be his disciple. At the Lord's command, Peter and other fishermen with him put out their nets and caught so many fish that their boats began to sink. Peter then fell at Christ's knees, crying, "Go away from me, Lord, for I am a sinful man." Many biblical details are absent in this print, and the narrative is expressed with only its most essential elements. Peter kneels with his arms stretched toward the solid, haloed figure of Christ, who stands like a beacon. Schmidt-Rottluff set the stage most simply in the background by depicting two men with their catch. These naked fishermen and the masklike face of Christ highlight the influence of primitivism and the incorporation of African and Oceanic art and culture that was typical of Die Brücke. The extremely shallow and abstracted perspective in *Peter Fishing,* made apparent by the aerial view of the boat, is a quality that distinguishes Schmidt-Rottluff's woodcuts from those of his colleagues.

■ JRW

PLATE 81

Max Pechstein,
German, 1881–1955

*Give Us This Day
Our Daily Bread,*
from *Das Vater
Unser (The Lord's
Prayer)* series

1921
Hand-colored woodcut
23⅞ × 16¼ inches
596 × 413 mm
86-06
Signed in pencil by artist
and publisher

Max Pechstein © 2011 Artists
Rights Society (ARS), New York /
Pechstein Hamburg / Toekendorf /
VG Bild-Kunst, Bonn

PLATE 81. Max Pechstein,
*Give Us This Day Our
Daily Bread,* from *Das Vater
Unser (The Lord's Prayer)*
series, 1921. Hand-colored
woodcut.

Vibrant orange pops visually against the
dense black angles of arms and elbows jutting
across this crowded table. Max Pechstein's
Give Us This Day Our Daily Bread (Plate 81)
is one of twelve hand-colored woodcuts in
the series *Das Vater Unser (The Lord's Prayer),*
completed in 1921. Filled with images of

FIGURE 65. Max Pechstein, title page to *Das Vater Unser (The Lord's Prayer)* series, 1921. Hand-colored woodcut.

men and women in prayer, the series is a moving demonstration of how artists in the early twentieth century used religious subject matter to pursue spiritual renewal and to reconcile their anxieties and hopes when confronted with a life-threatening breakdown of social order.[1] Like many German expressionists, Pechstein served in the military during World War I and then endured the desolation wreaked by Germany's political upheaval and economic collapse.

Pechstein's twelve woodcuts exemplify the flat black forms and primitivist styles explored by Die Brücke, to which Pechstein belonged for six years until he became estranged from the group in 1912. Yet his masterful application of design principles to incorporate symbolic imagery with text and his judicious choice of color further transform this traditional prayer into a modern devotional experience (see "The Religious Print" essay).

The shallow, altered perspective constructed by tilting the table toward the viewer creates a sense of immediacy and inclusion in the scene. The bold orange, squarely framed by the warm flesh tones of the men's faces, is tempered by the cool blue in their dark clothing. Pechstein left the platter on the table white, bringing attention to its central placement and the importance of the fish—a symbol for Christ—as "our daily bread." The fish motif also references biblical stories and miracles, such as Christ calling Simon Peter (see *Peter Fishing,* by Karl Schmidt-Rottluff, Plate 80) and the multiplication of the fishes to feed the masses. Even the text at the top of the print is meaningfully integrated, as the men seem to gaze on the words of the prayer as much as they turn toward God. Similarly, the integration of text and image is emphasized on the title page of the series (Figure 65), in which the top figure's arms and body echo the pattern of the large V in "Vater."

In *Forgive Us Our Trespasses* (Figure 66), a crowd of worshipers kneels before God; some cry out in awe, perhaps in shame. The repetition of geometric shapes creates an almost frenzied mood, yet the calm face of all-seeing God emerges from billows of clouds. God's omnipotence is conveyed with beams of vision that emanate from God's eyes. Color on the bottom and sides of the print are juxtaposed by Pechstein's use of white paper in the upper left to highlight God's divinity. The striking faces of this print, and also the face of God in *Our Father, Who Art in Heaven* (Figure 5), show a strong influence of African and Oceanic masks and sculpture. In 1914, Pechstein spent time in the South Sea islands of Palau and found inspiration for his work among the indigenous people and their arts.

Berlin publisher Fritz Voigt printed two editions of Pechstein's twelve large woodcuts. Fifty hand-colored sets were produced in addition to two hundred impressions of each block printed with black ink. The Thrivent Financial Collection of Religious Art holds a complete hand-tinted set and an uncolored example of *Forgive Us Our Trespasses* (Figure 67). Pechstein's large format and collage-like marriage of image and text resemble popular advertising posters in the nineteenth and early twentieth centuries. The strong graphic shapes combined with vivid color and the large size of each print are decidedly progressive.

■ JRW

Above: FIGURE 66. Max Pechstein, *Forgive Us Our Trespasses,* in *Das Vater Unser (The Lord's Prayer)* series, 1921. Hand-colored woodcut.

Left: FIGURE 67. Max Pechstein, *Forgive Us Our Trespasses,* in *Das Vater Unser (The Lord's Prayer)* series, 1921. Woodcut.

Note

1. Reinhold Heller, *Brücke: German Expressionist Prints from the Granvil and Marcia Specks Collection* (Evanston: Mary and Leigh Block Gallery, Northwestern University, 1988), 226–27.

PLATE 82

**Emil Nolde, German,
1867–1956**

Prophet

1912

Woodcut

16⅜ × 12¾ inches
415 × 324 mm (sheet)

97-26

Schiefler–Mosel 110,
Ackley 71a

Titled and signed in
pencil, full margins, thin
brown oatmeal paper

Emil Nolde © Nolde Stiftung
Seebüll

This somber face inspires thoughtful meditation on the profound wisdom and mysterious faith of God's prophet. His sunken cheeks, furrowed brow, and penetrating gaze evoke a deeply emotional, messianic portrait. In the words of Hamburg art collector and critic Gustav Schiefler (1857–1935): "Everything: beard, hair, background lines, appear in him to be reflected from an inner fire."[1]

Emil Nolde briefly joined Die Brücke in 1906 at Karl Schmidt-Rottluff's request. He remained with the group only until the end of 1907, but his friendship with these artists continued, and he shared many of their artistic philosophies.

Nolde's *Prophet* exemplifies the fresh artistic vision of Die Brücke as it rejuvenated the medieval invention of printmaking by hand-carving raw woodblocks and pressing images with original techniques. Nolde apprenticed as a carver in a furniture factory and came to the block with an understanding that forms could organically emerge as he cut the wood. The face of his prophet appears to materialize from the natural grain of the timber, present in the ink to the left of the forehead and in the lower right corner. In *Scribes* (Figure 68), Nolde similarly exposed the nature of the copperplate and the artistic processes of etching and aquatint as part of the print's final appearance. The thick aquatint rings across the hand and arm of Christ remain from an earlier, abandoned project, and long scratches across the scholars who challenge him (Mark 2:6–7) hint that this print has a history beyond the surface of the subject.[2]

FIGURE 68. Emil Nolde, *Schriftgelehrte (Scribes)*, 1911. Etching and aquatint.

Impressions of *Prophet* were printed with varying amounts of ink and on different paper types, making each one unique. Nolde spread the ink thickly in some areas but left other areas drier, allowing the grain of the wood to create a sense of bold brushwork. Faint marks on the back of the paper show that the impression in the Thrivent Financial collection is a *Reiberdruck*. Instead of a printing press Nolde used a tool to rub the back of the paper, pressing it against the woodblock just as the earliest European printmakers did in the fifteenth century. In some areas the ink began to seep slightly through the paper, to be picked up by Nolde's tool and streaked across the page. The handcrafted brown paper Nolde selected for this impression naturally buckled during the printing process, forming ripples at the bottom of the page that emphasize the wood grain and relief-like character of the image, further contributing to the influence of materials on the overall aesthetic.

This print recalls early modern devotion, in particular Sebald Beham's sixteenth-century woodcut *Head of Christ, Wounded with Thorns* (Plate 21) with its strong connection to St. Veronica's sudarium. Yet without a crown of thorns on its subject, Nolde's portrait may be seen as either an Old Testament prophet or as an image of Christ, who is called "prophet" in Christian tradition. This visual, archetypal bridge between the Hebrew Bible and the New Testament finds its scriptural parallel in Acts 3:22, which justifies Christ through the words of Moses, who said, "The Lord your God will raise up for you from your own people a prophet like me" (Deuteronomy 18:15). Considered by art historians to be a paragon of expressionism, Emil Nolde's *Prophet* transcends subject matter, style, and medium to become a modern icon in both theme and expressionist printmaking.[3]

■ JRW

Notes

1. Clifford S. Ackley,
   Timothy O. Benson,
   and Victor I. Carlson,
   *Nolde: The Painter's
   Prints* (Boston:
   Museum of Fine Arts,
   Boston, in association
   with the Los Angeles
   County Museum of
   Art, 1995), 223.
2. Ibid., 205–6.
3. Ibid., 223.

PLATE 82. Emil Nolde,
Prophet, 1912. Woodcut.

PLATE 83

Franz Marc, German, 1880–1916

Versöhnung (Reconciliation)

1912
Woodcut
11¹⁵⁄₁₆ × 16⅛ inches
304 × 420 mm (sheet)
01-08
Lankheit 837, II/ii
Full margins, Japan paper

Franz Marc was a founding member of the expressionist movement Der Blaue Reiter (The Blue Rider), along with the Russian artist Vassily Kandinsky (1866–1944). Similar to Die Brücke and other expressionists, Der Blaue Reiter eschewed naturalism in an effort to visualize feeling and evoke an emotional response in viewers. Unique to Der Blaue Reiter was each artist's personal expression of a deep-rooted, spiritual worldview. Marc grew up in a devout Protestant home, and his confirmation training led him, at the age of seventeen, to briefly consider joining the clergy.[1] Instead, art became the means by which he manifested his spiritual life.

As political tensions mounted prior to World War I, Marc came to believe that animals possess a natural purity of spirit that is lacking in humans, and animals appear in much of his artwork. In *Versöhnung* a dog, the traditional symbol of love and fidelity, sits and prayerfully bows its head. On bended knee, a woman clutches her chest and hangs her head. Behind her, a man tentatively reaches out to touch her arm. Around this trio, a complex construction of abstract shapes and lines represents the tension and conflicting emotions that can accompany the confession and forgiveness of a personal reconciliation.

Marc's lyrical woodcut exists in a close relationship between language and art, which was common in modern printed materials. It illustrates a poem titled "Versöhnung" by Else Lasker-Schüler (1869–1945), one of the few women active in the expressionist movement. Marc had read "Versöhnung" in an early issue of the magazine *Der Sturm*. Moved, he tried to capture the spirit of the poem in this picture. In the summer of 1912, Marc was asked to submit woodcuts to *Der Sturm*. He sent this one, which was published in September that year with a second printing of Lasker-Schüler's poem.[2] The moon and stars in the sky and the radiant lines that beam from the figure of the woman allude to the poem's opening words: "A great star will fall into my lap. Let us keep watch through the night…"[3] Although Marc's woodcut does not depict an exclusively religious subject, it does embody aspects of a rich spiritual life. Lasker-Schüler was Jewish, and "Versöhnung" may refer to Yom Kippur, the Jewish Day of Atonement; on that day one asks forgiveness not just of God but of anyone who has been knowingly or unknowingly harmed.

Marc and Lasker-Schüler became friends and continued to correspond regularly for several years. Looking forward to his release from military service, Marc wrote home to his wife Maria from Verdun: "Amidst all the boundless images of horror and destruction among which I now live, this thought of homecoming has a kind of halo around it."[4] That afternoon, March 4, 1916, Franz Marc became a victim of the First World War. Lasker-Schüler's poem "Gebet" (Prayer) was dedicated to the artist.

■ JRW

Notes

1. Susanna Partsch, *Marc* (Cologne: Taschen, 2001), 7.
2. Betty Falkenberg, *Else Lasker-Schüler: A Life* (Jefferson, N.C.: McFarland and Company, Inc., 2003), 80.
3. Ibid.
4. Ibid., 90.

PLATE 84. Max Beckmann,
Descent from the Cross,
1918. Drypoint.

PLATE 84

Max Beckmann,
German, 1884–1950

Descent from
the Cross

1918

Drypoint

18⅞ × 13 inches
479 × 330 mm (sheet)

84-29

Signed in pencil, full
margins

Max Beckmann © 2011 Artists
Rights Society (ARS), New York /
VG Bild-Kunst, Bonn

Christ's stiff, emaciated body and distended limbs confront the dreadful reality of the Crucifixion story in a new artistic style. Max Beckmann, along with George Grosz and Otto Dix, was a leading proponent of what would be labeled in the 1920s Die Neue Sachlichkeit, or "The New Objectivity," in avant-garde art. While stylistically rooted in expressionism, these artists' approach to subject matter has been described as "anti-expressionist" for its tendency toward irony and hopeless cynicism over spiritualism.[1] In 1912, Beckmann stood in opposition to Die Blaue Reiter and publicly disagreed with Franz Marc's attempt to express nature's inner spirit, claiming that objectivity of external characteristics should be central in art. Although *Descent from the Cross,* and the figure of Christ in particular, cannot be described as realistic in the traditional sense, Beckmann's distortion points to physical truth rather than any underlying spiritual essence.

After Beckmann served in the medical corps during World War I, his objective style shed its origins in French impressionism and became truly abstract. His abandonment of traditional proportion and perspective from 1916 to 1918 has been largely attributed to the horrors he witnessed on the battlefield. In *Descent from the Cross,* the severely tilted ladder, smaller toward the top, counters the otherwise shallow sense of perspective, accentuated by the unnatural scale of Christ's massive, flattened body. Twisted and wracked with rigor mortis, the figure of Christ and

the broken arms of the men who hold him certainly recall the physical devastation of warfare.

During this period Beckmann explored themes of guilt and redemption through a series of religious paintings, including *Adam and Eve, Christ and the Woman Taken in Adultery,* an unfinished *Resurrection,* and *Descent from the Cross,* of which this print is a reverse image. He drew inspiration for these works from German Renaissance painters such as Matthias Grünewald (c. 1470–1528).[2] The darkened sun, visible here in the upper right corner, pays homage to the mid-fifteenth-century Tegernsee altarpiece in Munich, which at that time was attributed to another of Beckmann's favorite painters, Gabriel Malesskircher (c. 1425–1495).[3] The diminished size of the kneeling figures in *Descent from the Cross* resembles the common practice of painting donors into medieval altarpieces.

To create the print, Beckmann chose drypoint, a technique in which the image is scratched into the copperplate. The immediacy of this direct interaction with the metal suits Beckmann's objective approach, as his simple, attenuated lines underlie the inky, abrasive burr inherent in drypoint to form this highly charged depiction of the dead Christ.

Considered an atrocious disregard for the sanctity of Christ's Crucifixion, Beckmann's painted version of *Descent from the Cross* appeared in the Nazi-sponsored exhibition of "degenerate art" in Munich in 1937.

■ JRW

Notes

1. Linda C. Hults, *The Print in the Western World: An Introductory History* (Madison: University of Wisconsin Press, 1996), 625.
2. Stephan Lackner, *Max Beckmann* (New York: Harry N. Abrams, 1991), 54.
3. Ibid.

PLATE 85

**Käthe Kollwitz,
German, 1867–1945**

Mary and Elizabeth

c. 1928

Woodcut

15⅓ × 18 inches
390 × 457 mm (sheet)

96-07

Klipstein 234,Va

Signed in pencil,
Japan paper

Mary and Elizabeth is the only religious theme explored by Käthe Kollwitz.[1] Described as a "dramatic artist who dealt in human emotions," Kollwitz employed gesture and facial expression to convey feeling.[2] Conventional depictions of Mary's visitation with Elizabeth (Luke 1:39–56) show the two women greeting each other. Kollwitz's version honors this tradition but places Elizabeth and Mary in an especially close embrace. Elizabeth pulls Mary near her and, cheek to cheek, seems to whisper in Mary's ear. Elizabeth's right hand tenderly caresses Mary's belly, and the gentle curve of her long fingers intimates the shape of a mother's growing womb. Mary delicately bows her head and innocently receives the older woman's affection. Their closed eyes emphasize a sensual rather than visual familiarity shared by two expectant

mothers. Kollwitz captures a precious and universally feminine experience.

Käthe Kollwitz was attracted primarily to the graphic arts, and to prints in particular, for their inherent democracy. Her lithographs, like *Abschied und Tod (Leave-taking and Death)* (Figure 69), tend to express the same immediacy as her numerous drawings, which were usually studies for prints.[3] The accessibility and intimacy of prints were especially appropriate to portray the socially conscious yet deeply personal themes of war and death that dominate her work. Death was a familiar subject for Kollwitz, whose son Peter was killed in World War I, and the theme of death as it relates to war and to children remained pervasive throughout her career.

Mary and Elizabeth is similar in style to *War,* a series decrying the calamity of warfare that Kollwitz first attempted in etching and lithography before turning to the austere white-on-black effects offered by the woodcut.[4] As in that series, Kollwitz carved the block to stress the mass of Mary and Elizabeth, rather than their outlines, but adapted her technique to soften this special moment between the two women. Like Die Brücke artists, Kollwitz utilized the woodblock's natural grain and cut hundreds of thin, horizontal lines to highlight the tender female figures, as if lifting them from within the black ink. Here there is no tragic implication but only the hope that emerges from the promise of life.

■ JRW

Notes

1. Carl Zigrosser, *Kaethe Kollwitz* (New York: H. Bittner and Company, 1946), 14.
2. Ibid., 7.
3. Ibid., 5.
4. Linda C. Hults, *The Print in the Western World: An Introductory History* (Madison: University of Wisconsin Press, 1996), 624.

FIGURE 69. Käthe Kollwitz, *Abschied und Tod (Leavetaking and Death),* c. 1923–24. Lithograph.

Plate 85. Käthe Kollwitz,
Mary and Elizabeth,
c. 1928. Woodcut.

PLATE 86. George Wesley
Bellows, *The Crucifixion*,
1923. Oil on canvas.

PLATE 86

George Wesley
Bellows, American,
1882–1925

The Crucifixion

1923
Oil on canvas
59½ × 65½ inches
1511 × 1664 mm
84-40
Signed at lower left

Rhythmic brushstrokes, acute and heightened emotion, and illuminated depth of space pull the viewer into this powerful depiction of Christ's Crucifixion. Christ's body commands our attention thematically and visually with its stark light color against a dark, stormy sky. The Gospel of Luke describes that when Jesus took his last breath, darkness fell over the earth, a great earthquake shook, and the temple curtain ripped in two; then "Jesus, crying with a loud voice, said, 'Father, into your hands I commend my spirit.' Having said this, he breathed his last" (Luke 23:44–46). By expertly angling the perspective of the central Crucifixion upward, and placing the large frontal figures to the side, George Wesley Bellows leaves an intuitive space for the viewer to enter the scene at the base of the painting. The crosses, lightning, and bodies of the spectators all seem to construct a large circle around the figure of Christ. The composition also appears to rest on a central horizontal line around Christ's midsection, which further contributes to immediacy and inclusion for the viewer.

Rich, royal purple worn by a kneeling female figure at the foot of Jesus' cross (probably Mary Magdalene) references the robe Christ wore when he was mocked by the crowds of people before his execution. The drama is built up in a symphony of subtle grays, browns, and purples, which gives the whites of Christ's body a visual prominence, almost illuminating the scene. The nude male in the lower right corner is probably a representation of Adam; his placement and depiction hold an art historical precedence from medieval altarpiece triptychs, and his gesture alludes to the fall of humanity, while Christ arises as humanity's salvation and redemption. The white-haired, bearded man in the lower right foreground may be intended as an Old Testament patriarch or prophet. The specific identities of many intriguing figures (such as the curious group of men on the far left and the female in green at center) and their iconographic arrangements and costumes warrant further study.

The realistic portrayal of Christ's body in this painting is reinforced by a preparatory crayon drawing, also in the Thrivent Financial collection, *Study for "The Crucifixion"* (Figure 70). Bellows was very intentional about the accuracy of the anatomical rendering of the body and in conveying the weight of a man's form hanging from the crucifix—muscles flexed in resistance, head slumped back and upward, perhaps from exhaustion, perhaps in final words to God.

George Wesley Bellows lived in an exciting time amid many great artists, and he was a passionate advocate of American artists and their work. Among contemporaries such as Edward Hopper, Marsden Hartley, Charles Demuth, and Georgia O'Keeffe, Bellows emerged as perhaps the most eloquent realist painter. He is associated with American realist movements of the early twentieth century known as "the Eight" and the Ashcan School. His brushstroke and use of color were viscerally expressive, his compositions luminous and brilliant. During his lifetime, Bellows was technically unrivaled. The graphic arts were vital in the shaping of his oeuvre; he enjoyed drawing from a young age and created many fine original prints.

Bellows chose subjects for his landscapes, portraits, and genre scenes that spanned the social and economic classes of his time. Social commentary abounds in his works, which depicted the kaleidoscope of American culture. From sporting clubs, prize fights, and bars, to circuses and prayer meetings, to the tennis lawns and polo fields of the wealthy, Bellows presented American life in its myriad forms. He and like-minded

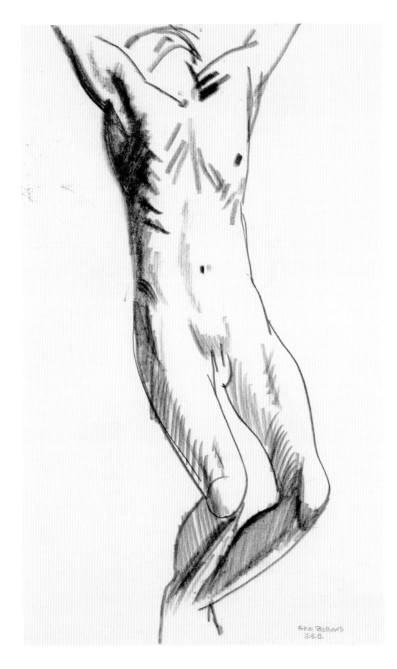

FIGURE 70. George Wesley Bellows, *Study for "The Crucifixion,"* 1923. Crayon.

Provenance

Estate of
Emma S. Bellows.

Note

1. Michael Quick, *The Paintings of George Bellows* (New York: Harry N. Abrams, 1992), 84.

contemporaries, such as Hopper and Robert Henri (teacher to both men), sought to paint everyday conditions realistically. Whether the scene was a boxing match, a polo game, or the Crucifixion, Bellows's keen sense of realism, ability to capture the gritty nature of life (especially in urban scenes), and acute awareness of the nuances of human emotion are evident.

Considered one of his most ambitious canvases, *The Crucifixion* was painted in 1923, two years before the artist's death from complications related to appendicitis. It likely

reflects his response to the violence and barbarism of World War I. This is Bellows's only religious painting and is consistent with his late painting style, which explored his own application of color techniques of sixteenth-century Italian artists; he enthusiastically wrote about the two-color technique in this painting to his teacher Robert Henri in 1923.[1]

The Crucifixion remained in the ownership of the artist's family (first with his wife, Emma Bellows, then in her estate through their daughter Jean Bellows Booth) until it was acquired for the Thrivent Financial Collection of Religious Art in 1984. The painting recently returned to the Minneapolis home office of Thrivent Financial for Lutherans from Luther Seminary in St. Paul, Minnesota, where it had been displayed in the chapel on loan since 1996. *The Crucifixion* has been widely exhibited in the United States and Europe, including:

- New York and Paris in 1924

- Art Institute of Chicago in 1925 and 1946

- Metropolitan Museum of Art, New York in 1925

- Columbus, Ohio in 1930

- World's Fair in Cleveland, Ohio in 1932

- Century Club in New York City in 1939

- Minneapolis Institute of Arts in 1984

- Los Angeles Museum of Art and the Whitney Museum of American Art in 1992–93.

Several of these venues were associated with retrospective exhibitions of Bellows's work.
■ JRL

PLATE 87

Oskar Kokoschka,
Austrian, 1886–1980

The Resurrection

1916
Lithograph
20½ × 16½ inches
521 × 419 mm (sheet)
85-57
Wingler–Welz 81
Signed in pencil, full
margins, Van Gelder
Zonen paper

Oskar Kokoschka © 2011
Foundation Oskar Kokoschka /
Artists Rights Society (ARS), New
York / ProLitteris, Zürich

PLATE 87. Oskar Kokoschka, *The Resurrection,* 1916.
Lithograph.

Oskar Kokoschka was never a member of any
specific expressionist group like Die Brücke
or Die Blaue Reiter, but he worked indepen-
dently to revolutionize art in a similar way.[1]
He used his paintings, drawings, and lithographs as a means to make the immaterial,
living forces within an object visible to the
eye. The spontaneous, frenzied application
of Kokoschka's lithographic crayon in
The Resurrection generates a nexus of energy
and mass that invokes a heightened sense of
spirituality and thus an expressionist vision.
The disordered world is given clarity through
Christ's triumph over death as he emerges
from his tomb in a field of white.

Like many expressionists, Kokoschka
deeply explored the work of old masters,
including those of the seventeenth century.[2]
His drawing style evinces a spontaneity of
composition and line reminiscent of etchings
by Rembrandt. For example, the multidirec-
tional sets of parallel lines used to model and
shade the rocky terrain in *The Resurrection*
are similar to those in *Abraham's Sacrifice*
(Plate 63) by the Dutch master. The iconography is also adapted from conventional early
modern Resurrection scenes: Christ holds a
standard with a banner in one hand, with the
other hand raised in benediction. Traditionally,
the figures around Christ's tomb include the
guards (either asleep or shocked and physically thrown by the force of the Resurrection)
and the women and disciples who have come
to mourn. The simply drawn men, women,
and children in Kokoschka's version do
not fit these typical roles, but rather appear
to represent humanity in awe of Christ's
miraculous Resurrection.

Kokoschka volunteered for military
service at the outbreak of the First World
War. He was wounded in the head and
chest in 1915 and convalesced during 1916.
The Resurrection is from a series of lithographs
narrating Christ's Passion that he created
that year.

■ JRW

Provenance

Carl Hitzeroth
(1879–1950; Lugt 565b).

Notes

1. Linda C. Hults, *The
   Print in the Western
   World: An Introductory
   History* (Madison:
   University of Wisconsin
   Press, 1996), 615–16.
2. Alfred Werner,
   "Kokoschka: Modern
   Old Master," *The
   Kenyon Review* 28, no. 1
   (January 1966): 52.

Plate 88. Georges
Rouault, *Le Christ en
Croix (Christ on the Cross)*,
1936. Color etching and
aquatint.

Plate 88

Stretched on the cross, Christ's body fills the entire frame of this luminous print, emphasizing his humanity. On each side, compassionate mourners reverently pray and console themselves in the presence of their suffering Messiah, while the sky, flush with the radiant colors of a setting sun, conveys the profound divinity of Christ's sublime sacrifice.

Georges Rouault's large aquatint *Le Christ en Croix (Christ on the Cross),* with its shards of saturated color and thick black outlines, is reminiscent of medieval stained glass and recalls the artist's apprenticeship in a glass painter's workshop during his youth. Rouault was France's primary expressionist printmaker, and his work shares affinity with Fauvism, though he was never involved with that early twentieth-century group.[1] Led by painters Henri Matisse (1869–1954) and André Derain (1880–1954), the Fauves ("Wild Beasts") favored vibrant, often unexpected color combinations and dramatic and spontaneous brushstroke. In *Le Christ en Croix,* Rouault emulated the bold brushwork possible in painting by working the plate with sugar-lift aquatint technique. The rich layers of color achieved with assistance from his expert printer, Roger Lacourière, complete the effect, creating a print that looks like a modern painting of a Gothic church window.

A similar result occurs in *Christ et la Sainte Femme (Christ and the Holy Woman)* (Figure 71), from Rouault's *Passion* series. Watercolors were painted by hand onto this printed image, making the impression in the Thrivent Financial collection unique and exceptionally personal. The blurring

between artistic media in both of these works contrasts with Rouault's German expressionist contemporaries, like Emil Nolde (Plate 82), who tended to exploit printmaking's graphic qualities rather than disguise them.[2] Yet Rouault's conflation of media and powerful Christian subject matter, drawn from his own devout Catholicism, revived traditional religious imagery with new artistic techniques to evoke a timeless and poignant emotional response.

■ JRW

Georges Rouault, French, 1871–1957

Le Christ en Croix (Christ on the Cross)

1936
Color etching and aquatint
25½ × 19⅜ inches
646 × 492 mm (plate)
85-01
Chapon/Rouault 286c, Wolfsy 284
Numbered 164/175, full margins, Montval paper

Georges Rouault © 2011 Artists Rights Society (ARS), New York / ADAGP, Paris

Figure 71. Georges Rouault, *Christ et la Sainte Femme,* 1936. Aquatint and watercolor.

Notes

1. Linda C. Hults, *The Print in the Western World: An Introductory History* (Madison: University of Wisconsin Press, 1996), 632.

2. Ibid., 633.

PLATE 89

Pablo Picasso,
Spanish, 1881–1973

David et Bethsabée
(David and
Bathsheba)

1947

Lithograph

25¾ × 19 inches
654 × 483 mm

93-29

Bloch 439,
Mourlot 109 I/X

Numbered 13/50, signed
in pencil, full margins,
Arches paper

Pablo Picasso, the great towering presence in twentieth-century art, brought remarkable innovation to the history of modern art. His extraordinarily prolific work progressed through several distinct periods as he participated in and was the originator of major avant-garde movements. He was one of the founders of Cubism, and his oeuvre spanned various artistic media, including painting, collage, sculpture, ceramics, drawings, and prints. His works on paper remain among the most significant and captivating examples in the twentieth century.

Daniel-Henry Kahnweiler, the renowned modernist art dealer, introduced Picasso to the work of German Renaissance artist Lucas Cranach; he gave Picasso a photocard of Cranach's *David and Bathsheba* painting from 1526 (now in the collection of the Staatliche Museen zu Berlin–Preussicher Kulturbesitz). This sixteenth-century painting was the compositional inspiration for the notable series of lithographs Picasso created titled *David et Bethsabée.*[1]

The biblical story of David and Bathsheba begins in 2 Samuel 11:2. David looks down from his roof and sees a beautiful woman bathing below. He is told she is Bathsheba, the wife of Uriah the Hittite. He instantly falls in love and sends for her, and she becomes pregnant with his child. David subsequently arranges for Uriah to be killed in battle and makes Bathsheba his own wife. David broke the Tenth Commandment by committing adultery, and God punishes his sinfulness by taking in death the child that David and Bathsheba conceived. David repents fully, and the couple is blessed with a second child, Solomon.

This story has historically been used to illustrate the theme of the "power of women"

in art. Other biblical and historical pairings such as Samson and Delilah, Judith and Holofernes, Aristotle and Phyllis, and Salome and Herod have served as warnings against the seductive power of love and desire, as well as demonstrations of the historical misogynistic belief that woman is temptress and seductress, capable of dominating and persuading even the most powerful of men. Lucas Cranach created several works with the power of women theme; *Solomon's Idolatry* (Plate 15) is a portrayal of the theme by one of Cranach's contemporaries. Picasso's tumultuous relationships with women and his numerous erotic artworks are well known, and it is not surprising that during his long career he would have been attracted to this theme.

Often the erotic visual potential of the female nude in art is exploited, thus emphasizing the sexualized component of the power of women theme. Yet in Picasso's lithograph Bathsheba is fully clothed; only her ankles and feet are exposed as she is washed by a female attendant. This servant's breasts are partially revealed as she bends over, but the leering King David focuses not on her but on the modestly attired Bathsheba. She is also fully dressed in Cranach's painting, perhaps accurately highlighting the culpability of David at this moment, for at this stage in the story Bathsheba is innocent.[2] Picasso exploits the idea with David towering voyeuristically over the entire scene, his massive head and harp larger than life.

Picasso developed this image through ten states. The early states showed rich, wide black ink on a white ground and progressed to thinner white lines on a densely black background. Ten states of this print were created on the same zinc plate, reworked between each state. There was also a related single state (essentially the sixth state from the zinc plate) that was transferred to a stone and reworked, then printed in an edition of fifty. Picasso then returned to the zinc plate and reworked it heavily for the final states. The lithograph in the Thrivent Financial Collection of Religious Art is a first state impression from the zinc plate.

■ JRL

Notes

1. Jeremy Howard,
   Cranach (London:
   Colnaghi, 2009), 12.
2. Ibid.

Plate 89. Pablo Picasso,
David et Bethsabée, 1947.
Lithograph.

PLATE 90. Sybil Andrews,
*Station VII: Jesus Falls for
the Second Time,* from
Stations of the Cross series,
1977. Color linocut.

PLATE 90

Sybil Andrews,
English, 1898–1992

*Station VII:
Jesus Falls for the
Second Time,*
from *Stations of
the Cross* series

1977

Color linocut

13⅕ × 16³⁄₁₆ inches

342 × 412 mm

98-08.5

White 69

Numbered 10/60,
titled and signed in pencil,
tissue paper

Sybil Andrews © 2011 Glenbow-
Alberta Institute

Sybil Andrews was in the Grosvenor School, a group of English printmakers led by Claude Flight between the First and Second World Wars. Working with linoleum blocks rather than wood, members of the Grosvenor School adapted and evolved elements from Cubist and Futurist avant-garde movements to emulate the energy and repetitive rhythm of an industrial and populous age, and celebrate the vitality of modern life.[1]

In 1947, Andrews immigrated to British Columbia, Canada, a year after she had begun to craft this *Stations of the Cross* series. Working out of narrative order, she created *Station II* and *Station XIII* in 1946 and periodically returned to the series over more than thirty years until the production of *Station IX* in 1978. Only ten of the fourteen traditionally recognized stations were completed before the artist's death in 1992, and whether she considered the series finished is unclear today.

Station VII: Jesus Falls for the Second Time is typical of the series in its style and color. The narrative, too, is consistently reduced to its most essential elements, a practice Andrews believed was fundamental to linocut print-making.[2] With legs and back braced, Simon of Cyrene heroically hoists the cross from Christ, who has collapsed beneath its weight. The dramatic tension of the scene is described through a subtle vortex in the area of Christ's

halo, around which the physical action occurs. The arching forms of Simon's back and legs seem to draw strength from this still point, in dynamic opposition to Christ's back and arms, which press against the stones that pave the difficult road ahead. Simon's buttressing arm mimics those of Christ, its power countered by the parallel form of the thick crossbeam.

Andrews used multiple linoleum blocks to create a range of colors and indicate depth for what are largely two-dimensional shapes. Each block was carefully planned and cut to carry a particular color to certain areas on the paper. When the colors were printed in order and correctly aligned on the paper, their shapes combined to produce a complete composition. Andrews compared color blocks to a "madrigal in music," and she cut the linoleum in a way that allowed colors to overlap and harmonize on the paper's surface.[3] In *Station VII,* she skillfully layered three colors to sculpt the folds of Simon's loincloth and Christ's sleeves and to create texture in the cobblestones and the wood grain of the cross. The series was printed on a fine, thin tissue paper that further accentuates texture and depth.

The abstraction of forms in *Station III: Jesus Falls for the First Time* (Figure 72) is more intense than in the other works of *Stations of the Cross.* Christ has fallen to his knees and his head hangs low, crowned with a wreath of long thorns. His back heaves against the thick black cross that dominates the upper left corner of the scene. Two Roman soldiers pull on his shoulders, urging him to stand. The interlocking geometric shapes and sharp angular representation of the soldiers' backs and necks recall elements of Futurism, which infuses human figures with machine-like qualities.

Andrews's decision to dramatically offset the red block boosts the sense of rhythm and energy in *Station III*. A unique artist's proof of this print in the Thrivent Financial collection (Figure 73) demonstrates the artist's experimentation with color and repetition, hallmarks of Grosvenor School linocuts.[4] In the margin of the proof Andrews penciled "red block missing," although

scrutiny suggests that the red ink is still present but almost completely covered by black. In her final version of the print, the reiteration of shape created by the red and black blocks is most evident in the crown of thorns; this draws attention to the figure of Christ. The doubled and overlapping soldiers break down perception of natural space, an effect intensified by the juxtaposition of the complementary colors red and green, which produces a feeling of vibration. The addition of the red block confounds the visual experience and challenges the viewer to understand what is happening within the picture. Andrews's avant-garde approach evokes a modern response to a subject traditionally used for devotion and deep, emotional contemplation of Christ's suffering.

■ JRW

Notes

1. Clifford S. Ackley, *Rhythms of Modern Life: British Prints, 1914–1939* (Boston: MFA Publications, 2008), 15.
2. Peter White, *Sybil Andrews* (Calgary: Glenbow Museum, 1991), 73.
3. Ibid., 74.
4. Ackley, 77.

Above: FIGURE 72. Sybil Andrews, *Station III: Jesus Falls for the First Time,* from *Stations of the Cross* series, 1962. Color linocut.

Below: FIGURE 73. Sybil Andrews, *Station III: Jesus Falls for the First Time,* from *Stations of the Cross* series, 1962. Artist's proof. Color linocut.

PLATE 91

**Marc Chagall,
Russo-French,
1887–1985**

Moses, from *Songes*

1981

Etching and color
aquatint

20⅜ × 14⅞ inches
519 × 378 mm

98-27

Numbered 35/50,
signed in pencil,
wove paper

Notes

1. Ruth Mellinkoff,
*The Horned Moses
in Medieval Art and
Thought* (Berkeley:
University of California
Press, 1970), 1.
2. Susan Compton,
"Chagall, Marc," in
The Dictionary of Art, ed.
Jane Turner (New York:
Grove, 1998), 6: 383.

Marc Chagall's colorful print was made in the late twentieth century, but his figure of Moses is based on iconography hundreds of years old. Moses holds two stone tablets outlining God's law, while two horn-shaped rays appear on his head. In Latin Scripture, when Moses descended Mount Sinai with the Ten Commandments, Jerome translated the Hebrew word *qeren*, which means "horned" or "rays of light," to *cornuta*, meaning "horned." As a result of this mistranslation, Moses was often depicted with horns in medieval Christian art.[1] Later, when theologians corrected this error, artists adapted the iconography into hornlike rays of light, as in Cornelis Cort's *Moses and Aaron before Pharaoh* (Plate 45). Chagall's print demonstrates that this tradition endures in imagery of Moses to the present day.

Moses is one of twenty etchings in a suite of both secular and religious prints titled *Songes,* meaning "dreams" in French. Chagall made black and white etchings as early as 1922, and he began experimenting with color printing techniques around 1948. Color allowed Chagall to bring to printmaking what he considered his "trade" in painting and stained glass.[2]

In this print, he layered areas of yellow, blue, and orange behind energetically etched black lines. The soft colors highlight the spirit of the image, which is more a symbolic representation of Moses' theological function than a true biblical narrative. An earthy shade of orange accentuates the mass of black that forms Mount Sinai, rising next to the monumental figure of Moses and providing a powerful frame for the Ten Commandments. A contrasting, complementary blue tints the sky, while areas of yellow highlight an angel, the face of the prophet, and the crowd of tiny people. This trio of yellow symbolically links God's message from the heavenly realm through Moses to humankind. Chagall left most of Moses' face and the tablets uncolored and white, reflecting the divine power of God's word and the blessed countenance of one who has spoken with God.

■ JRW

PLATE 91. Marc Chagall,
Moses, from *Songes,*
1981. Etching and color
aquatint.

Glossary

aquatint: an intaglio technique related to etching in which a plate is coated with acid-resistant grains of resin; areas of nonlinear tone are produced when printed.

burin: basic tool used to incise lines into an engraved plate.

burr: the ridge of copper displaced by the drypoint needle, which blurs the inked line in early impressions and thus creates softness and rich tone. Burr wears away quickly from the pressure of the printing press.

drypoint: an intaglio method in which the line is scratched into the plate with a needle.

edition: a set number of impressions printed from a matrix.

engraving: an intaglio method in which the lines are cut into the plate with a burin.

etching: an intaglio method in which the lines are cut into the plate using acid.

foreshorten: to portray an object at a steep angle, as an effect of perspective or angle of vision.

gouache: paint made from opaque pigments dissolved in water and thickened with a glue-like substance.

ground: an acid-resistant coating applied to a plate for etching. Lines are drawn through the ground with an etching needle, and when the plate is bathed in acid, those lines are "bitten," or etched, into the plate.

illuminated manuscript: a book or page from a book embellished with gold, silver, or colored designs. Also can refer to a *miniature*, an independent illustration that adorns a book.

impression: a unique instance of a printed artwork created when a matrix is inked and pressed on a sheet of paper or another support (e.g., vellum).

intaglio: a class of printing that uses metal plates. Ink lies in engraved or etched lines or recesses beneath the surface of the plate, which is otherwise wiped clean; the intense pressure of a printing press is required to effectively transfer the ink to paper.

linocut: a relief printing method in which the negative space of an image is carved away in a block of linoleum that then acts as a stamp when inked and pressed.

lithograph: a class of print made by drawing or painting a greasy medium on a flat surface, usually fine-grained limestone or a zinc plate, which is then treated to set the image. When printed, the surface is first wet with water, which settles on the unmarked areas; oil-based ink is rolled onto the surface and, repelled by the water, adheres only to the drawn marks. The ink is then transferred to the paper to create the printed image.

matrix: in printmaking, the object or surface worked by an artist (e.g., woodblock, metal plate, etc.) that is subsequently inked and pressed to paper to produce an original print.

oeuvre: the complete body of artwork produced by an artist.

original print: a work of art on paper created on a matrix by an artist, as opposed to images reproduced through fully mechanical (e.g., photomechanical) processes.

parchment: a writing support material made from prepared animal skin, also known as vellum.

pentimenti: literally "repentances" in Italian, these marks by the artist appear as errors in a finished artwork; they remain in the work after the artist has made corrections and thus serve to indicate compositional process.

plate: a metal matrix, usually intaglio; may also refer to a specific image within a series of prints.

plate tone: a printing technique in which ink is not fully removed from the surface areas of an intaglio plate when it is wiped; this remaining ink is transferred to the paper and creates tonal effects.

proof: trial impressions pulled before the matrix is complete. Also called a "trial proof" or "artist's proof," these refer to impressions set aside by the artist outside of an edition.

provenance: the history of ownership for a work of art.

recto: the front of a piece of paper that bears an artwork.

Reiberdruck: a printing method used before the invention of the printing press (and by modern artists interested in reviving early printing techniques) in which the paper is applied to the matrix and rubbed with a tool to transfer the ink.

relief: a class of printing in which a matrix (often wood) is carved so that the negative space of the image lies below the surface; ink is applied to the surface of the matrix, which is then pressed to paper, functioning like a stamp.

reproductive print: a printed image that recreates the design of another work of art—usually a painting but also possibly a sculpture, drawing, or another print.

state: an impression, or grouping of impressions, that reflects a particular instance of the matrix. Any impression that indicates additional work has been done on the matrix constitutes a different state.

tempera: paint in which pigments are dispersed in a substance, like egg yolk, that mixes with water.

verso: the back of a sheet of paper.

watermark: a mark that identifies the manufacturer of a sheet of paper, visible when the sheet is held up to light; helps determine the date or origins of a print or drawing.

woodcut: a relief method in which the negative space of an image is carved in a block of wood that acts as a stamp when inked and pressed.

Bibliography

Abbe, Mary. *"The Saints: Image and Devotion in Religious Prints."* Star Tribune (Minneapolis–St. Paul), December 23, 2007, 4F.

Ackley, Clifford S. *Rembrandt's Journey: Painter, Draftsman, Etcher.* Boston: MFA Publications, 2003.

———. *Rhythms of Modern Life: British Prints, 1914–1939.* Boston: MFA Publications, 2008.

Ackley, Clifford S., Timothy O. Benson, and Victor I. Carlson. *Nolde: The Painter's Prints.* Boston: Museum of Fine Arts, Boston, in association with the Los Angeles County Museum of Art, 1995.

Alberti, Leon Battista. *On Painting.* London: Penguin, 2004.

Andersson, Christiane, and Charles W. Talbot. *From a Mighty Fortress: Prints, Drawings, and Books in the Age of Luther, 1483–1546.* Detroit: Detroit Institute of Arts, 1983.

Andrews, Keith. "Goudt, Hendrik." In Grove Art Online. Oxford Art Online. http://www.oxfordart-online.com.

Barringer, Tim. *Reading the Pre-Raphaelites.* New Haven: Yale University Press, 1999.

Bartrum, Giulia. *German Renaissance Prints, 1490–1550.* London: British Museum Press, 1995.

———, with Günter Grass, Joseph Leo Koerner, and Ute Kuhlemann. *Albrecht Dürer and His Legacy: The Graphic Work of a Renaissance Artist.* Princeton: Princeton University Press, 2002.

Bartsch, Adam. *Le Peintre graveur.* 21 vols. Vienna, 1803.

Benesch, Otto, and Eva Benesch, eds. *Drawings of Rembrandt.* 2 vols. London: Phaidon Press, 1974.

Bénézit, Emmanuel. *Dictionnaire Critique et documentaire des peintres, dessinateurs, sculpteurs et graveurs, nouvelle edition.* Paris: Grund, 1976.

Béraldi, Henri. *Les Graveurs du dix-neuvième siècle.* 12 vols. Paris: Librairie L. Conquet, 1885–92.

Bindman, David, and Deidre Toomey. *The Complete Graphic Works of William Blake.* London: Thames and Hudson, 1978.

Binyon, Laurence. *The Engraved Designs of William Blake.* New York: Da Capo Press, 1967.

Block, Jane, and Stephen H. Goddard. *Les XX and the Belgian Avant-Garde: Prints, Drawings, and Books ca. 1890.* Lawrence: Spencer Museum of Art, University of Kansas, 1992.

Blum, André. *L'Oeuvre gravé d'Abraham Bosse.* Paris, 1924.

Boerner, C. G. *Kleine Szenen in großer Landschaft.* Düsseldorf: C. G. Boerner, 1998.

Boorsch, Suzanne, and Nadine M. Orenstein. "The Print in the North: The Age of Albrecht Dürer and Lucas van Leyden." *The Metropolitan Museum of Art Bulletin* 54, no. 4 (1997): 1, 13–60.

Bowron, Edgar Peters, Michael Clarke, and Andrew Butterfield. *Titian and the Golden Age of Venetian Painting: Masterpieces from the National Galleries of Scotland.* Houston: Museum of Fine Arts, Houston, 2010.

Brown, Jonathan. *Jusepe de Ribera: Prints and Drawings.* Princeton: Princeton University Press, 1973.

Brown, Michelle P. *Understanding Illuminated Manuscripts: A Guide to Technical Terms.* Los Angeles: J. Paul Getty Museum, 1994.

Cazort, Mimi. "Gandolfi." In *The Dictionary of Art.* Ed. Jane Turner. New York: Grove, 1998.

Chapon, François, et al. *Rouault, oeuvre gravé.* Monte Carlo: A. Sauret, 1978.

Compton, Susan. "Chagall, Marc." In *The Dictionary of Art.* Ed. Jane Turner. New York: Grove, 1998.

"Corporate Chart: Our Top 101 Active Corporate Art Collectors." *Art + Auction* XI, no. 3 (October 1988): 168–75.

de Montaiglon, Anatole. "Catalogue raisonné de l'oeuvre de Claude Mellan d'Abbeville." *Mémoires de la Société d'emulation d'Abbéville* 8 (1852–57): 291–559.

DeWitt, Lloyd. "The Raising of Lazarus." In *Jan Lievens: A Dutch Master Rediscovered.* Ed. Arthur K. Wheelock Jr. Washington, D.C.: National Gallery of Art, 2008.

Dickey, Stephanie. "Jan Lievens and Printmaking." In *Jan Lievens: A Dutch Master Rediscovered,* 54–67. Ed. Arthur K. Wheelock Jr. Washington, D.C.: National Gallery of Art, 2008.

Dürer, Albrecht. *Dürer's Record of Journeys to Venice and the Low Countries.* Ed. Roger Fry. New York: Dover Publications, 1995.

Ebertshauser, Caroline H., Herbert Haag, Joe H. Kirchberger, and Dorothee Solle. *Mary: Art, Culture, and Religion through the Ages.* New York: Crossroads Publishing Company, 1998.

Eichberger, Dagmar. "Dürer's Nature Drawings and Early Collecting." In *Dürer and His Culture.* Ed. Dagmar Eichberger and Charles Zika. Cambridge: Cambridge University Press, 1998.

Eisenstein, Elizabeth L. "Some Conjectures about the Impact of Printing on Western Society and Thought: A Preliminary Report." *Journal of Modern History* 40, no. 1 (March 1968): 1–56.

Falkenberg, Betty. *Else Lasker-Schüler: A Life.* Jefferson, N.C.: McFarland and Company, Inc., 2003.

Farmer, David Hugh. *Oxford Dictionary of Saints.* Oxford and New York: Oxford University Press, 2004.

Fisher, Jay McKean. *The Prints of Édouard Manet.* Washington, D.C.: International Exhibitions Foundations, 1985.

Foucart, Jacques, and Pierre Rosenberg. "Some 'Modelli' of Religious Scenes by Dirck Barendsz." *Burlington Magazine* 120, no. 901 (April 1978): 198–205.

Galichon, Émile. "Des Dessins de M. Ingres." *Gazette des Beaux-Arts,* Paris (May 15, 1861): 344–61.

Gardner, Helen, Fred S. Kleiner, and Christin J. Mamiya. *Gardner's Art through the Ages.* Belmont: Thompson/Wadsworth, 2005.

Georgel, M. Pierre. "Bulletin: Item 21." *Société de l'Histoire d'Art Français* (1968): 163–89.

Gillis, Eric, and Patrick Florizoone. *James Ensor.* New York: C. G. Boerner, Inc., 2003.

Giovani-Visani, Maria. *Giulio Clovio: Miniaturist of the Renaissance.* New York: Alpine, 1980.

Goncourt, Edmond de. *La maison d'un artiste.* Paris: G. Charpentier, 1881.

Griffiths, Antony. *Prints and Printmaking: An Introduction to the History and Techniques.* Berkeley: University of California Press, 1996.

Guercino and Nefta Barbanti Grimaldi. *Il Guercino, Gian Francesco Barbieri, 1591–1666.* Bologna: Tamari, 1957.

Guérin, Marcel. *L'Oeuvre gravé de Manet.* Paris: Da Capo, 1944.

Harrison, Colin. "Bosse, Abraham." In *The Dictionary of Art.* Ed. Jane Turner, 468. New York: Grove, 1996.

Hayes, John H. "Moses." In *The Oxford Companion to the Bible.* Ed. Bruce M. Metzger and Michael D. Coogan. Oxford: Oxford University Press, 1993. http://www.oxford-reference.com.

Heller, Reinhold. *Brücke: German Expressionist Prints from the Granvil and Marcia Specks Collection.* Evanston: Mary and Leigh Block Gallery, Northwestern University, 1988.

Herwaarden, J. van. *Between Saint James and Erasmus. Studies in Late-Medieval Religious Life: Devotions and Pilgrimages in the Netherlands.* Studies in Medieval and Reformation Thought 97. Leiden: Brill, 2003.

Hind, Arthur M. *A Catalogue of Rembrandt's Etchings, Chronologically Arranged and Completely Illustrated.* London: Methuen and Company, Ltd., 1923.

Hinterding, Erik. *The History of Rembrandt's Copperplates, with a Catalogue of Those That Survive.* Zwolle: Waanders Uitgevers, 1995.

Hollstein, F. W. H. *Dutch and Flemish Etchings, Engravings, and Woodcuts, ca. 1450–1700. Volume IV: Brun—Coques.* Amsterdam: M. Hertzberger, 1949.

———. *German Engravings, Etchings, and Woodcuts, ca. 1400–1700.* 65 vols. Amsterdam: M. Hertzberger, 1954.

Howard, Jeremy. *Cranach.* London: Colnaghi Gallery, 2009.

Hults, Linda C. *The Print in the Western World: An Introductory History.* Madison: University of Wisconsin Press, 1996.

Ives, Colta Feller. *The Great Wave: The Influence of Japanese Woodcuts on French Prints.* New York: Metropolitan Museum of Art, 1974.

Ives, Colta Feller, and Giovanni Domenico Tiepolo. *Picturesque Ideas on the Flight into Egypt.* New York: G. Braziller, 1972.

Jacobowitz, Ellen S., and Stephanie Loeb Stepanek. *The Prints of Lucas Van Leyden and His Contemporaries.* Washington, D.C.: National Gallery of Art, 1983.

Jacoby, Joachim W., Ger Luijten, Robert Zijlma, and F. W. H. Hollstein. *The New Hollstein: German Engravings, Etchings, and Woodcuts, 1400–1700.* Rotterdam: Sound and Vision Interactive, 1996.

Johnson, R. S. *Old Master Prints and Drawings, 1450–1800.* Chicago: R. S. Johnson Fine Art Catalogue, 1994.

Kantor, Jordan. *Dürer's Passions.* Cambridge: Harvard University Art Museums, 2000.

Kaplan, Wendy, ed. *Encyclopedia of Arts and Crafts.* London: Quantum Publishing, 1998.

Kashey, Robert J. F., and Martin L. H. Reymert. *Christian Imagery in French Nineteenth-Century Art, 1789–1906.* New York: Shepherd Gallery, 1980.

Klipstein, August. *The Graphic Work of Käthe Kollwitz.* New York: Galerie St. Étienne, 1955.

Koerner, Joseph Leo. *The Reformation of the Image.* Chicago: University of Chicago Press, 2004.

Lackner, Stephan. *Beckmann.* New York: Harry N. Abrams, 1991.

Landau, David, and Peter W. Parshall. *The Renaissance Print, 1470–1550.* New Haven: Yale University Press, 1994.

Lankheit, Klaus. *Franz Marc: Katalog der Werke.* Cologne: M. DuMont Schauberg, 1970.

Laver, James. *Costume and Fashion: A Concise History.* New York: Thames and Hudson, 2002.

Le Blanc, Charles. *Manuel de l'amateur d'estampes, contenant le dictionnaire des gravures toutes les nations, dans lequel sont décrites les estampes rares, précieuses et intéressantes avec l'indication de leurs différents états et des prix auxquels ces estampes ont été portées dans les ventes publiques.* Vol. 2. Paris: Émile Bouillon, 1854–88.

Lehrs, Max. *Geschichte und kritischer Katalog des deutschen, niederländischen und französischen Kupferstichs im XV. Jahrhundert.* Vienna: Gesellschaft für vervielfältigende Kunst, 1908–34.

Leistra, J. E. P. "Jacob de Wit." In *The Dictionary of Art.* Ed. Jane Turner. New York: Grove, 1998.

Lieure, J. *Jacques Callot.* Paris: Editions de la Gazette des Beaux-Arts, 1924–27.

Lindberg, Carter. *A Reformation Reader.* Oxford: Blackwell Publishing, 1996.

Lubbock, Jules. *Storytelling in Christian Art from Giotto to Donatello.* New Haven: Yale University Press, 2006.

Luther, Martin, and Wilhelm Pauck. *Luther: Lectures on Romans.* Louisville: Westminster John Knox Press, 2006.

La Magasin Pittoresque 1833–34. Paris: Aux Bureaux d'Abonnement et de Vente.

Marshall, Nancy Rose, and Malcolm Warner. *James Tissot: Victorian Life/Modern Love.* New Haven: Yale University Press, 1999.

Martineau, Jane, and Andrew Robison. *The Glory of Venice: Art in the Eighteenth Century.* New Haven: Yale University Press, 1994.

"Mary, Gospel of the Birth of." In *The Oxford Dictionary of the Christian Church.* Ed. F. L. Cross and E. A. Livingstone. Oxford: Oxford University Press, 2005. http://www.oxford-christianchurch.com.

Mayor, A. Hyatt. *Prints and People: A Social History of Printed Pictures.* New York: Metropolitan Museum of Art, 1971.

Meder, Joseph. *Dürer-Katalog; ein Handbuch über Albrecht Dürers Stiche, Radierungen, Holzschnitte, deren Zustände, Ausgaben und Wasserzeichen.* Vienna: Verlag Gilhofer und Ranschburg, 1932.

Melion, Walter S. "Theory and Practice: Reproductive Engraving in the Sixteenth-Century Netherlands." In Timothy A. Riggs and Larry Silver, eds., *Graven Images: The Rise of Professional Printmakers in Antwerp and Haarlem, 1540–1640.* 47–69. Evanston: Mary and Leigh Block Gallery and Northwestern University Press, 1993.

Mellinkoff, Ruth. *The Horned Moses in Medieval Art and Thought.* Berkeley: University of California Press, 1970.

Melot, Michel, Antony Griffiths, and Richard S. Field. *Prints: History of an Art.* New York: Rizzoli, 1981.

Menil, Dominique de. *Builders and Humanists: The Renaissance Popes as Patrons of the Arts.* Houston: University of St. Thomas Art Department, 1966.

Metropolitan Museum of Art (New York) and Germanisches Nationalmuseum Nürnberg. *Gothic and Renaissance Art in Nuremberg, 1300–1550.* Munich: Prestel-Verlag, 1986.

Metzger, Bruce M., and Roland E. Murphy, eds. *The New Oxford Annotated Bible, with the Apocryphal/Deuterocanonical Books.* New York: Oxford University Press, 1994.

Metzger, Christof, Tobias Güthner, Achim Riether, and Freyda Spira. *Daniel Hopfer: ein Augsburger Meister der Renaissance: Eisenradierungen, Holzschnitte, Zeichnungen, Waffenätzungen.* Munich: Staatliche Graphische Sammlung, 2009.

Michaux, Lisa Dickinson. *Herschel V. Jones: The Imprint of a Great Collector.* Minneapolis: Minneapolis Institute of Arts, 2006.

Nash, Susie. *Northern Renaissance Art.* New York: Oxford University Press, 2009.

National Gallery of Art, Alan Shestack, and Lessing J. Rosenwald. *Fifteenth-Century Engravings of Northern Europe from the National Gallery of Art.* Washington, D.C.: National Gallery of Art, 1967.

Panofsky, Erwin. *The Life and Art of Albrecht Dürer.* Princeton: Princeton University Press, 1995.

Parshall, Peter W. "Imago Contrafacta: Images and Facts in the Northern Renaissance." *Art History* 14, no. 4 (December 1993): 554–79.

———. "Lucas van Leyden and the Rise of Pictorial Narrative." Ph.D. thesis, University of Chicago, 1974.

———. "Lucas van Leyden's Narrative Style." *Nederlands Kunsthistorish Jaarboek* 29 (1978): 185–238.

Parshall, Peter W., and Rainer Schoch. *Origins of European Printmaking.* New Haven: Yale University Press, 2005.

Partsch, Susanna. *Marc.* Cologne: Taschen, 2001.

Perkins, Alex. "History of Jesus College Chapel." http://chapel.jesus.cam.ac.uk/chapel/history.html.

Perlove, Shelley, ed. *Pursuit of Faith: Etchings by Rembrandt from the Thrivent Financial Collection of Religious Art.* Dearborn: University of Michigan, Dearborn, 2010.

Perlove, Shelley, and Larry Silver. *Rembrandt's Faith: Church and Temple in the Dutch Golden Age.* University Park: Pennsylvania State University Press, 2009.

Picasso, Pablo, and Fernand Mourlot. *Picasso Lithographs.* Boston: Boston Book and Art Publisher, 1970.

Prelinger, Elizabeth. "Pierre Roche and the 'belle gypsographie.'" *Print Quarterly* X, vol. 2 (March 1993): 138–55.

Print Council of America. *What Is an Original Print?* New York: Print Council of America, 1961.

Quick, Michael, with Jane Myers, Marianne Doezema, and Franklin Kelly. *The Paintings of George Bellows.* New York: Harry N. Abrams, 1992.

Rassieur, Tom. "Chapters in Rembrandt's Life as a Printmaker." In *Pursuit of Faith: Etchings by Rembrandt from the Thrivent Financial Collection of Religious Art.* Ed. Shelley Perlove. 34–45. Dearborn: University of Michigan, Dearborn, 2010.

Refoule, F. "Evagrius Ponticus." In *New Catholic Encyclopedia.* 5: 644–45. New York: McGraw-Hill, 1967.

Ribera, José de, Craig Felton, and William B. Jordan. *Jusepe de Ribera, Lo Spagnoletto, 1591–1652.* Fort Worth: Kimbell Art Museum, 1982.

Riggs, Timothy A., and Larry Silver, eds. *Graven Images: The Rise of Professional Printmakers in Antwerp and Haarlem, 1540–1640.* Evanston: Mary and Leigh Block Gallery and Northwestern University Press, 1993.

Robinson, William W. "Nicolaes Maes as a Draughtsman." *Master Drawings* 27, no. 2 (Summer 1989): 146–62.

Rodney, Nanette B. "Salome." *The Metropolitan Museum of Art Bulletin,* New Series, 11, no. 7 (March 1953): 190–200.

Roper, Lyndal. "Martin Luther's Body: The 'Stout Doctor' and His Biographers." *American Historical Review* 115 (April 2010): 351–84.

Rosenberg, Jakob. *Rembrandt: Life and Work.* London: Phaidon Press, 1964.

Schapire, Rosa. *Karl Schmidt-Rottluffs graphisches Werk bis 1923.* Berlin: Euphorion Verlag, 1924.

Schiefler, Gustav, and Christel Mosel. *Emil Nolde; das graphische Werk…neu bearbeitet, ergänzt und mit Abbildungen versehen.* Cologne: Verlag M. Du Mont Schauberg, 1966, 1967.

Schiller, Gertrud. *Iconography of Christian Art.* Trans. Janet Seligman. London: Lund Humphries, 1972.

Schmidt, Peter. "The Multiple Image: The Beginnings of Printmaking, between Old Theories and New Approaches." In Peter W. Parshall and Rainer Schoch, *Origins of European Printmaking.* 37–56. New Haven: Yale University Press, 2005.

Scribner, Bob. "Ways of Seeing in the Age of Dürer." In *Dürer and His Culture.* Ed. Dagmar Eichberger and Charles Zika, 107–9. Cambridge: Cambridge University Press, 1998.

Sellink, Manfred, and Marjolein Leesberg. *Philips Galle, Part 1. The New Hollstein Dutch and Flemish Etchings, Engravings, and Woodcuts, 1450–1700,* Rotterdam: Sound and Vision Publishers, 2001.

Shaw, James Byam. "A Sketch for a Ceiling by Domenico Tiepolo." *Burlington Magazine* 101, no. 681 (December 1959): 447–51.

———. *The Drawings of Domenico Tiepolo.* Boston: Boston Book and Art Shop, 1962.

Silver, Larry, Elizabeth Wyckoff, and Lilian Armstrong. *Grand Scale: Monumental Prints in the Age of Dürer and Titian.* Wellesley, Mass.: Davis Museum and Cultural Center, Wellesley College, 2008.

Smith, Elise Lawton. *The Paintings of Lucas Van Leyden: A New Appraisal, with Catalogue Raisonné.* Columbia: University of Missouri Press, 1992.

Smith, Jeffrey Chips. *The Northern Renaissance.* London: Phaidon Press, 2004.

Spear, Richard E. *The "Divine" Guido: Religion, Sex, Money, and Art in the World of Guido Reni.* New Haven: Yale University Press, 1997.

Strauss, Walter L. *The Complete Engravings, Etchings, and Drypoints of Albrecht Dürer.* New York: Dover Publications, 1973.

———. *The Illustrated Bartsch.* New York: Abaris Books, 1978.

———, ed., with Max Geisberg. *The German Single-Leaf Woodcut, 1500–1550.* New York: Hacker Art Books, 1974.

Sumowski, Werner. *Drawings of the Rembrandt School.* New York: Abaris Books, 1979.

Tavernier, Auguste. *James Ensor: Illustrated Catalogue of His Engravings, Their Critical Description, and Inventory of the Plates.* Brussels: P. van der Perre, 1973.

Turner, Nicholas. "Guercino." In *The Dictionary of Art.* Ed. Jane Turner. New York: Grove, 1998.

Vallance, Aymer. *William Morris, His Art, His Writings, and His Public Life: A Record.* London: George Bell and Sons, 1897.

Van Gelder, Dirk. *Rodolphe Bresdin: Catalogue raisonné de l'oeuvre grave.* Vol. II. La Haye, Netherlands: Martinus Nÿhoff, 1976.

Van Mulders, Christine. "Galle." In *The Dictionary of Art.* Ed. Jane Turner. New York: Grove, 1998.

Vasari, Giorgio. *Vasari's Lives of the Most Eminent Painters, Sculptors, and Architects.* Trans. Mrs. Jonathan Foster. London: G. Bell, 1891 [1568].

Veldman, Ilja M., Ger Luijten, and F. W. H. Hollstein. *The New Hollstein Dutch and Flemish Etchings, Engravings, and Woodcuts, 1450–1700.* Roosendaal, The Netherlands: Koninklijke Van Poll, in cooperation with the Rijksprentenkabinet, Rijksmuseum, 1993.

Voelkle, William M., Roger S. Wieck, and Maria Francesca P. Saffiotti. *The Bernard H. Breslauer Collection of Manuscript Illuminations.* New York: Pierpont Morgan Library, 1992.

Voragine, Jacobus de. *The Golden Legend: Readings on the Saints.* Trans. William Granger Ryan. Princeton: Princeton University Press, 1993.

Vos, Rik. "The Life of Lucas van Leyden by Karel van Mander." *Nederlands Kunsthistorish Jaarboek* 29 (1978): 459–507.

Waal, H. van de, P. Wardle, and Rudolf Herman Fuchs. *Steps towards Rembrandt: Collected Articles, 1937–1972.* Amsterdam: North-Holland, 1974.

Wentworth, Michael Justin. *James Tissot: Catalogue Raisonné of His Prints.* Minneapolis: Minneapolis Institute of Arts, 1978.

Werner, Alfred. "Kokoschka: Modern Old Master." *Kenyon Review* 28, no. 1 (January 1966): 38–53.

Wheelock, Arthur K. Jr., ed. *Jan Lievens: A Dutch Master Rediscovered.* Washington, D.C.: National Gallery of Art, 2008.

White, Christopher. *Rembrandt as an Etcher: A Study of the Artist at Work.* New Haven: Yale University Press, 1999.

White, Peter. *Sybil Andrews.* Calgary: Glenbow Museum, 1991.

———. *Sybil Andrews: Colour Linocuts.* Calgary: Glenbow Museum, 1982.

Wingler, Hans Maria, and Friedrich Welz. *O. Kokoschka, das druckgraphische Werk. Systematisches Verzeichnis der Druckgraphik nach Bildthemen.* Salzburg: Verlag Galerie Welz, 1975.

——— and ———. *O. Kokoschka, das druckgraphische Werk II, 1975–1980.* Salzburg: Verlag Galerie Welz, 1981.

Winzinger, Franz. *Albrecht Altdorfer, Graphik: Holzschnitte, Kupferstich, Radierungen.* Munich: R. Piper and Company, 1963.

Wofsy, Alan. *Georges Rouault, the Graphic Work.* San Francisco: Alan Wofsy Fine Arts, 1976.

Zigrosser, Carl. *Kaethe Kollwitz.* New York: H. Bittner and Company, 1946.